# Narrative Dynamics in Paul

# Narrative
# Dynamics in Paul

*A Critical Assessment*

BRUCE W. LONGENECKER, EDITOR

Westminster John Knox Press
LOUISVILLE • LONDON

© 2002 Westminster John Knox Press

Most scripture quotations are the author's own translations. Scripture quotations marked NRSV are from the New Revised Standard Version of the Bible, copyright © 1989 by the Division of Christian Education of the National Council of the Churches of Christ in the U.S.A., and used by permission.

*Book design by Sharon Adams*
*Cover design by Mark Abrams*

*First edition*
Published by Westminster John Knox Press
Louisville, Kentucky

This book is printed on acid-free paper that meets the American National Standards Institute Z39.48 standard. ∞

PRINTED IN THE UNITED STATES OF AMERICA

02 03 04 05 06 07 08 09 10 11 — 10 9 8 7 6 5 4 3 2 1

**Library of Congress Cataloging-in-Publication Data**

Narrative dynamics in Paul : a critical assessment / Bruce W. Longenecker, editor.
    p. cm.
    Includes bibliographical references and indexes.
    ISBN 0-664-22277-3 (pbk.)
    1. Bible. N.T. Epistles of Paul—Criticism, Narrative. 2. Narration in the Bible. 3. Paul, the Apostle, Saint. I. Longenecker, Bruce W.

BS2650.52.N37 2002
227'.066—dc21                                2002071340

# Contents

# PART I

# Introduction to the Narrative Study of Paul

# 1

# Narrative Interest in the Study of Paul

*Retrospective and Prospective*

BRUCE W. LONGENECKER

## THE RISE OF INTEREST IN NARRATIVE
## FEATURES OF PAUL'S THEOLOGY

Narrative analysis of scripture has shown itself to be a vibrant and productive discipline since the 1970s. This is especially true with regard to the full-bodied historical narratives of the Tanach (the Old Testament or Jewish scriptures) and the gospel narratives of the New Testament. At times it has been helpfully applied to genres other than historical narratives, such as the Johannine apocalypse (Revelation) in which narrative aspects are clear. For the most part, however, the Pauline corpus has been relatively immune from narrative study for obvious reason: Paul wrote letters, not narratives. As J.C. Beker wrote in his 1980 classic work *Paul the Apostle*, 'Paul is a man of the proposition, the argument and the dialogue, not a man of the parable or story',[1] and it is this view that has dominated Pauline studies throughout the post-Enlightenment era of biblical investigation.

In the last two decades of the twentieth century, however, an interest in narrative features of Paul's thought began to emerge, with significant figures in the Pauline guild proposing that 'story' was an integral and generative ingredient in Paul's theological formulations. The discourse of Paul's letters, it is claimed, is best understood as the product of an underlying narrative bedrock. Paul's epistolary

---

1. J.C. Beker, *Paul the Apostle: The Triumph of God in Life and Thought* (Philadelphia: Fortress Press; Edinburgh: T&T Clark, 1980).

discourse is like a membrane that is tightly stretched over a narrative framework, revealing many narrative contours from beneath.[2] His letters do not simply offer independent snippets of 'truth' or isolated gems of logic, but are discursive exercises that explicate a narrative about God's saving involvement in the world. Academic and ecclesiastical interpreters, it is suggested, have all too often failed to see the narrative forest of Paul's theology for the discursive wood of his letters. Whereas Pauline scholars had for long debated matters pertaining to the content and persuasive strategies within Paul's letters, or the contexts in which those letters were written, interest in narrative aspects of Paul's letters began to focus attention on the 'pre-textual' ingredients that factored into and influenced Paul's reflections at any given point—those ingredients being narrative in character.

If the final decades of the twentieth century saw the enhancement of Paul's credentials as a 'narrative theologian', it is merely one example of the rise of interest in narrative within the theological disciplines in general. Since the 1960s, leading scholars in philosophical theology have argued that human existence is experienced in narrative terms. The same is true of philosophers of cognitive science, who progressively speak of story as the fundamental organisational principle of the mind.[3] As one scholar expressed it, any attempt 'to offer a full description of human being must come to terms with the narrative structure of human identity',[4] or as another claims, '[T]he movement of the story is the medium in which selfhood swims'.[5] If assertions of this kind have foundation,[6] then it is only natural to surmise that the discipline of theology itself must be conceived as fundamentally a narrative enterprise.[7] Should we expect Paul's theological articulations to fall outside of this generalisation simply because the genre of his writings is epistolary rather than narrative?

Philosophical theologians with an interest in narrative occasionally articulated views that resonated deeply with the growing narratival interests of

2. Here I am borrowing (and adapting) much of the imagery and terminology of S. Thompson, *The Apocalypse and Semitic Syntax* (Cambridge: Cambridge University Press, 1985) 108.

3. For instance, M. Turner, *The Literary Mind: The Origins of Thought and Language* (Oxford: Oxford University Press, 1996).

4. G.W. Stroup, *The Promise of Narrative Theology* (London: SCM Press, 1981) 87.

5. D. Cupitt, *What is a Story?* (London: SCM Press, 1991) 54. Cf. J.D. Crossan (*The Dark Interval: Towards a Theology of Story* [Niles, Ill.: Argus, 1975] 45): 'We live in story like fish in the sea.'

6. And the subsequent issue is whether the narrative dimension of human existence follows a narrative dimension of 'reality' or whether it is an imposition of narrative order on chaotic and disordered 'reality'. The latter view is famously held by F. Kermode, *Genesis of Secrecy: On The Interpretation of Narrative* (Cambridge, Mass.: Harvard University Press, 1979). For a detailed engagement with Kermode's perspective, see esp. F. Lentricchia, *After the New Criticism* (London: The Athlone Press, 1980) 29–60, esp. 30–39.

7. O. Davidsen (*The Narrative Jesus: A Semiotic Reading of Mark's Gospel* [Copenhagen-Aarhus: Aarhus University Press, 1993] 360) writes that theological discourse is Christian discourse 'only if it is founded on the narrative kerygma'.

Pauline scholars. W.A. Kort, for instance, suggested that narrative *produces* theological discourse rather than being a *by-product* of theological discourse:

> It is not as though narrative and text are neutral containers or occasions for a religious or theological content and agenda. Religious meaning does not antedate and cannot be divorced from narrativity.[8]

For Kort and others, claims about ultimate realities derive from narrative rather than narrative deriving from detached 'truths'. To what extent, then, might Paul's theological discourse itself be the product of a storied perception of reality?

Issues of this sort have of late been put firmly on the agenda in the study of Paul. Much of the impetus for the contemporary study of narrative ingredients in Paul's thought can be traced to the groundbreaking work of Richard Hays. Hays' two main works in the 1980s can be thought of as companion volumes in a single narrative project. Each in its own distinctive fashion provides methodological foundations for and suggestive insights into narratological features of Paul's theology. For our purposes, only his first monograph will be considered, since it is more closely related to the main narratological enterprise that sprang up in its wake.[9]

Hays' first monograph, *The Faith of Jesus Christ* (1983), with its revealing subtitle *An Investigation of the Narrative Substructure of Galatians 3:1–4:11*,

---

8. W.A. Kort, *Story, Text, and Scripture: Literary Interests in Biblical Narrative* (University Park: Pennsylvania State University Press, 1988) 3.

9. In the second of his narratological explorations, *Echoes of Scripture in the Letters of Paul* (New Haven, Conn.: Yale University Press, 1989), Hays argued that prominent scriptural narratives concerning God's sovereignty over creation and covenantal faithfulness to Israel played crucial roles in forming Paul's theological perspective and expression. Although Paul does not write in narrative genre, his thinking processes are narratively configured, so that scriptural narratives provide both the occasion for and the constraints on Paul's theologising, even when explicit 'proof-texting' is not evident. The theological patterning and values embedded within scriptural narrative guide Paul's thought process without explicit articulation. Accordingly, Hays writes (*Echoes*, 15); 'Paul repeatedly situates his discourse within the symbolic field created by a single great textual precursor: Israel's Scripture.' In this way, Hays' second major project showcases the potential of a narrative approach to Paul, broadening the key 'narrative ingredients' in Paul's thought to include Jesus, God, and Israel.

Even his third major work, *The Moral Vision of the New Testament: A Contemporary Introduction to New Testament Ethics* (San Francisco: HarperSanFrancisco, 1996), is largely animated by narrative interests. Hays distilled three focal images of New Testament moral identity (community, cross, new creation), arguing that these images are themselves summaries of 'the story told in (or presupposed) by Scripture' while at the same time governing 'the interpretation of individual texts by placing them within a coherent narrative framework' (195).

focussed on the story of Jesus as a generating feature of Paul's theology.[10] As he himself demonstrates, Hays has several twentieth-century predecessors in this narrative exploration. Some (e.g., Amos Wilder, Stephen Crites, James Sanders, William Beardslee) seemingly stumbled on a narrative quality in Paul's thought almost unwittingly in the course of pursuing other interests. Others, however, offered detailed interpretations of Paul that suggested the fundamental role of narrative in his thinking even if these scholars did not articulate their findings in terms of narrative.[11]

Despite precursors, however, it was Hays who put the issue of narrative contours explicitly on the agenda of Pauline study. In doing so, Hays was concerned to offer something of a methodological basis for the narrative study of Paul. So he inquires:

> [I]n the case of Paul, where we encounter texts discursive in form, how is it possible to discern the shape of the narrative structure which, as we have proposed, underlies the argumentation? . . . Does it make sense to say that a *story* can function as a constraint on the logic of an *argument*?[12]

For Hays, a narrative substructure is not 'behind' the text, detachable from it, but 'beneath' the text, undergirding it, supporting it, animating it, and giving it coherence, while also constraining its discursive options. Hays found resources for his project in the work of various theorists, such as Paul Ricoeur

---

10. Chico, Calif.: Scholars Press, 1983; 2nd edn, Grand Rapids: Wm. B. Eerdmans Publ. Co., 2001. Hays' case is enhanced by the reading 'faith of Jesus Christ' in places where the ambiguous Greek phrase πίστις 'Ιησοῦ Χριστοῦ has traditionally been read as 'faith in Jesus Christ'. His interest in determining the narrative potentiality and constraint of the story of Jesus on Paul's letter to the Galatians was followed up more generally by S. Fowl, *The Story of Jesus in the Letters of Paul* (JSNTSup 36; Sheffield: Sheffield Academic Press, 1990), who demonstrates the way in which a narrative substructure frequently provides Paul with primary resources for his ethical discourse.

11. For instance, a good number of scholars throughout the early twentieth century considered Paul's christology to be patterned on the suffering, dying, and rising divinity of the Hellenistic mystery religions: e.g., W. Bousset, R. Bultmann. Others have understood Paul's theology to be animated by Jewish eschatological expectations that were permeated by a narrative of divine sovereignty: e.g., A. Schweitzer (profiling eschatological 'mysticism'), E. Käsemann (elaborating 'the righteousness of God'), and J.C. Beker (accenting an 'apocalyptic macro-symbol'). C.H. Dodd sought to demonstrate that early Christian preaching was itself narratively configured and that Paul perpetuated this feature of apostolic tradition, elaborating its implication in his epistolary expositions. And O. Cullmann's contention that salvation history enlivens Paul's theology profiled the same narrative character of his thought.

12. Hays, *The Faith of Jesus Christ*, 20; 2nd edn, 21. Cf. similarly B. Witherington III, *Paul's Narrative Thought World: The Tapestry of Tragedy and Triumph* (Louisville, Ky.: Westminster/John Knox Press, 1994) 2.

(differentiating 'episodic' and 'configurational' dimensions of narrativity), Robert Funk (differentiating 'foundational language' and 'primary reflectivity'), and Northrop Frye (differentiating 'mythos' and 'dianoia'). Of these, Hays is most dependent on Frye, identifying 'mythos' as the plot or linear sequence of events depicted in a narrative and 'dianoia' as the 'theme' or meaning of that sequence.[13] This leads Hays to conclude the following three points:

1. There can be an organic relationship between stories and reflective discourse because stories have an inherent configurational dimension (dianoia) which not only permits but also demands restatement and interpretation in non-narrative language.
2. The reflective restatement does not simply repeat the plot (mythos) of the story; nonetheless, the story shapes and constrains the reflective process because the dianoia can never be entirely abstracted from the story in which it is manifested and apprehended.
3. Hence, when we encounter this type of reflective discourse, it is legitimate and possible to inquire about the story in which it is rooted.[14]

According to Hays, the procedure for discerning narrative substructures within discourse is twofold: '[W]e may first identify within the discourse allusions to the story and seek to discern its general outlines; then, in a second phase of inquiry we may ask how this story shapes the logic of argumentation in the discourse'.[15] Hays' work on the relation between narrative and discourse laid the first solid foundations for a contemporary brand of narrative approach to Paul.[16]

Hays' differentiation of two distinct aspects in Paul's thinking (i.e., 'substructure' and 'reflective discourse') resembles the work of others. For instance, 1983 also saw the appearance of Daniel Patte's 'Structural Introduction to the Pauline Letters' (as the subtitle announced).[17] In it, he distinguished between ideas articulated within a text and the convictional world or

---

13. Hays, *The Faith of Jesus Christ*, 21–22; 2nd edn, 22–24. Cf. N.R. Petersen (*Rediscovering Paul: Philemon and the Sociology of Paul's Narrative World* [Philadelphia: Fortress Press, 1985] 47–53), who distinguishes between 'poetic sequence' and 'referential sequence'.

14. Hays, *The Faith of Jesus Christ*, 28 (1st and 2nd edn).

15. Hays, *The Faith of Jesus Christ*, 28; 2nd edn, 29.

16. Narrative approach of different kinds are pursued by D. Trobisch ('How to Read an Ancient Letter Collection: Prolegomena to a Narrative Critical Study of the Letters of Paul', SBL International Conference 1999, Lahti [21/7/99]), who gives it a canonical twist, and by Petersen (*Rediscovering Paul*), who gives it a sociological twist.

17. In *Paul's Faith and the Power of the Gospel* (Philadelphia: Fortress Press, 1983).

'symbolic universe' underlying those ideas.[18] The convictional world is defended by means of articulated ideas, although it remains 'in the background of a discourse'; it 'provides the principle of organization of an argument and . . . , therefore, is not directly apparent. Because of its function, it *undergirds* the argument'. Patte's main interest was not in any aspect of the text per se but in the structures of the convictional world from which the theological discourse of a text emerges.

So too, in his 1985 work *Rediscovering Paul*, Norman Petersen set himself the task of working though Paul's 'theologizing to the symbolic universe it presupposes', defining 'symbolic universe' as 'a primary (pre-reflective) form of knowledge' to which 'theology' is 'a secondary (reflective) form that is dependent on it [i.e., the symbolic universe]'.[19] Consequently, for Petersen

> 'theology' is a form of conceptual 'machinery' by which the symbolic universe is maintained . . . a form of systematic reflection upon it. . . . Like all machineries for universe-maintenance, theology responds to the experience of problems in living within the inherited symbolic universe, whether these problems originate in failures of the universe or in competing representations or interpretations of it.[20]

In the early 1990s, N.T. Wright advocated a model mapping out the processes of human cognition in a way that placed narrative at the heart of the matter, sandwiched between a 'symbolic universe' (or 'worldview' as he prefers to call it) and theological articulations.[21] For Wright, 'worldviews' operate at a 'presuppositional, pre-cognitive stage',[22] operating 'like the foundations of a house: vital, but invisible'. Worldviews find expression primarily through stories ('worldview-by-means-of-story'): 'worldviews provide the *stories* through which human beings view reality. Narrative is the most characteristic expression of worldview, going deeper than the isolated observation or fragmented remark'. According to Wright, through stories 'one can in principle discover how to answer the basic questions that determine human existence: who are we, where are we, what is wrong, and what is the solution?'[23] Answers to these questions

---

18. See esp. *Paul's Faith*, 3–27.

19. *Rediscovering Paul*, 30.

20. *Rediscovering Paul*, 60.

21. *The New Testament and the People of God* (London: SPCK, 1992), esp. chapters 2 and 5. Wright notes (123 n. 5) the overlap of his use of 'worldview' with P.L. Berger and T. Luckmann's use of 'symbolic universe' (*The Social Construction of Reality: A Treatise in The Sociology of Knowledge* [Garden City, N.Y.: Doubleday, 1966]).

22. *The New Testament and the People of God*, 122. The quotations that follow are taken from 122–37 (with emphases usually removed), where a full elaboration of the model appears.

23. Other means of expressing a worldview are symbols (which reinforce the divide between insiders and outsiders) and actions (which reflect intention and motivation, often 'speaking louder than words').

are provided by a narrative that supports subsequent beliefs and convictions. The stories that give expression to a worldview are not *illustrative* of beliefs but are *generative* of them, giving form to them, being located 'at a more fundamental level than explicitly formulated beliefs, including theological beliefs'.[24]

Here, then, is a broad mapping of the relationship between narrative and nonnarrative aspects of human cognition in a tripartite scheme (worldview, narrative [along with other forms of articulation: e.g., symbols, action], and beliefs). Applied to Paul, Wright argues the following:

> Within all his letters, though particularly in Romans and Galatians, we discover a larger implicit narrative. . . . Paul presupposes this story even when he does not expound it directly, and it is arguable that we can only understand the more limited narrative worlds of the different letters if we locate them at their appropriate points within this overall story-world, and indeed within the symbolic universe that accompanies it.[25]

For Wright, as for others, narrative contours in the Pauline cognitive landscape are not simply the product of deeper theological processes but are themselves generative of theological articulations.

In 1994, Ben Witherington similarly distinguished between three aspects in the fabric of Pauline theologising:

> (1) Paul's symbolic universe, which entails those things that Paul takes to be inherently true and real, the fixed stars in Paul's mental sky; (2) Paul's narrative thought world, which is Paul's reflections on his symbolic universe in terms of the grand Story. This undergirds (3) Paul's articulation of his theology, ethics, and so forth, in response to the situations he must address.[26]

Polemicising against those who outline Paul's theology according to a neatly packaged 'collection of topics . . . arranged in a logical order', Witherington speaks of 'a fundamental Story out of which all his discourse arises',[27] a narrative

---

24. *The New Testament and the People of God*, 38.

25. *The New Testament and the People of God*, 405. In the corporate consultation of this project (see 'Interests of the Present Project' below), Wright announced that he would want to qualify this statement somewhat, so that Romans and Galatians are not the only prime examples of implicit narratives at work in Paul's letters.

26. *Paul's Narrative Thought World*, 6 n. 7. Whereas Hays employs a bipartite scheme in modelling Paul's cognitive landscape, Wright and Witherington employ a tripartite scheme.

27. Witherington, *Paul's Narrative Thought World*, 2, elaborated further there. For instance, Witherington speaks of the macro-Story as primarily grounded in the Hebrew scriptures, and as having been influenced by his understanding of later traditions (Jewish, Graeco-Roman, Christian), by his theological reflection, and by the experiences of God in Christ shared by Paul and other early Christians.

organisational phenomenon that may not always be articulated explicitly in Paul's letters.[28]

The language of narrative is now emerging in Pauline scholarship with sufficient frequency that it is no longer novel to speak of a narrative dimension in Paul's theologising. Narrative is now mentioned regularly in diverse contexts in the study of Paul. These include erudite gatherings of leading scholars in their efforts to synthesise Paul's theology;[29] helpful introductions to Paul's thought, life and letters;[30] and informed studies of Paul's theology.[31] Not all of these share the detailed methodological rigour exhibited in the work of Hays and Wright, finding the language of 'narrative' to be useful in the study of Paul without much methodological scaffolding. Nonetheless, despite their varied investment in and use of the term 'narrative', the term itself is rapidly becoming commonplace in analyses of Paul's letters and theology.

Many who find a narrative dimension in Paul's letters differentiate between various narrative components, identifying a variety of distinct stories (e.g., God, Israel, and Jesus). These narrative components are frequently said to inform and influence each other in different ways at different times, thereby resulting in Paul's distinct theological discourse at any given moment. This 'internarrational' aspect will be explored further below but needs to be noted here, since it is a significant feature of contemporary interest in narrative and Paul.

We have seen, then, that narrative is gaining a foothold among a significant number of prominent Pauline scholars. Narrative is increasingly becoming a tool for analysing *how* Paul's mind worked in order better to appreciate *what* he said and *how* he said it. When assessing the nature and processes of Paul's theological reflection (not merely the theological product of that process), nar-

---

28. Witherington (*Paul's Narrative Thought World*, 4) speaks of there being not only 'clear expressions' but also simple 'hints' of narrative theology undergirding Paul's letters.

29. See for instance the final articles in the first volume of the SBL Pauline Theology group's efforts; J.M. Bassler (ed.), *Pauline Theology, Volume 1: Thessalonians, Philippians, Galatians, Philemon* (Minneapolis: Fortress Press, 1991).

30. Besides Witherington's *Paul's Narrative Thought World*, see D. Horrell, *An Introduction to the Study of Paul* (Continuum Biblical Studies Series; London: Continuum, 2000) 55–56.

31. Besides those already mentioned, J.D.G. Dunn (*The Theology of Paul the Apostle* [Edinburgh: T&T Clark, 1998] 17–18) entertains the notion that the 'multilayered character' of Paul's discourse might profitably be viewed as a product of a 'narrative theology' from which that discourse emerges, although he prefers a 'dialogical' model. F.J. Matera (*New Testament Christology* [Louisville, Ky.: Westminster John Knox Press, 1999] 86) contends that a narrative structure gives coherence to Paul's varied statements 'about God, Christ, Israel, the gentiles, and creation'.

rative has increasingly come into play, probing the mechanisms of 'theologis-ing' that lies behind the theological content of Paul's letters.[32]

## THE INTERESTS OF THE PRESENT PROJECT

The suggestion that narrative features in Paul's texts are the tip of a narrative iceberg makes the narrative project in Pauline scholarship both abstruse and tan-talising: abstruse, since tracking extracompositional components and processes is an enterprise inevitably subject to conjectural supposition; tantalising, since it promises entry into the very 'machinery' of Paul's theological reflection. The prospect of advances in our understanding of Paul makes the claims of those who advocate a narrative approach to Paul suggestive and attractive. For this reason, assessing the approach in its infancy is of pressing concern.

The chapters that follow in this book comprise the first attempt by a group of Pauline scholars to assess the merits and demerits of the narrative approach to Paul. The interpreters have not been asked to participate because of a prior commitment to a narrative Paul. Most of the participants in this project have never previously declared an explicit view on a narrative approach to Paul, nor were they canvassed for their views prior to their inclusion in the project. No attempt was made to ensure that a balanced consensus would emerge. Only three things unite the participants in this project: (1) their credentials as Pauline scholars of repute, (2) their position within the closely knit scholarly community of British New Testament studies, and (3) their interest in assess-ing the narrative approach in its infancy.

An assessment of the narrative approach to Paul requires common point of access to ensure that the participants' potential diversity of interest and opin-ion is kept within workable parameters. In this regard, a decision was taken early on to structure the project according to a particular enumeration of nar-rative ingredients within Paul's 'thought world'. Proponents of the narrative

---

32. If narrative features underlie Paul's epistolary discourse, this may well have important implications in other areas of investigation into early Christianity. It would, for instance, waylay the temptation found all too often in contemporary work on the Gospels to credit later Christian figures (e.g., the author of Mark's gospel) with the first exercises in early Christian narrative theology. In *The Real Jesus* (San Francisco: HarperSanFrancisco, 1997), L.T. Johnson identifies twelve narrative features of Paul's discourse, rightly concluding in the following manner: 'These Pauline statements occur outside a narrative framework. We would not recognize them as part of a "story" without extant narratives where they also occur. . . . [Nonetheless] Paul can assume . . . that the Roman church, which he had never met, had as firm a possession of these basic aspects of the Jesus story as did his own Corinthian community' (120; cf. also 158).

study of Paul frequently differentiate several narrative ingredients, although their taxonomies vary. Wright, for instance, prefers to speak largely of a single story operative in Paul's thinking: the 'story of God, Israel and the world as now compressed into the story of Jesus',[33] or 'the story of Israel understood as the story through which the creator God is restoring the creation, and with it the race of Adam and Eve'.[34] Matera identified three narrative ingredients within a larger unfolding story: 'the story of Israel', 'the story of Christ', 'the story of his [Paul's] own life'.[35] Like Wright, Witherington wants to maintain the integrity of an overarching macro-Story, but Witherington finds it advisable to do so by identifying four distinct microstories within it:

> (1) the story of a world gone wrong; (2) the story of Israel in that world; (3) the story of Christ, which arises out of the story of Israel and humankind on the human side of things, but in a larger sense arises out of the very story of God as creator and redeemer; and (4) the story of Christians, including Paul himself, which arises out of all three of these previous stories and is the hinge, crucial turning point, and climax of the entire larger drama, which more than anything else affects how *the* Story will ultimately turn out.[36]

For his part, Dunn identifies five distinct narrative ingredients:

> [W]e could readily speak of the substructure of Paul's theology as the story of God and creation, with the story of Israel superimposed upon it. On top of that again we have the story of Jesus, and then Paul's own story, with the initial intertwining of these last two stories as the decisive turning point in Paul's life and theology. Finally, there are the complex interactions of Paul's own story with the stories of those who had believed before him and those who came to form the churches founded by them.[37]

---

33. *The New Testament and the People of God*, 79.

34. *The New Testament and the People of God*, 407.

35. Matera, *New Testament Christology*, 86. In his *The Origins of Christian Morality* (New Haven, Conn.: Yale University Press, 1993), W. Meeks discusses three critical 'stories' in the formation of early Christianity: those of Jesus, Israel, and the cosmos (196, 205).

36. Witherington, *Paul's Narrative Thought World*, 5. This enumeration corresponds with that of J. Goldingay, who considers 'biblical theology' to be a narrative enterprise. Goldingay argues that a New Testament theological narrative incorporates the following features: Who is God? Who is Israel? Who is Jesus? Who is the church? ('Biblical Narrative and Systematic Theology', in M. Turner and J. Green [eds], *Between Two Horizons* [Grand Rapids: Eerdmans, 2000] 123–42, 127).

37. *The Theology of Paul the Apostle* (Edinburgh: T&T Clark, 1998) 18. Precisely these five stories are outlined as existing within Paul's thought by Cupitt (*What is a Story?*, 114–15).

This model of five fluid but identifiable stories has been selected as the structural model for this project. It is representative of the internarrational aspect that has preponderance among proponents of the narrative approach, and its proposed microstories permit effective delineation of subject matter. Of Dunn's five narrative components, the first four are fairly clear: (1) God and creation, (2) Israel, (3) Jesus, and (4) Paul.

The fifth narrative element requires further definition, however. Dunn defines it as 'the stories of those who had believed before him and those who came to form the churches founded by them'. The scope of this is potentially quite large, as Dunn's use of the plural 'stories' assumes. With this narrative level, Dunn envisages especially the earliest Christian communities in general, including both (1) predecessors who 'believed before him' in the Christian movement and (2) inheritors 'who came to form the churches' founded by those predecessors. Consequently, for purposes of this project, this fifth narrative element is described as 'The Stories of Predecessors and Inheritors'. But since Dunn's definition would seem to exclude the communities founded by Paul himself, the liberty has been taken of broadening the scope to include Paul's own communities (e.g., those of Galatia). Moreover, since the notion of 'predecessors in faith' will, in good Pauline fashion, also include Abraham, the scope of this narrative group expands further, to meet Paul's own theological interests.[38]

Having selected Dunn's five narrative components as the template to follow for the structure of this project, two further factors needed to be taken into consideration. First, it was decided that an analysis of narrative elements throughout the whole of the Pauline corpus would be an unrealistic option, threatening to be unwieldy. Some restriction in the scope of selected texts needed to be introduced. Second, an analysis of narrative relationships in a single Pauline text was thought to be an unhelpful option, threatening to be too restrictive. Proponents of the narrative approach regularly recognise that narrative features are influenced by contextual and rhetorical factors. In one sense, identifying narrative elements is preliminary to the more interesting task of discerning how they are combined on any particular occasion. Accordingly, the number of selected texts must be greater than one if the dynamics of Paul's narrative reflection are to be adequately assessed.

In light of these considerations, two Pauline texts have been chosen as test cases for this project: Galatians and Romans. Each is undisputedly written by Paul; each has significant content overlap with the other; each is the product of situational

---

38. For this reason, Andrew Lincoln, who accepted the commission to write about this conglomerate of stories, was permitted a longer word length.

differences; and each evidences the five narrative strands identified by Dunn. Moreover, as we have seen, Wright has identified these two letters as the most fertile for narrative interpretation: 'Within all his letters, though particularly in Romans and Galatians, we discover a larger implicit narrative.' While restricting analysis to these two texts is somewhat artificial, it will facilitate the main goal of this project (to determine the presence and significance of narrative elements in Pauline texts and thought) while incorporating within the assessment process the recognition that contingent factors affect Paul's theological articulations.

Within these parameters, and with a provisional draft of this introductory chapter in hand, contributors to this project have been asked to consider particular narrative ingredients in Galatians and Romans, deliberating on such questions as the following:

1. Do Galatians and Romans share a basic, identifiable, coherent story of 'X'? If so, how does this story impact on other stories in those texts? Which stories does it affect most prominently? Does it do so in a similar fashion in both texts?
2. If both Galatians and Romans do not share an identifiable story of 'X', are there distinct stories of 'X' in Galatians and Romans? If so, to what is the difference attributable? How do those stories impact on other stories in each text? Do they show similar characteristics in this regard?
3. What is the potential of the narrative approach to Paul?

Issues of this sort have not acted prescriptively in the articles that follow but served initially as a common starting point for the various contributors,[39] from which their own interests have developed in relation to their subject matter.[40]

One overarching issue pertaining to the narrative approach to Paul concerns the 'location' of the respective narrative ingredients. If narrative has a place in Pauline study, where do those narrative elements reside? Are they simply read off the page, being 'in the text' itself, available to any reader of the epistolary 'surface'? Or are they primarily 'beneath the text', forming something like a 'narra-

---

39. This starting point has some affinity with the methodological procedures articulated by Hays (*The Faith of Jesus Christ*, 28; 2nd edn, 29): '[W]e may first identify within the discourse allusions to the story and seek to discern its general outlines; then, in a second phase of inquiry we may ask how this story shapes the logic of argumentation in the discourse.'

40. Several contributors to this book offer their own retrospective on the rise of narrative interests in Paul in a way that coheres with the retrospective offered in this chapter. Since their retrospectives are integral to their respective arguments, the inevitable overlap was deemed acceptable. For a fuller version of my own assessment of the influences behind this approach, see my 'The Narrative Approach to Paul: An Early Retrospective', *CurBS* 10 (2002). The adjective 'early' signals my view that the approach will continue to bear productive fruit for the foreseeable future.

tive substructure' that is signalled in but largely assumed by the text? Or are they simply 'in front of the text'—that is, heuristic devices that aid interpretation by serving as organisational templates without claiming narrative to be necessarily essential to the subject matter itself? Since individual narratives might lie at different 'levels', it was deemed appropriate for the contributors to explore these matters in connection with the subject matter of their assignment, rather than assuming in advance that all of the proposed narratives lie at a particular level.

With these parameters established, a lineup of twelve contributors was arranged. Of them, five were asked to write initial articles on one of the five main stories: Dr Eddie Adams (on God and creation), Dr Bruce Longenecker (on Israel), Dr Douglas Campbell (on Jesus), Professor John Barclay (on Paul), and Professor Andrew Lincoln (on predecessors and inheritors). Since these scholars have already published in their designated areas,[41] they are well qualified to look afresh at Pauline texts with narrative interests in order to assess the distinctive contribution of a narrative approach.

These five contributions were then passed to five further contributors, each of whom was asked to critique one of the initial articles: Dr Barry Matlock (on Adams), Professor Morna Hooker (on Longenecker), Professor Graham Stanton (on Campbell), Dr David Horrell (on Barclay), and Professor Howard Marshall (on Lincoln). These ten contributions were circulated to each participant a month prior to an overnight consultation involving all participants, joined also by Tom Wright. On that occasion, they were asked to discuss the feasibility of the narrative approach by debating details, teasing out issues, exposing assumptions, discussing terminology, reflecting on potential strengths and weaknesses of this project, and considering the approach's prospects for the future. This corporate consultation was an essential feature of the project. It ensured that the contributions to this book are not simply essays on a common theme written independently by scholars in their offices and cobbled together within a single book cover as if to suggest an overall coherence. Each of the

---

41. E. Adams, *Constructing the World: A Study in Paul's Cosmological Language* (SNTW; Edinburgh: T&T Clark, 2000); B.W. Longenecker, 'Different Answers to Different Questions: Israel, Israel, the Gentiles and Salvation History in Romans 9-11', *JSNT* 36 (1989): 95–123, and *The Triumph of Abraham's God: Transformation and Identity in Galatians* (Edinburgh: T&T Clark, 1998); D.A. Campbell, *The Rhetoric of Righteousness in Romans 3:21–26* (JSNTSup 65; Sheffield: Sheffield Academic Press, 1992); J.M.G. Barclay, 'Paul: An Anomalous Diaspora Jew', in *Jews in the Mediterranean Diaspora: From Alexander to Trajan (323 BCE–117 CE)* (Edinburgh: T&T Clark, 1996) 381–95; A.T. Lincoln, 'Abraham goes to Rome: Paul's Treatment of Abraham in Romans 4', in M.J. Wilkens et al. (eds), *Worship, Theology and Ministry in the Early Church* (JSNTSup 87; Sheffield: Sheffield Academic Press, 1992) 163–79, and 'Tradition, Gospel and Audience in the Theology of Romans 1:18–4:25', in D.M. Hay and E.E. Johnson (eds), *Pauline Theology, Volume III: Romans* (Minneapolis: Fortress Press, 1995) 130–59.

ten initial contributions has been the subject of peer scrutiny and debate in the context of the corporate consultation, and each author has had the opportunity to rework his or her original contribution in the light of that consultative process. In this way, the consultative process added an extra dynamic to our individual offerings and took the creative process to a new level.

To cap off the exercise, Professor James Dunn and Professor Francis Watson were asked to assess the merits or demerits, the strengths and weaknesses, of this project in particular and of the narrative approach to Paul in general, in the light of the ten exegetical offerings and the corporate consultation. They were not asked to summarise the group's findings (not least since collective 'findings' were not part of this project's agenda) but simply to interact with broader issues raised by and within the project, unrestrained as the others had been by any particular narrative assignment.

If interest in the narrative dimensions of Paul's thought have risen dramatically since the early 1980s, the same was true for narrative theology in the 'systematic' disciplines throughout the late 1960s and 1970s. In 1981, in the wake of the groundswell of interest in narrative theology, G. Stroup wrote the following:

> During the last ten years a new approach to theological reflection has emerged under the rubric of 'narrative theology'. As is the case with most new proposals in theology, it remains to be seen whether narrative theology is only another fad in theological discussion or whether it is a substantive contribution to the task of making Christian faith intelligible in the contemporary world.[42]

Stroup, therefore, took it upon himself to explore the possibilities and potentials of the newly conceived narrative theology. Twenty years after Stroup, a similar paragraph could be written with regard to recent attempts to situate Paul within the camp of the narrative theologians. Are such proposals simply faddish, or might they represent a substantive contribution to the task of interpreting, understanding, and appreciating Paul? The following contributions seek to elucidate these issues. The contributors do not speak with one voice. They have not sought common ground for its own sake nor attempted to arrive at some bland uniformity based on the lowest common denominator. Their interests were uniform, but their tasks were distinct, and the way they carried out those tasks owes as much to the nature of the tasks themselves as to their individual approaches and independent starting points. We hope that the articles that follow will enhance the flourishing discipline of Pauline studies and act as early guides to the possibilities and pitfalls of approaching Paul's texts in narrative light.

---

42. Stroup, *Narrative Theology*, 6.

# PART 2

# Narrative Studies of Galatians and Romans

# 2

# Paul's Story of God and Creation

## The Story of How God
## Fulfils His Purposes in Creation

EDWARD ADAMS

My remit in this essay is to investigate the presence and significance of a suggested 'story of God and creation' in Romans and Galatians. I propose to undertake this task by applying a set of questions to each text. The primary question I will ask is, Can a story about God and creation be identified in the letter? If this question can be answered positively, then several follow-up questions may be posed: How does the story influence Paul's theological argumentation? How does the story illuminate the 'theme' or 'themes' of the letter? How does the story function for its recipients (or, What is its social significance)? But before I can address these questions, a few basic issues need to be settled. What is 'narrative', and what are its most typical characteristics? How should the story topic 'God and creation' be defined? Which textual features of the letters should count as the potential ingredients of a story with *this* topic? I begin, then, with these preliminary considerations.

## 'NARRATIVE' AND ITS DEFINING CHARACTERISTICS

If we are going to look for traces of narrative in the letters of Paul, we must make some effort to clarify what we are seeking to find. We need to be able to say what a story *is* and what its essential characteristics are.[1] The definition of

---

1. As the editor has indicated in his Introduction, no prior definition of 'narrative' or 'story' has been imposed upon the contributors to this volume. In this essay, I am using 'narrative' and 'story' interchangeably, as does the main theorist on which I draw, M.J. Toolan, in his book, *Narrative: A Critical Linguistic Approach* (London: Routledge, 1988).

'story' we choose for the task before us, it seems to me, should satisfy three criteria. First, it should be practically useful for this investigation. If it is going to serve as a genuinely helpful descriptive and analytical tool, it must be neither too general or bland to be of discriminatory use nor too specific to be applicable to forms of discourse other than those that are most *obviously* narrative (e.g., fairy tales, comic strips, conventional novels, gospels). Second, it should not be an arbitrary definition, formulated just to suit the particular needs of this exercise. Rather, it should be soundly based in established narrative theory. Third, it should resonate with our general experience and expectations of narrative. It ought to be sufficiently intuitive to gain a measure of common assent.

Defining 'story' has proved a difficult and precarious task even for theorists of narrative. Michael Toolan offers what he calls a 'minimalist' definition of narrative that, I hope, should not prove to be too controversial and that, I believe, will give us a solid foundation on which to build. He describes narrative as 'a perceived sequence of non-randomly connected events'.[2] As Toolan explains, this basic account makes three key points. The first is that a story is a sequence of *events*. An event, in narrative theory, is a 'change of state'. It presupposes an existing state or set of conditions and consists in an action or occurrence that brings about a change to that state or set of circumstances.[3] Events or 'changes of state' are crucial to narrative. Without them, there would be no story to recount. The second point is that a story is a series of *nonrandomly* linked events. A succession of facts or occurrences does not in itself constitute a narrative. The events described must be seen as *consequentially* linked and not merely sequentially ordered.[4] *Relationships* (whether of cause, motivation, contingency, or some other interconnecting principle) between the events must be identifiable. Thirdly, the nonrandom links between events should be *perceived*. According to Toolan, the activity of perceiving consequential relations in a sequence of events is 'the enabling condition for narrative'.[5] This activity, he insists, is performed by the receiver. It is the receiver's prerogative to decide whether a text or a set of textual features constitutes a narrative. It is not illegitimate to enquire whether the consequential connectedness perceived by the receiver was intended and planned by

---

2. Toolan, *Narrative*, 7.

3. Toolan, *Narrative*, 7. S. Chatman (*Story and Discourse: Narrative Structure in Fiction and Film* [Ithaca, N.Y.: Cornell University Press, 1978] 32, 44–45) divides 'events' into 'actions', in which an existent (a character or an element of setting) is the agent of the event, and 'happenings', where the existent is the patient.

4. Toolan, *Narrative*, 7.

5. Toolan, *Narrative*, 9.

the author or teller of the story. But this, for Toolan, is an additional speculation, beyond the identification of a text or elements in a text as 'story'.[6]

This description focuses on the most basic criteria that must be met for a text or certain features of a text to be considered narrative. But as Toolan recognises, readers require, indeed *demand*, more of narrative than simply a succession of nonrandomly linked events.[7] We can thus build on this foundational definition by adding to it characteristics most readers would regard as essential to or typical of narrative.[8] Three features in particular may be specified.

The first is *characters*. The presence of characters, most theorists would agree, is a fundamental requirement in narrative.[9] It is difficult to imagine how a story could be recognisably a 'story' without them. As readers, we look for the events recounted in a narrative to be caused or experienced by individuals to whom we can relate. Characters, at least in plot-driven narratives (as opposed to character-centred ones), often play familiar *roles*, such as protagonist and adversary, and fulfil certain expected *functions*. A highly serviceable scheme of character roles and functions is A.J. Greimas' well-known actant model.[10] Greimas identified six main participant roles or actants in stories: sender, subject, object, receiver, opponent, and helper. The six roles are usually set out diagrammatically as follows:

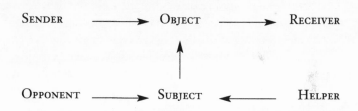

---

6. Ibid.

7. Toolan, *Narrative*, 8.

8. What follows assumes that readers have certain narrative expectations, definite ideas about what a story should contain and how it should proceed. Such expectations are shaped by readers' social, cultural, and literary conditioning. Narratives that do not conform to readers' expectations or actively subvert them (e.g., by resisting the desire for an ending or resolution) still depend on such intuitions for their impact. See further J. Culler, 'Defining Narrative Units', in R. Fowler (ed.), *Style and Structure in Literature: Essays in the New Stylistics* (Oxford: Blackwell, 1975) 123–42.

9. E.g., Chatman, *Story*, 19, 113.

10. For a summary and explanation of Greimas' model see R.B. Hays, *The Faith of Jesus Christ: An Investigation of the Narrative Substructure of Galatians 3:1–4:11* (Chico, Calif.: Scholars Press, 1983) 98–103. Greimas' mode of analysis builds on the earlier work of V. Propp, *The Morphology of the Folktale*, 2nd edn, trans. L. Scott (Austin: University of Texas Press, 1968).

Richard Hays made profitable use of Greimas' character typology in his groundbreaking study of narrative elements in Paul's christological argumentation in Galatians, *The Faith of Jesus Christ*.[11] The scheme has its practical limitations and theoretical shortcomings,[12] but its basic categories can be fruitfully exploited in an exercise such as the present one. In addition to having roles and functions, characters also possess certain *traits*.[13] A character's qualities are revealed either explicitly through the evaluative comments of the narrator or other participants in the story, or implicitly through the way in which the character acts in the events of the narrative. We can hardly expect complex characterisation in the argumentation of Romans and Galatians. Whatever character traits we may find are likely to be of a very basic kind.

A second feature most would regard as essential to narrative is *setting*. Toolan thinks that setting is less crucial to narrative than characters, but he states that the establishment of a clear setting is 'a strong psychological preference in most readers'.[14] As readers, we like to know where and when the events of a narrative happened (even a fictional one). We look for explicit topographical and chronological indicators to locate the story in space and time. The degree of specificity as to setting varies from genre to genre and story type to story type. Also, the degree to which setting contributes to the narrative differs from story to story.[15] It may simply provide a background to the story, but sometimes, Toolan points out, it can play a more active part in the tale. In some instances, a setting may become like a character; it can be 'quasi-animate'.[16]

A third quality most would consider to be intrinsic to narrative is *trajectory*. As readers we want a narrative 'to go somewhere'.[17] We expect some sort of development and a conclusion or climax. Aristotle famously stated in his *Poet-*

---

11. Hays, *The Faith of Jesus Christ*, 104–125. For another application to Paul's argumentation, see N.T. Wright, *The Climax of the Covenant: Christ and the Law in Pauline Theology* (Edinburgh: T&T Clark, 1991) 204–216.

12. Despite structuralist claims that such a model is applicable to *all* narratives, the schema is best suited to simple stories such as traditional folktales. It is much less useful for the study of complex and intricate plots and detailed characterisation. A theoretical problem with the model is that it reduces the *status* of characters in narratives to a functional one (i.e., it assumes that participants exist in a story only to fulfil certain plot requirements).

13. See Chatman, *Story*, 120–38.

14. Toolan, *Narrative*, 103.

15. Ibid.

16. Toolan, *Narrative*, 104. Toolan cites as examples of quasianimate settings the Chancery environment in *Bleak House* and Miss Havisham's dining room in *Great Expectations*.

17. Toolan, *Narrative*, 104.

*ics* that well-constructed plots should have 'a beginning and middle and end'.[18] He defined a beginning as 'that which is not a necessary consequent of anything else but after which something else exists or happens as a natural result'. An end is 'the natural result of something else but from which nothing else follows'. A middle 'follows something else and something follows from it'. [19] The notions of causality and finality entailed in this description are problematic, but these difficulties aside, Aristotle's basic dictum, I am sure, would command general assent.

Theoretical models of narrative trajectory tend to follow Aristotle's division of plot structure into 'complication' ('tying', δέσις) and 'denouement' ('loosing', λύσις), around a key turning point, a 'reversal' (περιπέτεια).[20] Michael O'Toole highlights the basic pattern. A story begins with an initial state of rest or condition of normality.[21] The equilibrium is disturbed by forces of some kind (physical, psychological, social, supernatural, etc.). The disequilibrium intensifies until it reaches an apogee. An action or intervention occurs to reverse the process, leading to the gradual restoration of the original state of normality or the establishment of a new equilibrium. This model would certainly not fit all narratives.[22] It works best for folktales and formulaic narratives (e.g., Hollywood blockbusters). But it is eminently recognisable as a 'classic' story structure.

On the basis of these core and typical features of narrative, a definition of 'story' can be formulated that I hope will meet the criteria set for this exercise:

> A story/narrative is a series of events that can be perceived as sequentially and consequentially connected. Typically, stories have characters, settings, and a trajectory.

With this definition in place, a basic interpretative principle may be proposed. If we can perceive within the variegated textual data that constitute Paul's letters a chain of interconnected events, with participants and elements of setting,

18. Aristotle, *Poetics*, 7.3. Beginning, middle and end are products of the composition process (the '*sjuzhet*', as the Russian Formalists called it), not elements of the basic story material itself (the '*fabula*'). Cf. Chatman, *Story*, 47.

19. Aristotle, *Poetics*, 7.4–7.

20. Aristotle, *Poetics*, 11.1; 18.1–3. Aristotle was speaking specifically of the structure of tragedy.

21. M. O'Toole, 'Narrative Structure', in R. Fowler (ed.), *A Dictionary of Modern Critical Terms*, rev. edn (London: Routledge, 1987) 158–59. Cf. Toolan, *Narrative*, 8.

22. It would be less applicable to what Chatman (*Story*, 48) calls 'revelatory' plots, in which a state of affairs is laid open rather than changed. Aristotle (*Poetics* 11.1–7) distinguished between 'reversals' (changes of situation) and 'discoveries' (changes from ignorance to knowledge). But he thought that the best plots contain both a reversal and a discovery and make the two coincident.

that form a coherent trajectory with beginning, middle and end, we may speak of the presence of a 'story'. The complete chain of events may not be present in any one section or portion of text (even though there are specific passages in Paul's epistles that clearly form self-contained 'narratives'; e.g., 2 Cor. 12:3–10; Gal. 1:13–2:14). The interconnections that make up the narrative trajectory may emerge in a number of distinct passages, and they may not necessarily appear in their logical, sequential order.

In line with Toolan's minimalist definition, we will not make Paul's *intention* to construct a narrative a condition for identifying a set of textual features as 'story'. However, we will certainly wish to address the question of whether the 'story' we might discern was to some degree planned by the author.

## TOPIC AND CONSTITUENTS
## OF THE PROPOSED STORY

My task in this essay is not only to consider whether we can isolate 'story' features in two of Paul's letters but also to explore a particular story with a particular content: a story of God and creation. As we have attempted to define the category 'story', so we must specify the topic 'God and creation'[23] and establish, in principle, the textual material out of which a 'story of God and creation' might be fashioned.

The story topic I have been assigned to investigate, 'God and creation', could be understood narrowly as referring to the story of God's *formation* of the world (taking 'creation' as a *process*). This interpretation would limit our database in Romans and Galatians to allusions to Genesis 1–2 and other references to God's generation of the universe and would restrict our story to an account of how God made the world. But such a topic, it is clear, holds little appeal for Paul. He is less interested in *how* God created than in the divine *purposes* in creation. God's original work of creation, reaching its climax in the making of humanity, as set out in Genesis 1–2, serves for Paul as the starting point (or departure point) for a development, not a self-contained story in its own right. On the other hand, the topic could be interpreted broadly as embracing God's comprehensive dealings with the world that God has made (taking 'creation' as a *product*), both the human world and the nonhuman world, with God as sustainer, sovereign, judge, and redeemer, as described in our texts. But this would plainly be far too wide a definition for the exercise

---

23. J.D.G.Dunn, on whose five-story model this whole project is structured, does not clarify what he means by 'the story of God and creation' (*The Theology of Paul the Apostle* [Grand Rapids: Eerdmans, 1998] 18).

on hand. The raw material for a story with such a topic would be virtually every theological statement in Romans and Galatians!

For the purpose of this study, I propose the following defininition of 'story of God and creation': *the story of how God brings to fulfilment his original purposes in creating humanity and the universe as a whole.*[24] This definition presupposes continuity between God's creative agenda and God's redemptive and eschatological activity in Paul's theological perspective. Such a story would have a specific and fixed reference point in God's creative work in the past (Genesis 1–2)[25] and would trace the progress and history of God's creative aims. It would incorporate a 'fall' event (Genesis 3),[26] an occurrence that jeopardises the advancement of God's creative ideals, and also redemptive events, if these events are depicted as restoring or completing God's intended plan for creation. A story of this kind would be narrow enough for us to investigate within present confines and yet (potentially) significant enough to be worthy of our investigation.

With the story topic defined in this way, it seems reasonable to stipulate that the primary textual data from which the constituents of the story may be derived should be 'Adam' motifs and Paul's uses of them to construct the human and cosmic plight, to explicate the Christ event, and to depict human and cosmic redemption. By 'Adam' motifs, I do not just mean explicit references to the figure of Adam and allusions to the story of Adam and Eve in Genesis 2–3, but also allusions to the creation account of Genesis 1 (especially the formation of humankind, male and female, in the image of God, and the creator's mandate to human creatures to rule over the earth, Gen. 1:26–28); echoes of Psalm 8 (especially the creation of human beings for glory and honour and the subjugation of the rest the world to humanity, Psa. 8:5–8); and allusions to subsequent Jewish speculation about Adam, his original state (his 'glory'), and the effects of his (and/or Eve's) transgression. Limiting ourselves to Adam motifs and their applications will obviously restrict the range of information from which a 'story of God and creation' can be reconstructed, especially in the case of Galatians, but it should help to maintain the quality and clarity of the evidence and leave us less open to (though not completely free from) charges of speculative analysis.

---

24. This definition almost certainly gives the story a narrower focus than Dunn intended.

25. As F. Watson states (*Text and Truth: Redefining Biblical Theology* [Edinburgh: T&T Clark, 1997] 225), the biblical notion of the creation of the world is one of the very few types of narrative event that would serve as Aristotle's absolute beginning.

26. I am using the term 'fall' here and elsewhere in this essay quite loosely, and am not importing into the investigation the later Christian doctrine of 'the fall'.

Having dealt with these issues of definition and method, we can now proceed to our epistles, beginning with Romans (concentrating on Romans 1–8). For obvious reasons, I will devote almost all my attention to this letter.

## PASSAGES IN ROMANS WITH CLEAR 'ADAM' MOTIFS

One passage in Romans deals explicitly and unambiguously with Adam: 5:12–21. There are four other passages in which, in my view, Adam motifs can be identified with a fairly high degree of confidence: 3:23; 7:7–13; 8:19–22; and 8:28–30. A reasonable case can be made for the presence of Adam themes in 1:18–32; 2:1–11 (specifically 2:7, 10); and 4:1–25 (specifically 4:13, 21). The allusions to Adam in these texts, however, are somewhat more controversial or less obvious than the proceeding set. In addition to all of these are a couple of passages that, I would argue, 'carry over' an Adam theme from a preceding passage: 6:1–23 and 7:14–25. At this stage of the exercise, we will concentrate on the five portions of text that are more clearly Adamic. If we can extricate a basic story of God and creation from these segments, we may then turn to the other passages to add to the narrative. Let us look, then, at the five key textual units in their discourse order.[27]

### Romans 3:23: Adam and Human Fallenness

In 3:23, Paul summarises the whole preceding argument of 1:18–3:20. He states that all sinned and are falling short of God's glory (πάντες γὰρ ἥμαρτον καὶ ὑστεροῦνται τῆς δόξης τοῦ θεοῦ). The glory in view here is probably the glory that, according to Psa. 8:5, God purposed for human creatures when God first made them. In Jewish Adam tradition, one of the results of Adam's failure was the loss or distortion of the glory he originally had.[28] Paul's wording almost certainly reflects this line of speculation. As Dunn opines, Paul seems to be thinking both of the glory lost in Adam's fall and of the glory that every individual is failing to achieve as a result.[29] In this verse, therefore, Paul alludes to the fall of Adam and uses this 'event' as a model for describing the sinfulness of all human beings. The effect of the echo is to imply that 'each of us has become our own Adam' (2 Apoc. Bar. 54:19).[30]

---

27. Space precludes any defence of my judgements on debated matters of interpretation in these and other passages.

28. E.g., Sir. 49:16; 2 En. 30:11–18; Apoc. Mos. 21:6.

29. J.D.G. Dunn, *Romans 1–8* (WBC 38a; Dallas, Tex.: Word, 1988) 168.

30. *2 Apoc. Bar.* 54:19, however, denies that Adam is the 'cause' of anyone's sin other than his own. In Rom. 5:12–21, Paul suggests that there is some sort of causal connection (which he does not make clear) between Adam's sin and subsequent human sin, and this idea of 'causality' may be submerged in Rom. 3:23.

## Romans 5:12–21: Adam's Rebellion and Christ's Reversal

In 5:12–21 Paul sums up the history of humankind prior to the coming of Christ and announces the new era of universal history that Christ has inaugurated. As Dunn states, the paragraph could be said to provide the 'programmatic text' for the whole letter.[31] Paul here employs the figure of Adam as a typological character ('Αδὰμ ὅς ἐστιν τύπος τοῦ μέλλοντος, 5:14) and sets him over against Christ. In comparing and contrasting Adam and Christ, Paul assesses the effects of Adam's rebellion for his offspring.

Adam and Christ are presented as fate-determining individuals, figures whose moral actions have had consequences for all. Adam, by his act of rebellion, allowed the destructive cosmic powers, sin and death, to gain their entrance into God's human creation and to establish their tyrannical reign over it (5:17, 21). Adam's trespass led to condemnation for all people. Christ, by his righteous and obedient deed (i.e., his death on the cross), has begun to reverse the effects of Adam's sin and to liberate the world from its enemy overlords, establishing in their place the reign of grace (5:21). Christ's death has brought grace and the gift of righteousness (5:17). What Christ achieved, Paul emphasises, more than compensates for Adam's transgression ('much more', 5:15, 17; 'abounded', 5:15; 'abundance of grace', 5:17; 'abounded all the more', 5:20 NRSV), and its positive effects more than outbalance the negative results of what Adam did.

Paul does not here call Christ 'the last Adam' (as he does in 1 Cor. 15:45), but his assertion that Adam is 'the type of the one who is to come' effectively accords Christ that role. As the new Adam, Christ deals with the problem created by the old Adam. But the second Adam does not begin where the first Adam began, retracing his steps as it were. The starting point for Christ's Adamic mission is the accumulation of sins of Adam's offspring (ἐκ πολλῶν παραπτωμάτων, 5:16). The task given by God to Christ is thus not simply to supplant Adam's disobedience with an act of obedience, but to undo the terrible consequences of Adam's failure.[32] In successfully completing this task, Christ makes available the gift of life (5:21). The 'eternal life' in view is probably the life God intended for human beings but that Adam and Eve forfeited (Gen. 2:9; 3:22). Through the new Adam, the creator's ambition for his creatures, that they have should life in all its fullness, is realised.

## Romans 7:7–12: Adam's Sin and God's Command

In 7:7–12, Paul argues that the law does not merely reveal sin; it is the instrument by which sin operates. Allusions to Genesis 2–3 in the passage have frequently

---

31. Dunn, *Romans*, 271.

32. N.T. Wright, *The Climax of the Covenant: Christ and the Law in Paul's Theology* (Edinburgh: T&T Clark, 1991) 38.

been noted. As Francis Watson states, the points of correspondence 'are so close that there can be little doubt that Paul had the Genesis story in mind throughout'.[33] There is little in these verses that does not apply to Adam (and Eve). In the key verses, 7:8–11, Paul suddenly shifts from talking about the 'law' (7:1–7) to speaking of the 'command' (ἐντολή). This more readily relates to the situation of Adam in the garden. The commandment given to Adam not to eat of the tree of knowledge of good and evil was meant to preserve life (εἰς ζωήν, 7:10) and carried with it the threat of death (Gen. 2:16–17; 3:22). But sin/the serpent found its opportunity in the commandment, exploiting God's decree to the primal pair to further its malicious ambitions. Sin/the serpent deceived Adam and Eve (ἡ ἁμαρτία… ἐξηπάτησέν με, 7:11; here the echo of Gen. 3:13 is very clear indeed: ὁ ὄφις ἠπάτησέ με) and used the command to produce in them 'sinful desire'.[34] As a result, they were denied access to the source of eternal life. Hence the command that promoted life proved to be a sentence of death (7:10).

With the first-person singular, Paul writes (not autobiographically but in retrospect with the benefit of gospel hindsight) as a human being in Adam. The experience of which he writes is that of 'Adam and after him all whom he represents'.[35]

## Romans 8:19–22: Adam's Sin and the Enslavement of Creation

In 8:18–30, Paul reaches the argumentative climax of Romans 1–8 (8:31–38 serving as a hymn celebrating the ultimate triumph and security of believers in Christ). He claims in 8:18 that the afflictions of the present are a stage on the way to the glory that will be. He develops this point in three subsections (8:19–22, 23–25, 26–27). In 8:19–22, he places believers' hardships within the context of the groaning of the wider creation (κτίσις in these verses is specifically the *nonhuman* creation). Paul alludes in these verses to Gen. 3:17–19, where God curses the ground (causing it to bring forth thorns and thistles) on account of Adam's sin. Paul, reworking the Genesis story (following and advancing a line of interpretation underway in his day), widens the scope of the curse to a comprehensive cosmic event. He tells how the creation, which he personifies as a sentient creature, was caught up 'unwillingly' (οὐχ ἑκοῦσα, 8:20) in Adam's sin. Although the sin was Adam's, the nonhuman creation, hav-

---

33. F. Watson, *Paul, Judaism and the Gentiles: A Sociological Approach* (Cambridge: Cambridge University Press, 1986) 152.

34. The idea that the first sin involved 'desire' or 'covetousness' is present in *Apoc. Mos.* 17:1–2; 19:3; *Apoc. Abr.* 24:10; Cf. Philo *Opif.* 152.

35. A.J.M. Wedderburn, 'Adam in Paul's Letter to the Romans', in *Studia Biblica 1978* (JSNTSup 3; Sheffield: JSOT Press, 1980): 413–30, 421.

ing been subjected to Adam (Gen. 1:28; Psa. 8:7), was made to share in his fall.[36] It was subjected to 'futility' (ματαιότης, 8:20), that is, it was prevented from reaching its created potential. Moreover, it was placed in bondage to 'decay' (φθορᾷ, 8:21), matching the reign of death over the human creation. But, Paul goes on to show, its present condition is not permanent; it is destined to share in the inheritance that awaits God's children. Even now, Paul claims, it looks forward with great hope and intense expectancy to its coming deliverance (8:19). Its present groaning is but the birth pangs of the glorious era to come (8:22).

The redemption set in store for creation, Paul states, is its liberation to obtain 'the freedom of the glory of the children of God' (8:21 NRSV). The formulation reflects an Adamic soteriology. The 'glory' to which reference is made is the pristine glory meant for Adam, eschatologically restored to redeemed humanity. When that glory is revealed, Paul implies, creation will be restored to its intended place, and God's children will be reestablished in their status as stewards of the created order and enabled to exercise their stewardship properly.

## Romans 8:28–30: The Divine 'Image' and 'Glory' Realised

Romans verses 8:28–30 forms the conclusion of the argument of 8:18–30. In 8:29–30, Paul spells out the saving purpose of God in relation to humanity. The goal of the whole redemptive process and the destiny toward which believers are heading is conformity to the image of God's Son (συμμόρφους τῆς εἰκόνος τοῦ υἱοῦ αὐτοῦ) and final 'glorification' (ἐδόξασεν). The language is that of Adam christology and soteriology. The thought expressed is this: Christ, the new Adam and the 'first-born of many brothers', has perfectly realised the 'image' of God in which human beings were created (Gen. 1:26–27). Those who are in Christ will be decisively stamped with that image so that the creator's original vision for humanity as a corporate entity will at last be actualised. The primordial glory will also be regained and perfected (cf. 8:21).

## A BASIC STORY OF GOD AND CREATION IN ROMANS

From these passages, it is not difficult to derive a 'story' in the sense defined above: a set of events in sequential and consequential connection, with characters, setting, and trajectory.

---

36. As Dunn (*Romans*, 471) states, this is the point of the awkward phrase διὰ τὸν ὑποτάξαντα in 8:20.

We have a series of *events* in consequential relation: the creation of human beings in God's image (8:29) and with God's glory (3:23; 8:21, 30) to have dominion over the rest of creation (8:20–21) and ultimately to possess eternal life (5:18, 21; 7:10); the command to Adam not to eat of the tree of knowledge (7:9–11); Adam's transgression (5:14ff.; 7:11) and fall from the divine glory (3:23); the entrance of sin and death into the human race (5:12); the subjection of the nonhuman creation to futility and decay (8:20); the ongoing failure of each of Adam's descendants to reach the divine glory (3:23); the Christ event and its reversal of the effects of Adam's sin (5:15ff.); and God's activity in the lives of redeemed humanity—culminating in the eschaton with the realisation of the divine image (8:29) and glory (8:21, 30), full possession of eternal life (5:21), and proper dominion over the created order (8:21). Of course, not all these events appear on the surface of Paul's argument. The original creation of humanity in the divine image, for example, is presupposed in 8:29 rather than explicitly affirmed.

*Characters* that participate in the events can be identified: God, humanity (a corporate character), Adam, Christ, sin and death (personified forces), and believers (a corporate character). These characters have *roles* and *functions* in the narrative that can be classified according to Greimas' actantial scheme. According to Greimas, a narrative is made up of three main sequences—an initial sequence, a topical sequence, and a final sequence—corresponding to Aristotle's beginning, middle, and end. In each sequence, all or most of the actant roles (sender, subject, object, receiver, opponent, helper) should be filled. In the *initial* sequence, a *subject* is appointed by a *sender* to convey an *object* to a *receiver*, but is prevented from doing so by an *opponent*, despite the aid given by a *helper*. The sequence thus ends in failure. In the *topical* sequence, a new *subject* is sent by the *sender* to resolve the problem set up at the end of the first sequence. The subject succeeds in his/her task, with the aid of a *helper*, overcoming the *opponent*, and communicating a new *object* (which will be the *helper* of the third movement) to the *receiver*. In the *final* sequence, the sender's original objective is accomplished.[37] From our passages, three basic sequences of this kind can be uncovered, the first focusing on Adam, the second on Christ, and the third on believers.[38]

In the first sequence, God is the sender, human beings are the receiver, and God's creative purposes for humankind (i.e., to fully express God's image, to

---

37. Hays, *The Faith of Jesus Christ*, 102.

38. These narrative movements do not conform exactly to Greimas' model, since Adam, as the subject of the first sequence, should be the receiver in the second sequence, and subject again in the third sequence. Cf. Hays, *The Faith of Jesus Christ*, 102–103. In our story, Adam as an actant disappears after the first sequence.

reflect God's glory, to have eternal life, to have dominion over the rest of creation) are the object. Adam is the subject, the one through whom the object is to be realised. Sin and death serve as the opponent. God's command (not to eat from the tree of knowledge) occupies the helper role (since it is intended to promote life). The sequence ends in failure. Adam disappoints in his intended role, and God's ambitions for humanity are thwarted. Sin and death hold humanity captive, and the failure of Adam is replicated by each of his descendants.[39]

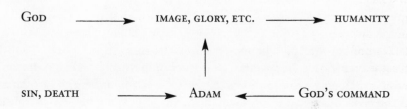

In the second sequence, God is the sender who acts to deal with the predicament that ended the first sequence. Christ is the subject, the divine agent appointed to resolve the problem. Humanity is the (potential) receiver. The abundance of grace and the gift of righteousness are the object. Sin and death again fill the opponent role, and Christ's obedience occupies the helper slot. The sequence ends in success, and the transaction executed paves the way for the fulfilment of the aborted first sequence. Christ accomplishes his task, triumphing where Adam failed. He begins the liberation of humanity from sin and death, and brings the gift of grace and righteousness that will enable believers to fulfil God's original creative ends.

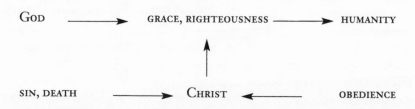

In the third sequence, God is the sender who carries to completion God's original objective. Humanity is the (potential) receiver and believers are the subject. God's purposes for humankind from the beginning are the object. Sin

---

39. The epoch from Adam's fall to Christ may be represented as a distinct movement in its own right. In this sequence, the law figures as a potential helper that is unmasked as a tool of the opponent (cf. 5:13, 14, 19; 7:7ff.).

and death are the opponent, and grace and righteousness, the helper. This
sequence brings the story to its 'end'. God's creative aims for humanity are
ultimately fulfilled in the final act of redemption.

As well as roles and functions, the participants have basic *traits*. God the
creator is characterised by grace (5:15) and (implicitly) by a commitment to
creation. Human beings are marked by their rebelliousness and sinfulness.
Adam is defined by his disobedience; Christ, by his righteousness and obedience. Believers, identified as God's sons or children, are not characterised by
qualities of their own but by the gifts they receive (5:15ff.) and the activity of
God in their lives (8:29–30).

Explicit elements of *setting* are much less detectable than characters. The
spatiotemporal locations of the events in the narrative (such as the garden of
Eden) are presupposed rather than articulated. However, the overall setting of
the whole story, the wider created order, is certainly clear. The larger creation
serves as more than the 'background' for the history of the creator's relationship with humanity. In 8:19–22 (a coherent narrative of God and creation in
itself), it becomes a story character in its own right. Indeed it is the central
character of this pericope (the word 'creation', κτίσις, occurs four times in
these verses, and in three of these instances it is the grammatical subject of the
clause of which it forms part). The nonhuman creation here, to use Toolan's
words, takes on 'quasi-animate' qualities. It is not portrayed as an 'active' character in the drama. In terms of the main events of the story, the creation is
'patient' rather than 'agent'—the object (or passive subject) of both God's sub-
jecting activity in the past and God's liberating act in the future. It is rather
depicted as a 'sensing' and 'feeling' participant. It 'groans' and 'suffers birth
pangs' (8:22). It 'earnestly expects' (8:19) and 'eagerly awaits' (8:19) the future
revelation of God's children. Significantly, groaning and eager anticipation are
predicated of believers in the verses that immediately follow. The linguistic
correlation establishes the idea of a bond of sympathy between creation and
believers: they both share the same suffering and anticipate the same hope.

The identification above of three distinct narrative sequences is evidence of
a story *trajectory*. The development follows the classic pattern of complication,
reversal, and denouement. A prior state of equilibrium is presupposed rather

than stated. The primordial state may be gauged from 5:12 and 8:19–20: a world free of the actualities of sin and death, futility and corruption. The world at this stage is assumed to be inherently good (though obviously not perfect). The state of rest is disturbed by the action of Adam. This causes the inimical forces 'sin' and 'death' to enter and tyrannise the human scene. The nonhuman creation is made to share in humanity's fall. The disequilibrium intensifies until it reaches the apogee of the 'many trespasses' of 5:16. The reversal is constituted by Christ who, in his obedience that culminates in his death on the cross, begins to unravel the effects of Adam's sin. The unravelling culminates in the revelation of the children of God. The story ends with a new equilibrium: the restoration and perfection of the whole created order and the accomplishment of the creator's objectives for humankind.

We have, then, in Romans 1–8, a basic and coherent 'story of God and creation' that meets our definition both of 'narrative' and the given story topic: a unified series of events with characters, setting, and trajectory, tracing the history of God's creative aims from their foundation at the beginning of creation, through their frustration due to Adam's fall and subsequent human fallenness, to their ultimate fulfilment in the eschaton. The focus of the story is Christ, who functions as a new Adam, sent to repair the damage done by the first Adam. As a result of the Christ event (5:21), what God purposed for human creation from the start is being and will be put into effect.[40]

Was this story intended by Paul? I would not wish to claim that the story was planned by Paul *exactly* as we have assembled it. It can hardly be supposed, after all, that Paul *intended* to follow Greimas' actantial scheme! What can be said, I think, is that the story we have perceived *arises* from Paul's intentions and is continuous with them. If all Paul's references and allusions to Adam were deliberate, as I would argue, then the story they produce must be viewed as grounded in his compositional aims. But did he weave Adam motifs into his argument with any degree of narrative consciousness? He could hardly have been unaware that the basic text on which he builds, Genesis 1–3, is narrative in form! He does not merely comment on Genesis 1–3; he adds to it and moves it forward, making connections between Adam and Christ, and Adam and believers. He also retells the Adam story, expanding the consequences of Adam's transgression, both for the human world and for the rest of creation, beyond those envisaged by the Genesis text itself (though in touch with Jewish speculation about

---

40. There remains the question, Are the creator's original purposes for humankind fulfilled in the salvation of a *portion* of humanity (i.e., believers) or in the ultimate restoration of *all* humanity? At the very least I think we can say that for Paul in this letter, the *potential* scope of Christ's redemptive work is just as universal and all-embracing as the actual scope of Adam's fall (5:12–21).

Adam). His handling of Genesis 3 in Rom. 8:19–22 is, in some respects, quite creative. Paul is not, therefore, just *mediating* a prior narrative. He is consciously *working* with it—reshaping, amplifying, and advancing the story. For these reasons, I would venture to suggest that the story reconstructed above originates in the *narratological* intentions of Paul.

## OTHER 'ADAMIC' PASSAGES

Having established the presence of a basic 'story of God and creation', we may look for further events, characters, and sequences of the narrative in the other Adamic passages. Space precludes discussion of all these texts, so I will give (brief) attention to two interlinked passages, 1:18–32 and 4:1–25, and merely touch on the others.

In 1:18–32, Paul describes the gentile plight (as part of his larger discussion of human sinfulness). He argues that the gentiles have wilfully neglected and rejected the knowledge of God available from the created world around them. Instead of glorifying God (1:21), the appropriate response of the creature to the creator, they have suppressed the truth they received and have sunk into religious, sexual, and moral corruption. God has given them over to this decline, manifesting wrath in the process.

A reasonable case can be made, I believe, for allusions to Genesis 1–2 in this passage.[41] The reference to God's act of creation in Rom. 1:20 recalls Gen. 1:1 and may signal a general allusion to the creation story. The order of created animals in Rom. 1:23 is reminiscent of Gen. 1:20–25.[42] The word 'image' (εἰκών) in Rom. 1:23 may refer to the creation of humanity in God's image in Gen. 1:27. The terms 'male' and 'female' (ἄρσην and θῆλυς) in Rom. 1:26–27 recall the created sexual distinction of Gen. 1:27. The statement in Rom. 1:32 that 'those who practice such things deserve to die' (NRSV) may point to the divine threat of death in Gen. 2:17.

These echoes suggest that Paul uses the creation accounts of Genesis as a yardstick with which to measure the gentile decline. With the Adam allusions, he seems to present the gentiles' fall into turpitude as a gathering movement away from the creator's original design: the gentiles distorted God's image, worshipped the subhuman creation instead of ruling over it, subverted the created distinction of male and female, and pursued practices that lead to death and not the eternal life for which God created them.

---

41. Wedderburn, 'Adam', 416.

42. N. Hyldahl, 'A Reminiscence of the Old Testament at Romans 1:23', *NTS* 2 (1955–56): 285–88.

Several scholars have argued that Paul has consciously modelled his account of the gentile plight on the sin of Adam in Genesis 3.[43] But this claim is extremely difficult to sustain. There is nothing in Genesis 3 to suggest that Adam rejected God's revelation in creation, became an idolater, engaged in illicit sexual practices, and fell into all kinds of wickedness.

What Paul does seem to be indicating, rather, is that Adam's downfall and the gentile ruin flowed from the same source: the creature's rejection of its creaturely status. Adam's sin arose from his desire to be like God (cf. Rom. 7:7-8); the gentiles' core transgression was to turn away from their creator. The sinful slide of the gentiles, as Paul sketches it, follows an entirely different course from Adam's fall in Genesis, but (he seems to be implying) it stems from the same root: creaturely rebellion against the creator.

In Romans 4, Paul takes up the example of Abraham to establish his thesis that God justifies by faith and not by the works of the law (3:27-30). The story of Abraham is strongly connected to the story of gentile rebellion in 1:18-32. By various links back to chapter 1, Abraham is portrayed as the reverse image of the disobedient gentiles.[44] The linkage is based on and deliberately evokes the Jewish tradition that Abraham was a pagan idolater who came to know God by reflecting on the created world around him.

Paul presents Abraham's faith, demonstrated in his reaction to God's promise of offspring, as creaturely trust in the creator. Abraham believed in the God 'who gives life to the dead and calls into existence the things that do not exist' (4:17).[45] Moreover, he 'gave glory to God' (4:20 NRSV). He thus did what the disobedient gentiles declined to do. In rejecting their creaturely estate, the gentiles repeated Adam's core error. Abraham, in this display of faith, not only reverses the rebellion of the gentiles but also that of Adam. Abraham is negatively the counterimage of Adam and positively 'the pattern of man as he was created to be'.[46]

The inheritance promised to Abraham and his spiritual offspring is not defined by Paul as the land of Palestine, as in the patriarchal narratives, but 'the world' (4:13). By extending the scope of the promise to global proportions, Paul almost certainly places the concept of inheritance within an Adamic

---

43. Most notably, M.D. Hooker, 'Adam in Romans 1', *NTS* 6 (1959-60): 297-306.

44. See further my 'Abraham's Faith and Gentile Disobedience: Textual Links Between Romans 1 and 4', *JSNT* 65 (1997): 47-66.

45. This is a statement of crucial importance to the theology of Romans. Here Paul correlates God's creative work, calling the nonexistent into existence, with his redeeming activity, raising the dead. See further E. Käsemann, *Commentary on Romans*, trans. G.W. Bromiley (Grand Rapids: Eerdmans; London: SCM Press, 1980) 121-24.

46. Dunn, *Romans*, 238.

framework. The blessing promised to Abraham to those who follow in the footsteps of his faith is nothing less than 'the restoration of God's created order, of man to his Adamic status as steward of the rest of God's creation'.[47]

Paul thus weaves the story of gentile failure in Romans 1 and the story of Abraham's faith in Romans 4 into the 'story of God and creation', adding to the larger narrative. The story of gentile decline adds a further dimension to the plot complication. The gentile plight illustrates how God's purposes in creation have been frustrated by human rebellion, the basic sin of the gentiles replicating the fundamental sin of Adam. The story of Abraham's faith is a kind of anticipatory reversal and denouement (prefiguring the topical and final sequence), showing how the creator's ideals for humanity are carried forward. By incorporating the Abraham story, which is the story of how God justifies the ungodly, into the 'story of God and creation', Paul indicates that God's act of justification does not constitute a departure from the creator's aims; it is a creative act that repairs the fractured relationship between creator and creature and effects the achievement of the creator's original objectives (cf. 8:30 NRSV, 'those whom he justified he also glorified').

The remaining Adamic passages add to the narrative as follows. The allusion to Psa. 8:5 in Rom. 2:7 and 2:10 shows that the basis of God's final judgement will be God's original creative agenda. The extension of the Adam/Christ contrast of 5:12–21 into chapter 6 indicates that the decisive break undergone by believers at baptism is the annulment of their solidarity with the old Adam (the 'old self' of 6:6). They are now united with the new Adam. The carrying forward of the Adam allusions established in 7:7–12 into 7:13–25 serves to identify the 'I' of 7:13–25 as the human being 'in Adam'. Paul demonstrates the powerlessness of the law to resolve the moral conflict within an Adam-oriented individual.

Paul thus relates large parts of his argument to his 'story of God and creation': his account of the gentile plight, his discussion of Jews and gentiles in the final judgement, his treatment of justification by faith, his teaching on incorporation into Christ and its moral consequences, and his discussion of the role of the law in the divine plan (cf. 5:13, 14, 19). The conclusion to which one is drawn is that Paul's narrative of God and creation is the main story line of Romans 1–8 of which other possible stories are subplots.[48]

---

47. Dunn, *Romans*, 213.

48. Paul does not appear to relate his discussion of God's dealings with Israel in Romans 1–11 to the 'story of God and creation' in Romans 1–8. Nevertheless, he does hint that God's covenant relationship with Israel operates within a more general creator-creature framework (9:19–24; 10:18; 11:23–24). It is significant that the discussion both of the problem of historical Israel in God's purposes and of Romans 1–11 as a whole closes with a doxology in 11:36 affirming God as the source (ἐξ αὐτοῦ), agent (δι' αὐτοῦ), and goal (εἰς αὐτόν) of the universe and its history (τὰ πάντα). By this, Paul seems to indicate that God's saving actions in Israel's history are part of God's all-embracing plan for the whole of creation.

# THE SIGNIFICANCE OF THE STORY

This brings us to the issue of the significance of Paul's 'story of God and creation' in Romans. Let us now address the three questions raised at the outset.

First, how does the 'story of God and creation' that we have identified influence Paul's argumentation? The story is woven into the argument of Romans 1–8. Although it is fully explicit only in 5:12-21 (and seemingly explicit in 8:19-22), the narrative runs though Paul's discourse from 1:18 to 8:30. On one level, the story helps to guide and direct the theological discussion. The beginning and end of the story occur at the beginning and end of the overall argument (1:20 and 8:19-22, 29-30). The concentration of Adam motifs in the opening and closing sections of the argument, 1:18-32 and 8:18-30, suggests that the story frames the overall presentation of Romans 1–8. The location of the topical and central sequence of the story, in which Christ reverses the misdeed of Adam, at the central section of the entire argument of Romans 1–8 (i.e., at 5:12-21, which both sums up 1:18–5:11 and paves the way for chapters 6–8) suggests that the main act of the drama is the pivot of the theological exposition. The story can thus be viewed as the substructure of Paul's whole argument of Romans 1–8.[49]

To suggest that the theological direction of Romans 1–8 is shaped, to a significant extent, by a story of God and creation could be taken to imply that it is guided by a *Heilsgeschichte*. 'Salvation history' designates a theological perspective that views God's redemptive purposes as unfolding steadily in a cumulative sequence of historical events. From this point of view, the Christ event is seen to stand in continuity with God's saving actions in previous history. The notion as applied to Paul has been subject to much criticism,[50] not least because it fails to do justice to the alleged 'apocalyptic' dimensions of his thought, which place emphasis on the fundamental newness of God's saving act in Christ and its discontinuity with God's historical actions in the past.[51]

The 'story of God and creation' we have uncovered in Romans is in some ways similar to a 'salvation history' in that it involves a series of events in consequential continuity heading toward a goal. But it should be differentiated

---

49. Cf. P.J. Achtemeier (*Romans* [Interpretation; Atlanta: John Knox Press, 1985] 14), who writes that Paul has chosen 'the story of God's dealings with his rebellious creation, as the structure within which to tell the Romans about his understanding of the meaning of that story'.

50. See Hays, *The Faith of Jesus Christ*, 55–62.

51. It should be recognised that both 'salvation history' and 'apocalyptic' are scholarly constructs. On the deeply problematic nature of the category 'apocalyptic' in Pauline studies, see R.B. Matlock, *Unveiling the Apocalyptic Paul: Paul's Interpreters and the Rhetoric of Criticism* (JSNTSup 127; Sheffield: Sheffield Academic Press, 1996).

from 'salvation history' in at least two important respects. First, our story of
God and creation follows the trajectory structure of complication and denouement around a 'reversal'. The sequence of events is thus not developmental (in
the sense that each event after the starting point builds positively on the previous one). There is a key turning point in the movement. In stories patterned
on a classic trajectory model, events before and after the reversal display a 'mir-
ror-like opposition in intensity and result'.[52] There is an overall teleological
advancement, but there are radical dichotomies within the sequence and a central event that has singular and decisive significance. Second, the story we have
reconstructed concentrates on God's role and activity as *creator* and brings
God's redeeming actions into the picture when they are seen to extend, continue, reinstate, or accomplish God's creatorial ambitions. The 'history' it
tracks is the history of God's purposes for creation. Strictly speaking it is a *creation history* rather than a salvation history.[53]

The second question is, How does the story illuminate the theme or themes
of the letter? The grand theme of Paul's letter to the Romans, it can hardly be
doubted, is the 'righteousness of God'. But the meaning of the phrase is much
debated. The identification of a 'story of God and creation' as an underlying
framework for Paul's theological discussion in Romans 1–8 has a bearing on
how the expression should be understood. Specifically, it lends weight to Käsemann's interpretation of the motif. According to Käsemann, God's righteousness is God's *own* righteousness (taking δικαιοσύνη θεοῦ as subjective
genitive), but it is a divine quality that has a 'gift' and a 'power' character.[54] It
is a power that goes out into the world and reclaims it for God's sovereignty.[55]
Käsemann argues that the divine righteousness operates in a universal arena.
It is not specifically tied to God's covenantal dealings with Israel. It rather
reflects the faithfulness of the creator to creation.

Käsemann's understanding of the theme fits well into a general understanding of Romans (or at least Romans 1–8) as strongly influenced by a 'story
of God and creation'. The revelation of God's righteousness in the gospel,
announced in 1:17 and 3:21, may be more clearly viewed as the revelation of
how God has acted to restore creation in the saving event of Christ.

The third question is, How does the story function for its intended readers? Social anthropologists point out that stories, both oral and written, play

---

52. O'Toole, 'Narrative Structure', 159.

53. I owe this point to my colleague, Professor Colin Gunton. For Paul, both creation and redemption stem from divine grace (Rom. 4:17).

54. E. Käsemann, '"The Righteousness of God" in Paul', in *New Testament Questions
of Today* (London: SCM Press, 1969) 168–82, 174.

55. Käsemann, 'Righteousness', 182.

an important role in the construction and preservation of group identity. Ethnic groups often use 'narratives of peoplehood' (which include reference to their origins, descent, shared heritage, and common destiny) in order to define themselves and set their boundaries.[56] Such narratives not only reproduce collective identities; they also create them.

What kind of community identity does Paul's 'story of God and creation' in Romans serve to fashion for its recipients? The story is a grand narrative that invites its readers to find their identity in the large sweep of the history of creation, from its beginnings to its culmination. It roots their social selfhood in God's plan to bring God's aims for the world to fulfilment. It is not a story that would easily generate or sustain a 'sectarian' social identity, a separatist response to the world outside the community.[57] To be sure, Paul's addressees are encouraged to see themselves as a 'saved people', but the salvation envisaged is one that is universal in scope (for the benefit of all humanity and not just a select part of it) and involves the reclamation of the whole universe for God. Readers are induced to see themselves as the beachhead of a restored world. The narrative creates for its addressees a sense of community belonging, but the community to which they belong (the church) is itself seen to 'belong' to a larger world, a world to which God remains committed and in which God is providentially involved, a world that, though presently fallen, is still God's creation, manifesting a cosmic, social, and moral order,[58] a world that God will bring to its originally intended glory. The story thus serves to construct for its readers an identity that is both particular and universal.[59]

## GALATIANS

We turn now at last to Galatians. 'God' figures prominently in this letter, and Paul makes several important theological comments about the 'world' and 'the

---

56. M. Al-Rasheed, *Iraqi Christians in London: The Construction of Ethnicity* (Mellen Studies in Sociology, 21; Lewiston, N.Y.: Edwin Mellen, 1998) 101 (and generally, 101–135).

57. I am using 'sectarian' here in the sociological sense defined by E. Troeltsch, *The Social Teachings of the Christian Churches*, vol. 1, trans. O. Wyon (London: Allen & Unwin; New York: Macmillan, 1931) 331–43.

58. Despite Paul's dismal analysis of humanity in 1:18–3:20, he maintains a comparatively positive view of the present world as divinely arranged and as reflecting God's power and deity. See my *Constructing the World: A Study in Paul's Cosmological Language* (SNTW; Edinburgh: T&T Clark, 2000) 151–93.

59. To speak of a 'universal identity' is somewhat paradoxical since social identities are usually understood to be inherently particular.

present age': that it is 'evil' (1:4), that it is influenced by 'elemental powers' (στοιχεῖα, 4:3, 9), that Christ gave himself to rescue believers from it (1:14), and that through Christ believers have been crucified to it and it to them (6:14; I take Paul's 'I' to be paradigmatic as well as autobiographical). Paul also talks about a 'new creation' (6:15) that stands in antithesis to the world crucified with Christ. However, at no point in the letter does Paul specifically define God as creator or the present world as God's creation. In the whole epistle, only one Adam motif may be identified. It occurs at 3:28.

In 3:26–28, Paul speaks of the new reality into which his readers have been baptised (many scholars think that he is drawing here upon a preformed baptismal tradition). In the new sphere of life entered into through baptism, he claims, 'there is neither Jew nor Greek, slave nor free, and there is no "male and female"' (οὐκ ἔνι Ἰουδαῖος οὐδὲ. Ἕλλην, οὐκ ἔνι δοῦλος οὐδὲ ἐλεύθερος, οὐκ ἔνι ἄρσεν καὶ θῆλυ). With the final pair, Paul clearly refers to the created sexual distinction of Gen. 1:27 (the change of wording in the third clause strongly suggests a deliberate allusion to the Genesis text). As we have seen, Paul alludes to the male-female distinction of Gen. 1:27 in Rom. 1:26–27. In that text, he affirms the differentiation. But here, he problematises it. The male-female clause of Gal. 3:28 has generated an immense scholarly debate, particularly in recent years. One issue at stake is whether the distinction negated is the divinely created *sexual* distinction itself or the humanly constructed *gender* categorisation arising from it, and whether Paul would, in any case, have been able to separate the two. Another is the precise force of Paul's negation. Is he saying that in Christ the distinction is rendered unimportant, that it is transcended but not undone, or that it is completely obliterated? Discussion of these and related matters is beyond us here. It suffices to make the simple observation that, in this text, the division of humanity into male and female at the original creation is seen either to constitute or to have generated a barrier to social unity, a barrier that is in some sense overcome 'in Christ'.

From this single verse, we clearly cannot derive 'a story of God and creation' in the sense defined at the outset of the discussion. Paul shows no concern in Galatians to develop a comprehensive universal history. As Hays comments, Paul traces his main story 'backwards no farther than Abraham and forwards no farther than the immediately controverted future of the Galatian churches'.[60] Our investigation of Galatians thus halts at the first hurdle. But we may indulge in a little 'what if' speculation. Gal. 3:28 hints that, were Paul to have developed a 'story of God and creation' in Galatians, it might have proceeded somewhat differently from that in Romans. Whereas in Romans a 'fall' (Genesis 3) that frustrates God's original design for creation is the problem

---

60. Hays, *The Faith of Jesus Christ*, 263.

to be resolved, a 'story of God and creation' arising from Gal. 3:28 might have had (aspects of) the original design of creation (Genesis 1–2) as part of the complication to be undone. Such a narrative would not fit with our definition of the story topic—the story of how God brings to fulfilment God's original aims in creating humanity and the universe as a whole—since the very presupposition entailed in our topic, that God's eschatological programme is *continuous* with God's original programme in creation, is called into question.

## CONCLUSIONS

To sum up, a coherent (and complex) 'story of God and creation' can be identified in Paul's letter to the Romans. This story, I have argued, helps to guide and shape Paul's argument and has significance for the debate over the meaning of the key theme of the letter, the 'righteousness of God'. The story serves to fashion the identity of its intended readers. It defines their identity in nonsectarian terms. A 'story of God and creation', in accordance with the definition worked out for this enquiry, cannot be perceived in Galatians.

That Paul related a story of God and creation in Romans but not in Galatians may be due, partly, to the different situational contexts of the letters and his different purposes in writing. As Hays points out, the limited scope of Paul's perspective in Galatians reflects the highly specific nature of the issue with which he was dealing.[61] But a shift in theological emphasis may also have played a part. In Romans, Paul accentuates the continuity between 'creation' and 'new creation', and in Galatians, the discontinuity. The former is more conducive to the development of a story of God and creation (as understood in this study) than the latter.

Finally, I must relate this study to the wider concerns of the narrative project of which it is part. One is naturally wary about drawing general conclusions from a fairly limited study, but as a participant in the larger discussion, I must take a view on the broader issues involved. I take refuge in the qualification that the following remarks are provisional judgements, subject to revision in the light of further discussion.

First, do narrative elements 'exist' in front of the text, in the text, or behind the text? This study suggests that narrative presence may be three-dimensional: narrative components may exist on all three proposed levels. The primary location of narrative elements, I would maintain, is the text itself: narrative constituents are *textual* features of Paul's discourse. But if, as in this study, story elements are uncovered by bringing a model of 'story' to the text, an 'in front

---

61. Hays, *The Faith of Jesus Christ*, 263.

of the text' dimension to narrative presence must also be acknowledged, since it is through the *interaction* of the model and the text that a narrative is identified. Moreover, if narrative constituents consist partly of intertextual 'allusions', we must also admit a 'behind the text' dimension to narrative existence, since such allusions require anterior texts and traditions and prior stories.

Second, can attention to narrative elements in Paul's letters give us insight into how his mind worked at a precompositional level? I would not wish to drive a wedge between the narrative features of Paul's textual compositions and the mental processes that lie behind them, but it seems to me that the former does not necessarily give us direct access to the latter. The cognitive route by which Paul arrived at a particular narrative construction was probably quite different from the path of the narrative trajectory. In Romans, Paul's 'story of God and creation' (I have suggested) broadly follows the trajectory of beginning, middle, and end, moving from Adam to Christ to believers. However, it seems highly likely that the process of reflection that led to this final patterning *began* with the Christ event, with Paul progressively weaving a larger story around it. It may be argued that the more deeply embedded and unobtrusive the narrative structure, the more likely it is to reflect Paul's deepest level of thinking. But this still leaves the problem that the evidence is *textual* and gives no *guarantee* of entry into a *precommunicative* stage of thinking. It seems wise to me, therefore, in narratological analysis of Paul's writing, to treat 'narrative' as a textual phenomenon rather than a mental phenomenon, and to use 'story' as a tool for analysing what Paul said on a given occasion rather than as an instrument for probing the innermost workings of his mind.

Third, do Paul's stories form the coherent centre of his theology? That is to say, can we extract from Paul's letters certain basic and fixed stories that may then be seen to be generative of all his theological statements and argumentation? My view is that Paul's stories reflect the same epistolary diversity and are subject to the same varying contextual influences as any other aspect of his discourse. When we look at a particular story Paul tells in a particular letter, such as the 'story of God and creation' in Romans, its form and content are quite distinctive to that letter, and the story is linked with the particular aims of the letter. I would resist, therefore, the attempt to subsume the whole of Paul's theology under one all-encompassing 'story'. A 'story of God and the world' might qualify as a potentially all-embracing narrative, but Paul's pictures of the world vary considerably, for example, between Romans and 1 Corinthians.[62] Any endeavour to merge them into a single story would blunt the edges of both presentations, and the end product would be wholly applicable to neither epistle.

---

62. This is one of my main arguments in *Constructing the World*.

Pursuit of the narrative contours of Paul's compositions is a valuable and illuminating exercise (as I hope this study has indicated), but it is no direct line into the recesses of his mind and no smooth and easy path to the core and centre of his theology.[63]

63. An earlier version of this essay was read as a paper at the Biblical Studies Research Seminar in the Department of Theology and Religious Studies, King's College London. I am appreciative of the helpful comments I received then. I am particularly grateful to my colleagues, Professor Judith Lieu and Dr Bridget Gilfillan Upton for their suggestions for improvement. Thanks too go to Professor John Barclay and Dr David Horrell for their comments on an early draft of the essay. Above all, I would like to thank Dr Barry Matlock for his careful reading of this piece (as well as several previous drafts of it!) and for his formal response.

# 3

# The Arrow
# and the Web

## Critical Reflections on a
## Narrative Approach to Paul

R. BARRY MATLOCK

Until quite recently, my mental lexicon of contemporary biblical criticism had only the following (half-joking) entry under Narrative Criticism of Paul: 'What you do when the Pauline text doesn't actually say what you need it to (i.e., you read it in light of the *underlying narrative*)'. So it is a good thing to be forced actually to think about the subject a bit, and in the company of others with contrasting points of view. Adams' fine paper is a good remedy for my cynicism. And while I am not quite ready to sign on to a narrative approach to Paul, it is, at least, a more studied sort of scepticism that I now exercise in the following.

As a preface to my critical reflections, I would note that I have chosen to give relatively greater emphasis to methodological discussion of the narrative proposal more broadly, rather than keeping to the particular end of the street that Adams and I are meant to be working ('the story of God and creation'). This is partly because there is relatively less action down on our end (not to grumble); also because I find myself quite happy with what Adams says on our subject. More basically, I am not myself inclined to offer here a narrative analysis of Paul—not because I reject such an approach but because I still have too many questions (and perhaps because my working tendencies still run in other directions). My perception is that I can best contribute to this project by constructively raising critical questions that might serve to clarify the nature and the potential of a narrative approach to Paul. But, all scepticism aside, it is in full commitment to this project that I attempt to place a few items on the agenda for discussion, anticipating at the same time that I will have much to learn from others.[1] I add here one final preliminary matter that I think necessary in order to avoid a mistaken impression: While below I take a critical stance toward various aspects of the narrative approach taken by Richard Hays and N.T. Wright, I have been greatly instructed by their suggestive works on Pauline theology, without which the discipline would be much the poorer.

## ASSESSING THE
## NARRATIVE METHOD

Any assessment of the broad proposal of a 'narrative' approach to Paul must still give a certain pride of place to the work that self-consciously inaugurates such an approach: Richard Hays' 1983 monograph *The Faith of Jesus Christ*.[2] Searching for 'the framework *out of which* Paul reacted to the pastoral problems that appear in his letters', Hays finds this to be 'constituted . . . by a "sacred story", a narrative structure'.[3] Hays attends specifically to compressed summary 'allusions' to or 'recapitulations' of this story, a story that 'operates as a constraint governing the logic of Paul's argumentation' and without which one is unable to 'follow' Paul's letters.[4] 'Story' in Hays' usage is 'the Christ-story', 'the gospel', and Paul's 'gospel' (or his 'theology', or the argumentative discourse of his letters), though not narrative in form, has a narrative '(sub)structure'.[5] The approach to narrative analysis chosen is the 'actantial' model of structuralist A.J. Greimas.[6] Hays' project, then, is more sharply delimited than the sort of grand narrative approach to Paul represented by, say, Oscar Cullmann, whose biblical-theological emphasis on 'a process of continuous development' poses a 'danger of reading Paul through a Lukan filter'.[7] Perhaps suggestive of the versatility of Hays' proposal, though, N.T. Wright is able to subsume Hays' narrative

---

1. As one working on the contemporary scene in Pauline studies, I applaud the foresight and leadership of Bruce Longenecker in orchestrating this collaborative exercise of assessing the narrative proposal.

2. R.B. Hays, *The Faith of Jesus Christ: An Investigation of the Narrative Substructure of Galatians 3:1–4:11* (SBLDS 56; Chico, Calif.: Scholars Press, 1983).

3. Hays, *The Faith of Jesus Christ*, 1, 5.

4. Hays, *The Faith of Jesus Christ*, 5–6, 7–8, 27, 29; see 1–30.

5. Hays, *The Faith of Jesus Christ*, 17, 20–21, 26–27.

6. Hays, *The Faith of Jesus Christ*, 92–103.

7. Hays, *The Faith of Jesus Christ*, 59–62.

approach into a 'grand narrative' perspective (arguably) not unlike that of
Cullmann so described.[8] Wright's employment of a narrative approach is part
of a creative and original project too complex to characterize here, but for present purposes it may be noted that, where narrative theory is concerned, Wright
is content simply to adopt Hays' Greimasian method wholesale.[9]

Stephen Fowl's *The Story of Christ in the Ethics of Paul* defines Pauline 'narrative'
quite strictly in terms of the narratives embodied in Christ-hymns like Phil.
2:6–11.[10] Methodologically, Fowl's interest in narrative is related to the 'narrative
ethics' of Alasdair MacIntyre and Stanley Hauerwas and concerns how moral discourse is 'sustained by the narratives employed by any given community to render an account of the way the world is and how the community fits into that world'.
Noting that there is no 'privileged method' for determining 'the practical force of
a narrative', Fowl focuses specifically on the analogical correlation between (christological) tradition and (ecclesiological) situation represented in Paul's use of such
hymns, whereby the story of Christ functions as an exemplar for the community.[11]

Representing yet another approach, 'narrative' in Norman Petersen's *Rediscovering Paul* revolves around the (quite unobjectionable) observation that 'letters have stories'.[12] Petersen distinguishes the 'referential sequence' (the
logical or chronological order of events) from the 'poetic sequence' (the order
of telling) of a letter's story, analysing the rhetorical function of such compositional features of the poetic sequence as 'plot', 'point of view', and 'closure'

---

8. N.T. Wright, *The Climax of the Covenant: Christ and the Law in Pauline Theology*
(Edinburgh: T&T Clark, 1991) 193–216; *The New Testament and the People of God* (London: SPCK, 1992) 69–80, 371–417. Hays himself hints at a 'grand narrative' reading
(*The Faith of Jesus Christ*, 244–45 n. 106, 263–64), which he actually adopts in 'Crucified with Christ: A Synthesis of the Theology of 1 and 2 Thessalonians, Philemon,
Philippians, and Galatians', in J.M. Bassler (ed.), *Pauline Theology, Volume I: Thessalonians, Philippians, Galatians, Philemon* (Minneapolis: Fortress Press, 1991) 227–46.

9. See Wright, *The Climax of the Covenant*, 204–205.

10. S.E. Fowl, *The Story of Christ in the Ethics of Paul: An Analysis of the Function of
the Hymnic Material in the Pauline Corpus* (JSNTSup 36; Sheffield: Sheffield Academic
Press, 1990); cf. Hays, *The Faith of Jesus Christ*, 17.

11. Fowl, *The Story of Christ in the Ethics of Paul*, 92–95, 198–207. Fowl's monograph
is not, then, a continuation of Hays' project (and makes no mention of Hays, in fact);
for his part, Hays pointedly wishes to say something about Paul in particular, not make
a general statement about the centrality of 'narrative' to human life and thought (see
*The Faith of Jesus Christ*, 19). But in hindsight, their broader interests may be seen as
complementary (cf. *The Faith of Jesus Christ*, 258–64).

12. N.R. Petersen, *Rediscovering Paul: Philemon and the Sociology of Paul's Narrative World*
(Philadelphia: Fortress Press, 1985) ix, 2, 43; in contrast, Hays is interested in 'the structure of the gospel story, not of Paul's personal story' (*The Faith of Jesus Christ*, 29).

13. Petersen, *Rediscovering Paul*, 1–30, 43–88.

as part of a broader exercise in historical-critical reconstruction in which the constructedness of the historical as well as the literary are both recognised.[13]

In the largest-scale narrative treatment of Paul to date, *Paul's Narrative Thought World*, Ben Witherington credits Hays, Petersen, Fowl, and Wright with helping shape his own narrative approach.[14] But Witherington does not explain what unites these disparate approaches beyond the term 'narrative' itself, nor yet what unites Paul's use of scripture, of Jesus tradition, and of autobiography in Witherington's own approach, which simply bypasses questions of method.[15]

While this overview has been brief, it is sufficient to make a first general observation about the narrative proposal. A safe conclusion is that narrative criticism of Paul's letters, at least as it has been modelled so far, is not any one thing. (Which is not necessarily to say that it should be.) A second general observation follows closely on: There is a need for methodological clarification. Witherington's approach offers no strictly methodological advances; Fowl's use of 'narrative' does not need (and thus does not offer) a detailed narrative-critical methodology (there is no 'privileged method'); and Petersen's approach would seem to be better classified as what has come to be called 'socio-rhetorical', rather than 'narrative', criticism. The work that gives the most extensive attention to methodological considerations is Hays' 1983 monograph, providing the model for Wright (among others). Hays subsequently remarks, 'Upon rereading *The Faith of Jesus Christ* ten years later, I remain unrepentant concerning the central thesis of my earlier work: Paul's theology must be understood as the explication and defense of a *story*', with Paul's πίστις Χριστοῦ phrases (taken by Hays as 'the faith of Jesus Christ') 'understood as summary allusions to this story'.[16] Nevertheless, he concedes, 'I am, however, somewhat repentant about the methodological overkill of the piece. Some of the

---

14. B. Witherington III, *Paul's Narrative Thought World: The Tapestry of Tragedy and Triumph* (Louisville, Ky.: Westminster/John Knox Press, 1994) 7 n. 11.

15. Cf. B.N. Fisk, review of Witherington, *Paul's Narrative Thought World*, in *JBL* 115 (1996): 552–54: 'The book cries out for a theoretical discussion of method and for clear explanations of the increasingly popular categories "story," "narrative," and "thought world." Witherington never explains why he considers under the same rubric ("story") OT narratives, wisdom speculation, traditions about the historical Jesus, and Paul's own experience of the risen Christ' (554).

16. R.B. Hays, 'ΠΙΣΤΙΣ and Pauline Christology: What Is At Stake?', in E.E. Johnson and D.M. Hay (eds), *Pauline Theology, Volume IV: Looking Back, Pressing On* (SBLSymS 4; Atlanta: Scholars Press, 1997) 35–60, 37.

17. R.B. Hays, 'ΠΙΣΤΙΣ and Pauline Christology', 37 n. 5 (cf. 'Crucified with Christ', 232 n. 13). Hays does not specify here what, methodologically, he would dispense with; however, in the reprint edition of his original monograph, which appeared after this essay was written (*The Faith of Jesus Christ*, 2nd edn [The Biblical Resource Series; Grand Rapids: Eerdmans, 2002]), Hays strongly distances himself from the structuralist methodology he originally employed (xxvi–xxvii).

methodological preliminaries I would now gladly consign to the flames.'[17] It may
have made sense—assuming a *theory* of narrative is what is wanted—for Hays, as a
doctoral student in the late 1970s and early 1980s, to turn to the narrative theory
of Greimas. This choice is less obvious, however, twenty years later, for one setting
out to select an approach to narrative among currently available options.[18] It is not
just that structuralism as a movement is no longer current.[19] Structuralism, narratology, and semiotics themselves have not stood still since the narrative theory of
the early Greimas.[20] For that matter, Greimas himself appears to have moved on.[21]
Indeed, one could make a good start at exploring alternative theories of narrative
in the work of two sympathetic but thoroughgoing critics of Greimas and structuralist narratology, namely, Fredric Jameson and Paul Ricoeur.[22] But then we

18. Greimas had been digested for biblical critics in D. Patte, *What Is Structural Exegesis?* (GBS; Philadelphia: Fortress Press, 1976) 36–52 (cf. Hays, *The Faith of Jesus
Christ*, 130 n. 36).

19. That is true enough, but a critic of structuralism might still acknowledge structuralist narratology as a high point of the movement. Cf. F. Jameson, *The Prison-House
of Language: A Critical Account of Structuralism and Russian Formalism* (Princeton, N.J.:
Princeton University Press, 1972) x–xi.

20. Neither the radical 'post-structuralism' of a Roland Barthes nor the more conservative 'open structuralism' of a Gerard Genette would leave undisturbed the classical
structuralist assumptions of Greimas' early theorising (the strict application of a Saus-
surean linguistic model to literature; the search for a universal 'grammar' of narrative; an
abstract, achronic approach). For an overview of developments in literary structuralism,
see A. Jefferson, 'Structuralism and Post-Structuralism', in A. Jefferson and D. Robey
(eds), *Modern Literary Theory: A Comparative Introduction*, 2nd edn (London: Batsford,
1986) 92–121. See also R. Scholes, *Structuralism in Literature: An Introduction* (New
Haven, Conn.: Yale University Press, 1974); J. Culler, *Structuralist Poetics: Structuralism,
Linguistics and the Study of Literature* (London: Routledge & Kegan Paul, 1975).

21. The inadequacy of the model Hays employs is asserted in the work of no less a
Greimas enthusiast than D. Patte; contrast *What Is Structural Exegesis?* with *Structural
Exegesis for New Testament Critics* (GBS; Minneapolis: Fortress Press, 1990), which
moves beyond the 'partial theories' of the 'early' Greimas to the 'meta-theory' of the
later Greimas (1–5, 130–32); Patte explicates this 'meta-theory' in *The Religious Dimensions of Biblical Texts: Greimas's Structural Semiotics and Biblical Exegesis* (Semeia Studies;
Atlanta: Scholars Press, 1990), where he draws attention to the inadequacy of precisely
those features of the early theory that he had himself earlier highlighted and that
Pauline critics have been so enamoured of, namely, the 'actantial model' and the con-
comitant analysis of plot sequences (see 12–14; 26–27 n. 4; 54–57).

22. See F. Jameson, *The Political Unconscious: Narrative as a Socially Symbolic Act* (London: Routledge, 1983); P. Ricoeur, *Time and Narrative* (3 vols., trans. K. McLaughlin
and D. Pellauer; Chicago: University of Chicago Press, 1985–88).

23. It may be recalled that Hays himself employed the concept of 'intertextuality'
in his *Echoes of Scripture in the Letters of Paul* (New Haven, Conn.: Yale University Press,
1989), though 'in a more limited sense, focusing on [Paul's] actual citations of and allusions to specific texts', pointedly steering clear of the likes of Kristeva and Barthes (15).
For a recent introduction to the concept of 'intertextuality', see G. Allen, *Intertextuality* (The New Critical Idiom; London: Routledge, 2000).

ought to ask whether it is really a theory of *narrative* that we want. How different would our treatment of Paul's letters look if we took as our central critical concept not 'narrative' but (another branch of Greimas' tradition) 'intertextuality'?[23] And even if we prefer to retain 'narrative', we should still ask whether it is a *theory* of narrative, exactly, that we need. Although it is no problem in principle to take a narrative perspective on (formally) nonnarrative texts such as Paul's letters, surely the application of a narrative theory like Greimas'—which presents us with a set of slots to be filled—needs a fair bit of narration on which to feed. It is no way around this to focus on summary 'recapitulations' that putatively 'manifest an obvious actantial structure'.[24] We can fill the slots, all right (Pauline critics are as clever as any, surely), but how much confidence may we place in the results? Perhaps the apparent attraction of a relatively simple, step-by-step method is difficult for Pauline scholars (always hungry for new methodological direction) to resist; but we should be sure that we do not settle for this model out of mere convenience.

Finally, to return to Hays and Wright, it is not clear to me that they can help themselves to Greimas' model of narrative while disavowing its theoretical basis.[25] To be sure, their disavowals are not in doubt. What is unclear is whether their use of Greimas' theory is compatible with it. Greimas' theory makes no secret of its antihumanism and antihistoricism. Can we nevertheless legitimately ask this theory to help us better appreciate the 'main emphases' of a narrative (so Wright)?[26] In fact, so odd is the marriage of Greimas with Hays and Wright that some explanation seems to be called for. It is striking that both Hays and Wright emphasise the covert nature of the 'narrative' aspect of Paul's letters. Says Hays, 'My thesis requires one crucial postulate about the character of the [Pauline] text: that it is strongly allusive. Its foundation and framework are for the most part hidden from view, implicit rather than explicit.'[27] According to Wright, Paul's letters present us with 'a larger implicit narrative, which stands out clearly as the true referential sequence behind the poetic sequence demanded by the different rhetorical needs

---

24. Hays, *The Faith of Jesus Christ*, 101.

25. Hays, *The Faith of Jesus Christ*, 16, 93; Wright, *The New Testament and the People of God*, 70.

26. Wright, *The New Testament and the People of God*, 73. One commentator on structuralism (Jefferson, 'Structuralism and Post-Structuralism', 92) describes its 'revolutionary' character in these terms: 'Structuralism is revolutionary because it can be adopted only as an alternative and not as an addition to traditional academic habits. It cannot be incorporated as a handy extra methodological tool to be resorted to when all else fails.' While I am inclined to be pragmatic where methods are concerned, I think it is fitting to ask for some alternative justification if one is to apply Greimas' actantial approach while denying the theoretical basis intended to justify it.

27. Hays, *The Faith of Jesus Christ*, 234; note also that the hidden logic that the narrative approach reveals is put forward as a corrective to the 'Lutheran' tradition (29).

28. Wright, *The New Testament and the People of God*, 405.

of the various letters', a larger story that 'Paul presupposes . . . even when he does not expound it directly'.[28] And Hays and Wright both draw particular attention to an aspect of narrative grammar supposedly revealed by Greimas' model (though Hays notes that this construction 'has never particularly engaged the attention of structuralist critics'): namely, a certain modulation between a first and a second Subject through the three plot sequences (Initial, Topical, and Final), which, says Hays, is 'of considerable importance for our analysis of the logic of Paul's argumentation'.[29] But so convenient is this 'narrative pattern' to the particular christological and biblical-theological cases argued by Hays and Wright that the value of their appeal to narrative theory as an independent 'methodological control' on their efforts is called into question.[30] Or at least one can see how a theory that purports to show that, despite appearances on the surface, the deep logic of narrative is on their side might appeal to Hays and Wright (hence my opening definition of 'narrative criticism' as only 'half-joking').[31]

I shift now to the task of identifying some positive contributions of Adams' paper, a number of which readily suggest themselves. To begin with, Adams gives equal recognition to the fact that, to be of any use, our definition of 'narrative' has to fit (nonnarrative) texts like the Pauline letters but that it cannot simply be cut to that measure without begging the question of its own cogency. Another positive feature is the methodological guidance Adams draws from the 'critical linguistics' perspective that he has employed with profit elsewhere.[32] Also, I think it is sensible to orient our topic of 'the story of God and creation' around the figure of Adam in order to get a handle on it.[33] I was

---

29. Hays, *The Faith of Jesus Christ*, 103; cf. Wright, *The Climax of the Covenant*, 205.

30. Hays, *The Faith of Jesus Christ*, 120.

31. Actantial analysis appears to facilitate the distinctive connections Wright draws between Israel and Jesus as messiah (see, e.g., *The New Testament and the People of God*, 382–83); as for Hays, it facilitates the connections he draws between πίστις and Jesus (see, e.g., *The Faith of Jesus Christ*, 114–15, 123–24). Although, as noted above, Hays retrospectively drops the structuralist methodology, blaming it, in fact, on the influence of H. Boers at Emory (*The Faith of Jesus Christ*, 2nd edn, xxvii), the particular use he originally made of it in his own right suggests an unsuccessful argument for the subjective genitive reading of πίστις Χριστοῦ (with the intriguing result that L.T. Johnson, in a new Foreword to the reprint edition, now finds this actantial argument more persuasive than its author does [xii–xiii]). (See the Afterword, below.)

32. As for Adams' limited use of actantial analysis, I take it that he is simply following what seems to be becoming a convention of 'narrative criticism of Paul', a convention I have simply asked that we take a careful look at before we perpetuate it.

33. Cf. the narrative typology of C.K. Barrett's classic protonarrative treatment of Pauline theology, *From First Adam to Last: A Study of Pauline Theology* (London: A. & C. Black, 1962).

pleased to find Adams bringing our theme of 'God and creation' in Paul into relation with Paul's 'righteousness (of God)' language in Romans, and in a way that I find congenial. But what is to me perhaps most impressive about Adams' treatment of our theme in Romans and Galatians is his contextual sensitivity, his resistance, that is, to any hasty assimilation of one letter to the other. Indeed, far from letting Romans fill in the 'missing' details of Galatians, Adams speculates on how differently a 'story of God and creation' might have gone within the horizons of Galatians, possibly undermining Adams' own presupposition of continuity between eschatological redemption and original creation that works so well for Romans. On this, I find that Adams' conclusion hits just the right note: 'My view is that Paul's stories reflect the same epistolary diversity and are subject to the same varying contextual influences as any other aspect of his discourse. . . . I would resist, therefore, the attempt to subsume the whole of Paul's theology under one all-encompassing "story"' (see page 42).

Like Adams, I would want to temper my claims with the realisation that they are made on the basis of a relatively small part of the picture—and from a rather slanted view, at that. But it strikes me that some far-reaching questions, in terms of assessing the 'narrative' proposal, can be spun out from the simple observation that the 'story' of Galatians starts from Abraham, not Adam—questions enabled by the narrative proposal itself, thus constituting a payoff of that approach. The reasons for this difference between Romans and Galatians are unclear. Adams finds hints of 'a shift in theological emphasis': 'In Romans, Paul accentuates the continuity between "creation" and "new creation", and in Galatians, the discontinuity' (see page 41). At any rate, something about the difference between a letter written to stave off a threat of gentile 'judaizing' (Galatians) and a letter written (among other things) to stave off a threat of gentile 'anti-Judaism' (Romans) called for a different biblical 'story'.[34] On this very point, C.K. Barrett asked whether we are not justified in combining Galatians 3 'with references made elsewhere to Adam', thus making 'a clear, connected, and complete story'.[35] This is certainly a sensible proposal, one that, in the nature of the case, cannot be ruled out. But a consideration precisely of the 'nature of the case' here is suggestive for a narrative approach to Paul. When is Paul's silence *silence*, and when is it the calm water concealing a submerged narrative? You could say that in Galatians Paul simply chooses not to tell part of the story. But how different would Galatians look if Paul just didn't have a Grand Story? Such a case of indeterminacy of interpretation, where the same text (not really the same) may

---

34. Cf. the similar line of questioning of Fisk, review of Witherington, 554.

35. Barrett, *From First Adam to Last*, cited from Hays, *The Faith of Jesus Christ*, 244 n. 106; although Hays does not commit himself, he leans toward Barrett's view (227, 244–45 n. 106, 263–64).

be taken to point in radically different directions without some neutral fact of the matter to adjudicate, can be quite revealing of interpretative predispositions.

This leads to a third general remark about the narrative proposal: We need to be more clear about the *aims* of a narrative approach to Paul. Here the rhetoric that has typified the approach stands out as particularly significant. In Hays' terms, Paul's 'foundational story' is the 'substructure' of his theology, that in which his theology is 'grounded' or 'rooted', that which 'undergirds' it, which, though 'partly submerged', breaks the surface intermittently in the form of 'allusive' phrases intended to 'recall' and 'evoke' the 'underlying' story.[36] Inasmuch as such foundationalist language takes itself literally, as though it named an object and located it spatially, it may be rife for deconstruction—which is not necessarily to place such language beyond use.[37] That is, such language may be seen to be practical, not theoretical. The metaphor of 'depth' versus 'surface' is an argumentative figure for commending or asserting one thing over another. The battle being fought over Paul in this particular case is (ironically) that between rhetoric and theology, or, in the terms made popular by J.C. Beker, the tension between 'contingency' and 'coherence'.[38] As Hays often reiterates, the 'narrative' he is after imposes a 'constraint' on Paul's argumentation. The narrative approach, on this model, identifies that which Paul brings ready-made, as it were, to his rhetorical encounters.[39]

If the aim of such a narrative approach is to rescue some sense of a coherent core to Paul's theology from those who would place too much emphasis on the exigencies of Paul's rhetoric, then it seems bound to fall short of persuasion. The reason is simple. One may just as well be struck by how Paul's argumentation acts as a constraint on his 'story'. The 'narrative' proposal may cohere well with a certain sort of 'theological' approach, but it can hardly be expected to have independent probative force for one tending to see the 'same' phenomena from an 'intertextual' and 'rhetorical' perspective. Would Abraham and Moses have had the same place in Paul's story apart from the controversies that brought them into his letters? Does normative and

---

36. Hays, *The Faith of Jesus Christ*, 6, 7, 8, 13, 38, and throughout; 'Crucified with Christ', 231–34.

37. On 'deconstruction' in the sense assumed, see S.C. Wheeler III, *Deconstruction as Analytic Philosophy* (Cultural Memory in the Present; Stanford, Calif.: Stanford University Press, 2000) 197–215 and 216–30.

38. See Hays, *The Faith of Jesus Christ*, 1–30, 247–66.

39. Hays ('Crucified with Christ', 233) writes, 'As [Paul] confronts pastoral problems in his churches, he responds to them by thinking through the situation in the light of the story, plotting the community's place within the unfolding narrative.'

determinative appeal to Paul's 'foundational story' sometimes become an effective replacement for the letters? To make Paul's story a 'constraint' on his argument is potentially to be in the thrall of Paul's own rhetoric, and to figure Paul's theology as 'narrative' is itself a trope (though one that takes itself simply to be mirroring the essence of Paul and his letters). A 'narrative' reading of Paul is both a type of approach and a type of *argument*. Hays' advocacy of a 'narrative' approach to Paul has tended to run two claims together, the foundationalist one criticised here and the more general appeal that we should attend to narrative features of Paul's letters, an appeal that has both found independent confirmation in the carefully defined work of Fowl and has been stretched rather thinly in the diffuse synthesis of Witherington. Given that 'narrative criticism' of Paul is not any one thing, and given the vast terrain over which it has attempted to range in one form or another, methodological clarification might assign some of the work to a refined 'narrative' approach (or approaches) and some to 'intertextuality', giving place both to 'theological' and to 'rhetorical' modes of analysis—and combinations as yet undreamed of.

I would raise as a final point for reflection the matter of the central metaphor under whose aspect we view Paul on the narrative approach we are assessing here, or on any revised or rival approach—the 'arrow' and the 'web' of my title. To focus the matter in this way is to draw attention to the otherwise hidden choices we might make in opting for some version of a narrative approach to Paul. I see three interrelated tendencies in variations of the narrative approach as modelled thus far. The first is the tendency to imagine Paul armed with a story waiting to be told instead of a story that lives in the telling. The second is the tendency to think in terms of a single, Grand Story instead of many stories, joining and separating, having the unity of an anthology, not that of a singular entity. The third tendency is to picture a linear, progressive, and forward-looking Story instead of stories that are more like parables, bearing down on the present moment of the community. Is scripture for Paul more like a line pointing forward (the arrow), or a set of concentric circles drawing one inward (the web)? (Perhaps we will want to say 'both', but the distinction may still prove illuminating.) This question implicitly raises the question of other tellers and other tellings, of whether we think more in terms of Paul's (and others') fidelity to a singular, ongoing story or of his respinning biblical stories around Christ, stories that could be told in quite other ways. Do we imagine Paul's hermeneutics as (in oversimplified terms) more 'early Jewish' or 'later Christian'? Perhaps a Grand Narrative perspective, so 'natural' to us, requires an apologetic impetus (Luke, Irenaeus) or even a technological shift (the Greek Bible in codex form) unknown to Paul.

This raises again the question of whether it would be better to take 'narrative' or 'intertextuality' as our central critical concept. Does a 'narrative' perspective predispose us to approach Paul's 'story' referentially, as a depiction of a certain grand movement of history (arguably, not the most helpful approach theologically)?[40] Could an 'intertextual' perspective restore to us a sense of the 'biblical story' for Paul as a vast theological and rhetorical reper- toire—narrative, poetry, prophecy, mystery—to be performed in endless vari- ation and improvisation on the themes of humanity, death, and transcendence? If there are potential problems with a narrative approach to Paul, they may not lie where we are perhaps prone to think, that is, with the issue of taking a 'nar- rative approach' to nonnarrative texts. A narrative interpretation is a function of paying a certain kind of readerly attention to Paul, and, as such, it does not ultimately stand or fall on the essentialistic question of suitability to the mate- rial (though again the question of anachronism looms large). It stands, instead, on the pragmatic question of the fruits of such a reading, including how it structures and determines our perception of Paul. There is, then, one final question about this focus on our metaphors: *Is it rhetoric or theology—or both?*

## AFTERWORD

Since writing the above, I am compelled by the appearance of a reprint edi- tion of Richard Hays' *The Faith of Jesus Christ* to break the silence I had kept here on an issue over which I have been engaged: namely, the πίστις Χριστοῦ debate—that is, whether this phrase is to be interpreted as 'faith in Christ' (the objective genitive reading) or as 'the faith(fulness) of Christ' (the subjective genitive reading).[41] I had originally left the matter to one side since, *in principle*, the narrative proposal and the subjective genitive reading of πίστις Χριστοῦ are separate matters (though, *in practice*, the two go together like ham and eggs, in a way that seems beyond mere coincidence). In a new Introduc- tion to the work, Hays himself separates his subjective genitive reading of

---

40. I have in mind the 'mythic' character of much of the Story in question, which for some will attenuate the sense in which it could be said, *without further ado*, to be 'paradigmatic' for us. Hays has revealed that 'the great adversary whose shadow looms over *The Faith of Jesus Christ* is Rudolf Bultmann' (*The Faith of Jesus Christ*, 2nd edn, xxv). But on this point, one knew where Bultmann stood—and from there he casts a long shadow. For renewed debate in this area, see T. Engberg-Pedersen, *Paul and the Stoics* (Edinburgh: T&T Clark, 2000).

41. See R.B. Matlock, 'Detheologizing the ΠΙΣΤΙΣ ΧΡΙΣΤΟΥ Debate: Cautionary Remarks from a Lexical Semantic Perspective', *NovT* 42 (2000): 1–23 (a first attempt to think outside the limits of the debate as it has been defined, arguing for the objec- tive genitive reading from a fresh methodological perspective).

πίστις Χριστοῦ from, and subordinates it to, his narrative proposal much more sharply than I would have anticipated, given the title of the work and his own earlier descriptions of it.[42] But in the form that Hays argues them, at least, I have difficulty seeing them other than as two sides of the same coin, hence his original attempt to use his particular approach to narrative as an independent argument for the subjective genitive reading.[43] It is as well to raise this issue here so that the reader may consider whether my disagreement with Hays over πίστις Χριστοῦ might unduly prejudice my view of the narrative proposal (though I stand by my critical questions above, where in any case I extend an olive branch here and there).

A substantial part of Hays' new Introduction is given over to identifying the 'dialogue partners' that he would now wish to engage, among whom I appear to number.[44] The invitation to dialogue is welcome, but it gets off to a rough start. Consider the following striking pair of sentences, together with the footnote that interrupts the first:

> Matlock . . . writes as though there were an objective science of lexical semantics that permits him to perform theologically 'neutral' interpretations of linguistic units,[63] in contrast to all the other foolish participants in the debate who have allowed theological considerations to warp their judgment. This is an astonishingly naive claim.

---

63. The very first paragraph of Matlock's article disclaims the possibility of ruling on 'a properly exegetical decision from some "neutral" standpoint above the fray' (Matlock, 'Detheologizing,' 1). He then proceeds for the next 23 pages to ignore this disclaimer. By page 2, he writes, "Ideally, lexical semantics might offer a more or less stable and agreed set of terms and principles for the analysis of word-meaning, worked out in general application[,] and thus "neutral," at least, to the specific interpretative issues arising over πίστις Χριστοῦ.' In light of the opening disclaimer, we expect this sentence to be followed by another to balance the 'ideally' with a 'however, in reality'—but the shoe never drops.[45]

I have faith that the reader will see the movement made between the first two sentences—from 'writing as though' to an 'astonishingly naive claim'—for what it is. Hays cites no instance of this 'claim' because it was never made;

---

42. See Hays, *The Faith of Jesus Christ*, 2nd edn, xxiii–xxix; in the annotated bibliography to his *The Letter to the Galatians* (NIB 11; Nashville: Abingdon Press, 2000), Hays gives the perfect one-line summary of his monograph: 'Argues for "the faithfulness of Jesus Christ" as an integral element of the gospel narrative that undergirds Paul's argument in Galatians' (198).

43. See again above, nn. 30, 31.

44. Hays, *The Faith of Jesus Christ*, 2nd edn, xxxv, xliv–xlvii.

45. Ibid., xlvi (the bracketed comma in the footnote restores the original).

it corresponds to nothing that I said (nor even, quite, to my underlying narrative). Hays, on the other hand, declares that 'the conventional judgments of
lexicographers and commentators since the Reformation have been mistaken'
on πίστις Χριστοῦ (foolish participants in the debate who have allowed theological considerations to warp their judgement?) and 'the balance of grammatical evidence strongly favors the subjective genitive interpretation' (a
theologically neutral interpretation of linguistic units?).[46] Presumably to fulfil all righteousness, Hays interrupts his attribution to me of a naive claim to
neutrality to note that I actually claim the opposite. And although he cannot
be expected just to take my word for it, his response leaves me disappointed to
find that I have already lost him so badly by page 2 of the article in question.
With my offending gesture to general lexical semantic concepts that are 'neutral' (mind the inverted commas) simply in the sense that they have developed
well outside the πίστις Χριστοῦ debate, I had in mind such matters as the
analysis of 'polysemy', whether and how one may distinguish the senses of a
polysemous word and what makes for good argument as to which sense is to
be preferred in a given case—matters introduced in that article and developed
in work in press and in progress.[47] I am genuinely surprised to find that Hays
expects falling footwear here—the wait may be a long one.

Judging from Hays' comments, which all seem to revolve around this point,
I believe I have unintentionally misled him in speaking of 'detheologizing' the
πίστις Χριστοῦ debate, which he takes to be a 'sure prescription for misinterpretation'.[48] His concluding word on my work is as follows: 'The attempt
to do non-theological exegesis of the New Testament is self-defeating. In fact,
Matlock's own interpretation of Galatians 2—to the extent that he offers us
one—is itself theological, despite his efforts to transcend theology'.[49] This last
realisation might have led one (correctly) to suspect that my talk of 'detheologizing' the debate is a more limited affair than ruling theological concerns
'out of court', as Hays represents me as doing.[50] In fact, unless Hays would
want to insist that there is nothing other than theological *preference* to distinguish a better or worse argument over Paul's *language*, I think he broadly
agrees with me on 'detheologizing' (though he might prefer another term).
Notice that to decide among the various linguistic options *solely* on the basis

---

46. Ibid., xlvii, 276.

47. See R.B. Matlock, '"Even the Demons Believe": Paul and πίστις Χριστοῦ,' *CBQ*
(forthcoming), a partial overview of research leading up to a monograph on πίστις
Χριστοῦ in Paul.

48. Hays, *The Faith of Jesus Christ*, 2nd edn, xlvi.

49. Ibid., xlvii.

50. Ibid.

of theological preference is an argument from consequences and is thus 'logically' invalid. I have avoided framing my argument in quite those terms because, '*theo*logically', space must be given to consequences (without making this the only consideration). At any rate, this unfortunate misunderstanding prevents Hays from seeing much point to what I am doing. Says Hays, 'Matlock's "exegetical" procedure is basically nothing more sophisticated than to look up the word πίστις in various lexicons, with particular emphasis given to [the Louw & Nida lexicon]'. Would that it were as simple as that. Actually, I had taken care to state that the Louw and Nida lexicon 'is not assumed to be the final authority' but rather 'the obvious starting point for semantic analysis of πίστις'—a simple first step that Hays seems still to have failed to take.[51] He continues, 'Can anyone seriously believe that the lexicographers are not making *theological* judgments. . . ?' Hays imagines the point of my use of Louw and Nida to be that it is presumed to be theologically neutral. Actually, the point is to try to grasp, generally, why the Louw and Nida lexicon is structured in the odd way that it is, compared to conventional lexicons—the linguistic awareness of polysemy and of semantic context that lies behind it—and how this might relate to πίστις, as such, and to our particular exegetical argumentation over πίστις Χριστοῦ. When that penny drops for Hays, it may be hoped that the quality of argument will rise.

To end on a more positive note, I congratulate Richard on this well-deserved reprint. The work hardly needs my commendation, given the new Foreword by Luke Timothy Johnson. But the enthusiastic praise of one who agrees with you, though sincere, is also self-praise. The praise of a critic carries a certain weight of its own. For it is possible to hold a work to be *importantly* mistaken in its central claims and worthy thus of serious and extensive critical attention. Such a work is Richard Hays' *The Faith of Jesus Christ*. If you have not read it, I hope that you will.

---

51. Matlock, 'Detheologizing the ΠΙΣΤΙΣ ΧΡΙΣΤΟΥ Debate', 8 n. 21.

# 4

# Sharing in Their Spiritual Blessings?

*The Stories of Israel in
Galatians and Romans*

BRUCE W. LONGENECKER

Any search for narrative components within Paul's theological reflection must early on come to grips with Paul's deliberations on the people of Israel. Of the various narrative taxonomies suggested by proponents of the narrative approach to Paul's thought processes, the 'story of Israel' must certainly have great potential as a significant theological resource. Even a cursory glance through the Pauline literature would indicate this. To give just one example, when describing Christ as 'our paschal lamb' in 1 Cor. 5:7 or recalling the wilderness wanderings of 'our ancestors' in 1 Cor. 10:1–11, Paul seems to expect that his predominantly gentile converts enjoy at least a basic familiarity with the scriptural narratives of the Hebrews' exodus from Egypt into the promised land. Whether this familiarity is attributable to Paul's prior instruction, to local synagogual influence, or whatever, Paul clearly assumes some fundamental cognisance with the story of Israel.

It seems likely, then, that an exegete whose sole aim is to demonstrate the narrative character of Paul's reflections on Israel would be labouring with an elephant but giving birth to a mouse. There is, however, one aspect of Paul's 'story of Israel' that goes right to the heart of any attempt to understand Paul's theology and/or theologising: that is, the content and character of that story. Granting a narrative character to Paul's reflections on Israel is not the same as assessing the stability of that story and determining its place within Paul's theological processes. These will be our primary interests in this essay.

In what follows I will be content to fall in line with the broad narrative approach to Paul, accepting its premises, terminology, and delineation of stories in order for the approach to offer what it may. In the first two exegetical sections of this essay, Romans and Galatians are examined in relation to the story of Israel. Although a complete analysis of pertinent passages in Romans and Galatians is not possible within the constraints of this exercise,[1] even a cursory analysis will uncover important aspects of Paul's handling of the 'story of Israel' on two occasions. In the third section, 'Synthesis', I argue that, while the 'story of Israel' is identifiable as a crucial component in the process of Paul's theological reflection, it is not textually stable in all respects in the extant texts of Paul. The implications of this are shown to require careful consideration with regard to our understanding of Paul's theological reflection. Finally, in light of the results of this exercise, Section 4 offers some reflections on the merits of a narrative approach to Paul.

In the analysis that follows, it will be important to recognise a schematic distinction between two forms of 'linearity': (1) 'covenantal linearity' and (2) 'organic linearity' (which might also be called 'participationistic linearity'). These are heuristic terms applied to Paul's letters in order to assess those texts with the greatest amount of precision; although they derive from certain features of Paul's letters, they are not Paul's own terms. Consequently the terms themselves are relatively insignificant and are useful only as shorthand pointers to larger concepts within Paul's letters. The term 'covenantal linearity' refers to a special relationship between God and the ethnic people of Israel, in which God has elected Israel as God's chosen people and has become involved especially with the course of Israel's history. The term 'organic linearity' refers to the participation of gentile Christians within the organic unfolding of God's elective grace upon ethnic Israel, so that the inclusion of gentile Christians within Israel's ongoing story is an integral part of that story line. As will be shown, differentiating between these two forms of linearity is a key consideration for the recovery of narrative dynamics in Paul's theology.[2]

# ROMANS

Romans incorporates the story of Israel to a much greater extent than any of Paul's other letters. In Romans, moments from Israel's past, present, and future are part of the warp and woof of Paul's theological agenda. While there is no sustained survey of Israel's history of the kind found in some speeches of Acts (e.g., Acts 7:2–53 [Stephen]; Acts 13:16–41 [Paul]), the highpoints in Israel's

---

1. Nor can I attempt to deal with the important works of other scholars whose proposals impinge on our topic in significant ways (most notably, N.T. Wright, J.M. Scott, F. Thielman, S.C. Keesmaat, T.W. Berkley, and a host of others).

2. For instance, the simple term 'linearity' is not precise enough for our purposes. As will be shown, in Galatians the story of Israel has linearity (i.e., ethnic Israel in relationship with God goes on to be redeemed by the Son of God) but is lacking an 'organic' component, unlike Romans.

past history are clearly outlined in 9:4–5, giving way to a sustained consideration of Israel's past, present, and future (Romans 9–11). In this way, in Romans
the 'story of Israel' touches on all the basic points in the overarching drama of
salvation history by means of a 'covenant linearity' in which God is proving
faithful to the chosen people even throughout the surprising twists and turns
of salvation history (i.e., 'Has God's word failed? By no means!' [9:6]).

It is not surprising, then, that the story of Israel is closely associated with
the story of God. In Romans, Paul maintains that a special relationship
has existed and continues to exist between God and Israel, a relationship
heuristically discussed here as one of 'covenant'. That relationship was established with 'the patriarchs' of Israel (9:5), resulting in the 'election' of Israel as
'beloved [of God] for the sake of the patriarchs' (11:28). The covenant relationship is evident in other features of Israel's history, recounted in 9:4 (NRSV,
cf. 3:1–2): 'adoption, the glory, the covenants, the giving of the law, the worship, and the promises'. Of these, Israel's reception of God's law is highlighted
elsewhere in the letter: The Jewish people were entrusted with 'the oracles of
God' (3:2 NRSV), and demonstrate a 'reliance on the law', boasting in their relationship to God (2:17; cf. 10:2). They 'know his [God's] will' and have been
'instructed in the law' (2:18 NRSV), in which they continue to 'boast' (2:23
NRSV).

The recognition of Israel's elected status lies alongside Paul's conviction
that her story has been marked out by failure to please God. Her 'zeal for God'
has not translated into a corporate lifestyle that enhances the reputation of
God. Instead, in a novel interpretation of Isaiah 52:5, Paul identifies Israel's
failings as the cause whereby God's name is blasphemed among the nations
(2:23–24). In the wake of the Messiah's ministry, Israel's zeal is 'not enlight-
ened' (10:2), having stumbled over the stumbling stone (i.e., Christ; 9:30–10:4;
cf. 10:18–21).

This conviction that Israel has not pleased God merges with Paul's conviction that Israel's story falls within the larger story of the cosmic power of Sin[3]
at work in God's own creation (3:9–20).[4] This conviction is evident in Rom.
5:12–21, where the 'world' that emerged from Adam's act of transgression
found a corrective neither in the establishment of a chosen people nor in the
giving of the law. Paul addresses the point more explicitly in Romans 7, where
he fuses the story of the 'fall' of Adam with a story of Israel (cf. also Paul's discussion of 'the Jew' of Romans 2–3 within the Adamic condition, and his sim-

---

3. The upper-case 'S' serves to indicate that Paul envisages the cosmic power of 'Sin'
as more than (but clearly related to) individual acts of human 'sin' and 'transgression'.

4. I will not comment here on whether Paul intended an allusion to Israel's sin in
Rom. 1:23; the general point is clear regardless of how one assesses this specific issue.

ilar use of 'I' in 3:7).[5] The one depicted in Romans 7 is zealous for God and eager to observe God's good law (cf. 9:31; 10:2). But this person is also one who, unlike the Christian (in Paul's taxonomy of things) has no external resources to deflect the invading influence of the power of Sin—the cosmic power that enslaves people and works them like marionette puppets, and the power spoken of in 3:9: 'All [people], both Jews and Greeks, are under the power of Sin.' Prior to the coming of the Messiah, the story of Israel is enmeshed within the story of a creation at odds with its creator. Paul even goes so far as to suggest that the giving of the law increased the problem of sinfulness, presumably within the boundaries of ethnic Israel (5:20).

Paul does not permit Israel's place within the story of fallen creation to undermine confidence in God's covenant faithfulness to Israel (3:3–4). In Romans 9–11 Paul defends God's faithfulness in the light of God's mysterious historical dealings. In these chapters Paul makes at least five main claims in relation to Israel's current disbelief,[6] the first three of which are as follows: (1) God's constancy is evident in the way God has always worked, calling some but not others (9:6–18); (2) salvation is currently enjoyed by a remnant of Israel (9:27–29; 11:1–6); and (3) God is free to make of Israel whatever God wishes, within God's broader purposes (9:19–26; 11:7–10). In this way, Paul believes he has defended God's reputation against the charge of 'indiscriminate behaviour' or infidelity towards those that have been chosen—lest those in Paul's communities think that God's fidelity towards them could also become jeopardised (contra his claims in Romans 8).

A fourth claim emerges from Romans 9–11: even unbelieving Israel is playing a role in God's redemptive story. In the penultimate stage of that story, Israel's 'trespass' allows salvation to go to the gentiles (11:11), thereby enabling the 'reconciliation for the world' (11:15). This is elaborated in the olive tree analogy, in which gentile Christians are likened to wild 'unnatural branches' that are enjoying the rich nutrients of a cultivated olive tree, and Jewish unbelievers are likened to 'natural branches' whose extraction from the root (i.e., the patriarchs) is not likely to be permanent (11:17–24). This imagery is strongly suggestive of a view of salvation history in which gentile Christians find themselves incorporated within the story of Israel's own salvation, heuristically labelled here 'organic linearity'.[7]

---

5. For a defence of this view, see my *Eschatology and the Covenant: A Comparison of 4 Ezra and Romans 1–11* (JSNTSup 57; Sheffield: Sheffield Academic Press, 1991) 225–45.

6. Of further import is Paul's claim that his ministry among the gentiles is intended to awake jealousy among the Jewish people and 'save some of them' (11:14; cf. 10:19).

7. Cf. J.P. Sampley, 'Romans and Galatians: Comparison and Contrast', in J.T. Butler, E.W. Conrad, and C.V. Ollenburger (eds), *Understanding the Word* (Sheffield: JSOT Press, 1985) 315–39, 331.

Paul's discussion of Israel in Romans 9–11 moves to a fifth claim: In the ultimate stage of God's redemptive story, 'all Israel will be saved' (11:26) by the eschatological deliverer (i.e., Jesus) who will root out their ungodliness (i.e., their lack of faith). Whereas the disobedience of gentile nations is currently being met by God's saving mercy, the disobedience of (unbelieving) Israel will be met by God's mercy at the eschatological culmination of salvation history. But underlying all this is the assumption that Israel is a distinct people arising from their election as God's beloved people (11:28–29). If Israel's story overlaps with the story of creation in the grip of the cosmic power of Sin, God's gracious grip on both Israel and creation is sovereign.

This story line informs the way Paul depicts his own story as well as that of his communities. Since the communities of (predominately) gentile Christians planted by Paul are sharing in the 'spiritual blessings' of the Jews (15:27),[8] some of the material resources of gentile Christian communities are being directed to support 'the poor among the saints at Jerusalem' (15:26 NRSV). This is taking place under Paul's oversight (15:25–28), in recognition of the fact that the emergence of Pauline churches around the Mediterranean basin is in some measure contingent on Jewish Christianity in Jerusalem, which provides a conduit to the rich theological resources of the Jewish people. Seemingly Paul here is again envisaging an 'organic' relationship between the story of Israel and that of gentile Christians.

Also linked to the story of Israel is the story of Jesus. Jesus' identity 'according to the flesh' is related to David from the outset of the letter (1:3 NRSV), just as he is referred to as 'the root of Jesse' towards the end (15:12 NRSV). If Jesus emerges from among 'the Israelites' (9:5), he is also the one who will redeem the unbelievers among them in the future (11:26–27).

Paul's merging of the stories of Jesus and Israel is also evident in the letter's prescript (1:1–7), where brief but significant narrative coupling of all five stories of this project is evident. Paul's own story as one called to be an apostle (1:1, 5–6) is linked with that of Jesus (Paul is 'a servant of Jesus Christ'), told in brief overview in 1:3–4. These stories themselves are associated with the stories of God (1:1, 7), the 'inheritors' (1:5–7), and Israel (by means of the figure of David, 1:3).

A more developed version of this narrative coupling is evident in Rom. 3:21–31, a primary theological centre of the letter. In this passage, the story of God is at the forefront, as the one who acts to effect salvation (God 'put forward' Jesus, 3:25

---

8. Although 'their' in the phrase 'their spiritual blessings' (τοῖς πνευματικοῖς αὐτῶν) refers in the first instance to Jewish Christians in Jerusalem, the assumption that spiritual blessings are 'theirs' cannot be fully explained without recognition of an ethnic dimension in Paul's reflections.

NRSV), linked with the story of Jesus as the one in whom the righteousness of God has been 'disclosed' (3:21 NRSV). Mention of 'all who believe' (3:22; cf. 3:30), of being 'justified by his grace' (3:24 NRSV), of the 'law of faith' (3:27 NRSV),[9] of righteousness 'by faith apart from works prescribed by the law' (3:28 NRSV), and of righteousness for 'gentiles' (3:29) introduces the stories of 'inheritors' and of Paul's mission, as does the personal referent of 3:31 NRSV: 'Do we then overthrow the law by this faith? By no means! On the contrary, we uphold the law.'

The story of Israel has also influenced Paul's discourse in this passage. First, the affirmation that 'God is one' (3:30 NRSV) is an intentional recitation of what pious Jews throughout the generations regularly confessed. This is part and parcel of the Jewish rejection of idol worship, referred to already in 2:23, which lies at the heart of the brighter moments of Israel's history. Second, the reference to 'boasting' in 3:27 seems to refer to the situation of 'the Jew' described in 2:17–24, wherein boasting in Jewish covenant identity 'with God, within the law' is repeatedly envisaged. Whatever the covenantal history of Israel was about, Paul does not envisage it to involve a stringent ethnocentric covenantalism that excludes gentiles from salvation and the glorification of God. Third, the controversial phrase 'the righteousness of God' is likely to contain some reference to God's covenant faithfulness to Israel (3:21–22, 25; cf. 3:4–7),[10] even if its full scope of meaning goes beyond that to include God's faithfulness to his creation. Finally, mention of God's forbearance in 'having passed over the sins previously committed' (3:25 NRSV) includes a gesture to the history of Israel. If, as is likely, these previously overlooked sins include those of the Jewish people prior to Christ (cf. 2:17–3:20), then Paul seems to envisage the sacrificial system in the pre-Christian 'story of Israel' as in some manner ineffective. Atonement for the sins of Israel has finally taken place by means of Jesus' own 'faithfulness' (πίστις, 3:22, 25)— that is, his obedience to God 'even to the point of death' (Phil. 2:8).[11]

The summary of the main 'argument' of Romans (15:7–13) is the third passage wherein an explicit convergence of Israel's story and the other four stories of this exercise is noticeable. If Jesus is from the race of 'the Israelites' (9:5) and will one day return to redeem unbelieving Israel (11:26–27), in the meantime he has also served a specific function in relation to the unfolding story of Israel by becoming

---

9. If νόμος here refers to the Mosaic law; for defence, see my *Eschatology and the Covenant*, 207–11.

10. See, for instance, R.B. Hays, 'Justification', in D.N. Freeman et al., (eds), *Anchor Bible Dictionary*, vol. 3 (New York: Doubleday, 1992) 1129–33; S.K. Williams, 'The "Righteousness of God" in Romans', *JBL* 99 (1980): 241–90.

11. This aspect of Paul's case in Romans (the 'faithfulness of Christ') requires greater defence than I am able to offer here. See further my *The Triumph of Abraham's God* (Edinburgh: T&T Clark; Nashville: Abingdon Press, 1998) 95–115.

a servant of the circumcised on behalf of the truth[fulness] of God in
order that he might confirm the promises given to the patriarchs, and
in order that the Gentiles might glorify God for his mercy (15:8–9 NRSV).

These verses are some of the most significant in Romans,[12] and they reveal in clear
and unqualified terms a convergence of all five stories considered in this project.
The story of Jesus, the 'servant of the circumcised', is affiliated with the story of
Israel. Those two stories together are related to the story of God, the God who is
faithful to the covenant people ('the truthfulness of God') and who confirms the
promises made to Israel's patriarchs. This convergence in the stories of God, Israel,
and Jesus informs the other stories of our project (Paul and 'inheritors'), in that
now the gentiles too are welcome to 'glorify God'. The praising of God's name by
the gentiles among God's people (15:9–12) is again suggestive of the inclusion of
gentiles within the story of Israel (e.g., 'Rejoice, O gentiles, with his people', 15:10
NRSV). Here, along with the olive tree analogy of Romans 11 and the claim that
gentile Christians are participating in the spiritual blessings of the Jews (15:27), is
a third occasion in Romans where an 'organic linearity' makes an appearance.

We have seen, then, that in at least three critical passages[13] Paul explicitly
weaves all five stories together in intricately woven lacework, with the story of
Israel playing a prominent role. In Romans Paul's theologising demonstrates
the integral relation of Israel's story to the other stories of this project. While
it may be too much to claim that Israel's story is a driving force behind the whole
of the letter, it is not too much to claim that at many critical points Paul's theologising both develops and is developed by a narrative of Israel. In that narrative, a 'covenant linearity' is clearly evident in which God's gracious dealings
with Israel throughout history are at the fore. At two or three significant points,
however, 'covenant linearity' is expanded to include 'organic linearity' in which
Israel's story is depicted as unfolding to include gentile Christians within it.

## GALATIANS

In the terminology of this project, it might be said that Paul writes the Galatian letter to counter a specific coupling of the story of Israel with those of

---

12. T. Söding ('Verheißung und Erfüllung im Lichte paulinischer Theologie', NTS
47 [2001]: 146–70, 167) capably articulates a growing conviction that this section is the
recapitulation not only of the paraenesis of Romans 12–15 but of the whole of the letter, with 15:8 functioning as the key statement ('der Kernsatz').

13. The letter's prescript, 1:1–7, which for many readers would have provided an
initial impression of Paul; 3:21–31, a central 'junction' in the letter's theological traf-
fic; the concluding summary of the main body of the letter, 15:7–13.

Christ and of Christians. The Galatian Christians were enamoured with the views of some 'agitators' who envisaged Israel's story to embrace those gentiles for whom the story of Christ had salvific significance. Paul's case in Romans follows similar lines, but what fills the space 'between the lines' is enormously different for Paul on the one hand and the agitators on the other, especially with regard to the observance of the law. While the agitators were probably interested in promoting observance of the whole law, it was particularly the circumcision of gentile Christians that motivated their efforts. Circumcision had long been a cardinal practice of Jewish history. Biblical and Jewish traditions traced this practice back to Abraham, the ultimate patriarch of Israel (e.g., Gen. 17:9–14; *Jub.* 15:11–14). For the agitators, the conviction that gentile Christians were incorporated into the story of Israel corresponds to the conviction that gentile Christians should practise circumcision. Paul, perceiving the agitators' stance to be an abandonment of the gospel, puts gentile circumcision at odds with Christ: 'If you let yourselves be circumcised, Christ will be of no benefit to you' (5:2 NRSV; cf. 3:26; 5:6; 6:15). If in Paul's letter to the Galatians there is a coupling of the story of Israel and the story of Christ, it is one that bypasses the agitators' own manner of coupling.

Just as Romans is animated by 'covenant linearity' with regard to ethnic Israel, so too is Paul's earlier letter to the Galatian Christians. What Paul and the agitators would have in common is the certainty that Israel's story is one of special relationship with God. This conviction lies behind Paul's describing the law as 'our pedagogue until (εἰς) Christ came' (3:24; cf. the slightly different imagery of 4:1–3).[14] The point at issue should not rest on whether 'pedagogue' carries positive (e.g., 'caretaker') or negative (e.g., 'disciplinarian') force. The primary feature of this depiction of the law is that it had a specific function with regard to Israel's national history. In the Graeco-Roman world, a pedagogue was one who acted on behalf of a father concerned with the proper upbringing of his child (and consequently I favour the positive overtones).[15] Against this background, Paul's likening of the law to a pedagogue (1) develops a familial metaphor that itself indicates an underlying recognition of a covenant relationship between God and Israel,[16] and (2) includes within its

---

14. The εἰς of 3:24 has temporal force, as here, rather than telic force (i.e., the law served as a pedagogue 'to lead us to Christ' [NIV]).

15. In her reply to this article, Morna Hooker is in agreement with me on this. With hindsight Paul likens Israel's situation under the oversight of a pedagogue as a form of 'confinement' (cf. 3:23), but this should not override the general force of the pedagogue imagery.

16. The same is true of Paul's comments in 3:19–20, where the giving of the law to Israel is envisaged in a manner suggestive of a covenant relationship, albeit in terms that contrast it with the exceeding significance of what God has done in Christ.

bounds the whole sweep of Israel's history under the law from the time of its reception at Sinai (cf. 3:19) to the coming of Christ (cf. 3:24).

Further evidence of 'covenant linearity' within Galatians comes from Paul's comments in 4:4–5 depicting that what God has done in Christ has had a direct bearing on the story of Israel: 'God sent forth his Son, born of a woman, born under the law, to redeem those who were under the law.' Christ has effected redemption for Israel (or at least provided the opportunity for her redemption). The same might be evident in 3:13, where the 'us' spoken of likely refers to ethnic Jews: 'Christ redeemed us from the curse of the law, having become a curse for us.' These two passages indicate a convergence of the stories of Israel and Jesus, with the story of Christian communities included in that convergence. In particular, in both 4:4–5 and 3:13–14 the redemption of Israel is a penultimate goal that facilitates the accomplishment of an ultimate goal. That ultimate goal, of course, is the salvation of the world, spoken of as the 'blessing of Abraham . . . upon the gentiles' and the reception of the Spirit in 3:14 and as the 'adoption as sons' (τὴν υἱοθεσίαν) in 4:5. But the ultimate goal is subsequent to a prior necessary condition: that is, the redemption of Israel (cf. Mark 7:27; Acts 15:15–17). Paul follows here a theological pattern well established in the Jewish theology of his day: the redemption of Israel is an initial component and indispensable part of God's eschatological act of cosmic salvation.[17] Although the phrase 'to the Jew first and also to the Greek' appears only three times in the extant Pauline corpus, and then only in Romans (1:16; 2:9–10), the conviction behind the phrase is just as much a part of Paul's presentation in Galatians. Consequently, Galatians as much as Romans exhibits a robust covenantal linearity, with the God who elected Israel to be God's special people being the same one who acted in Christ to provide for Israel's salvation.

It is easy to see how a sequential patterning of this kind could promote an understanding of the eschatological era as the full flowering of Israel's story. Such an understanding seems to have been held by the agitators, for whom the salvation of the nations in Christ likely equated to the final phase of Israel's history, in which the nations converge within Israel's worship of God. We know that Paul himself would take a somewhat similar path later in Romans, in which he depicts gentile Christians as participating in the spiritual blessings of the Jewish people (11:17–24; 15:7–13, 27). In Galatians, however, the situation is not so clear-cut. In Romans, 'covenant linearity' could at times include 'organic linearity'. In Galatians, however, this convergence in forms of linearity is debat-

---

17. Scholars continue to undervalue this feature of Galatians, with near-disastrous consequences. So, e.g., C. Roetzel (*Paul: The Man and the Myth* [Edinburgh: T&T Clark, 1999] 123) writes, 'In the heat of this decisive battle [for the Galatian Christians], Paul overextended himself, leaving himself open to the charge of denying the validity of God's promises to the historical people of Israel.'

able. There Paul goes to great lengths to avoid the depiction of 'in Christ' communities as participators in the fullness of the history of ethnic Israel.

In 3:15–18, for instance, Paul strains against all odds to depict Abraham in any possible way other than as the patriarch of ethnic Israel. To do this, he entertains a rather forced argument about Abraham's exclusive 'seed' being Christ (since 'seed' is singular; contra Gal. 3:29; Rom. 4:16–18) instead of a particular corporate people (3:16). In this way, Abraham and Christ are associated with each other in a manner that wholly bypasses Israel's constitution and constituents.[18] Christ is not the seed *par excellence*, with members of ethnic Israel being ordinary seed; instead, Christ is simply the *exclusive* seed, with no other seed envisaged (except, as he goes on to say in 3:29, through their inclusion in Christ).

Demonstrating the same point is Paul's use of the word 'covenant' in 3:15–17 (usually translated 'will'; cf. NRSV). Longstanding Jewish traditions rooted the giving of the Mosaic law within the broader context of God's covenant with Abraham and his physical descendants. That Paul was familiar with this pattern is clear from Rom. 9:4–5, where he employs it himself. In Galatians 3, however, Paul depicts the giving of the law as falling outside the boundaries of God's covenant promise to Abraham.[19] That promise concerned faith and Christ, and it cannot be annulled, qualified, or enhanced by later phenomena such as the giving of the law to an ethnic people, despite the angelic presence that adorned that event (3:19).[20] The giving of the law was one of the most momentous events shaping Jewish history, and Jewish traditions presupposed that particular history to be the primary arena of salvation history. But Paul seems intent on holding back the tide of these traditions, placing the giving of the law beyond the salvific 'covenant'. There is no attempt here to yoke the story of Israel with those of Christ and the people of Christian faith; in fact, Paul seems wholly intent to avoid such a coupling altogether. Israel's reception of the law was merely a parenthesis between

---

18. I am not claiming here that Paul bypasses the story of Israel in Galatians or that he ignores the history of Israel. Unfortunately, I have left Hooker with this impression; see her response, pages 91, 94–95.

19. It is, however, crucially important also to note Paul's insistence (3:21–22) that the law is not contrary to 'the promises of God'. In fact, it has served God's salvific purposes (e.g., it 'has imprisoned all things under the power of sin'). Later in a different way Paul emphasises the same point again, indicating that Christian love embodies what the law had always envisaged (5:13–14). In these ways, Paul is not a proleptic pseudo-Marcionite, seeing the God of salvation in Christ as somehow different from the God who gave the law to Israel. But nonetheless, even if the law is 'not opposed' to the promise (since the same God stands behind them both), Paul's comments in 3:15–18 set law and promise apart to the extent that the giving of the law to Israel is excluded from God's covenant promise to Abraham.

20. I see no reason to think that 'through angels' in 3:19 rules out God as the originator of the law, the angels being the source of the law. For defence of this important feature, see my *Triumph of Abraham's God*, 59.

the primary moments of salvation history—God's promise to Abraham and the coming of Abraham's exclusive seed, Jesus Christ.

A few verses later Paul reinforces these points. In 3:29, instead of defining those who belong to Christ as enjoying the spiritual blessings of the Jews (as in Romans), Paul defines them solely as descendants of Abraham, the 'pre-Israel' recipient of the promise (as in 3:15–18). Abraham is not a figure that permits organic linearity between Christians and Israel in this passage. Such a scenario is not on Paul's agenda; moreover, he seems intent on sidestepping that scenario altogether.

The passage that is most promising for an organic or participatory interpretation of gentile Christians in relation to Israel's history is 4:1–7, not least 4:4–5 where the Son of God is said to have entered into Israel's history to redeem those under the law. This feature must take pride of place in any description of covenantal linearity, as we have seen. But does it involve 'organic linearity' as we have defined it? Clearly Paul believed Israel's 'maturity' to be in Christ. But it is not clear that this 'maturity' involves a participationistic scheme in which the gentiles share in Israel's own and distinctive 'spiritual blessings'. Paul envisages the 'maturity' of other nations as also being in Christ (4:8–9). Israel and the nations are alike in their problem and their solution: the problem includes their position under the στοιχεῖα (the overseeing 'tribal deities', of which Israel's was the law) and the solution is inclusion in Christ. In this way, the 'story of Israel' is patterned in much the same way as the stories of other nations, despite the fact that, prior to the coming of Christ, Israel had enjoyed a level of intimacy with God that outstripped the other nations. The issue in Galatia was whether gentile Christians needed to include themselves within Israel's ongoing story, and if so, how that was to happen. Paul addressed these issues by insisting that gentile Christians are to envisage themselves as included within the story of Jesus Christ, the redeemer of Israel, whose sonship is the point of 'maturity' for all nations, Jews and gentiles alike. It would have been simple for Paul to state explicitly in 4:1–7 that gentile Christians were participating in Israel's maturity by their faith in the Messiah who had redeemed Israel. But he never makes this 'organic' point in relation to faith, which is a curious omission if this were indeed the central point of his argument.[21] Clearly

---

21. Two of my revered mentors, Professors Hooker and Dunn, offer counterarguments to my interpretation of Galatians, each one highlighting this passage in particular. I am not convinced, however, that Paul's use of pronouns in these verses plays so easily into their case. While some of the pronouns have potential to be read in relation to an 'organic' interpretation (e.g., 4:3; cf. 3:23–25), others do not (e.g., the 'our' of 4:6), unless Paul really intended to say in 4:6 that, because gentile Christians are sons, so God has consequently sent the Spirit into the hearts of Jewish Christians (an unusual form of 'organic linearity'!). To assign all of Paul's first-person plurals to Jews and second-person plurals to gentiles in 4:1–7 is a blunt interpretative tool that does as little justice to 4:1–7 as it does to 3:23–29. Clearly further debate on this passage would be

the gentile Christians share with Jewish Christians in the spiritual blessings of the 'new creation', but this need not be taken as 'organic linearity' since the inverse can also be said (i.e., Jewish Christians share the same with gentile Christians). Both are participants in the story of the new creation, not the unfolding story of ethnic Israel.

Neither can we infer in 4:1–7 that Paul envisages the 'inheritance' of the Spirit to be an integral aspect of the unfolding story of Israel (even if the giving of the Spirit was integral to God's eschatological activity). Paul has already noted that, according to scripture, the 'blessing' of the Spirit would be given through Abraham's seed to 'all the nations' (3:8). Paul says nothing about the Spirit being intended for Israel, with the gentiles gaining access to Israel's privileges through faith. Paul has already defined 'seed' with exclusive reference to Christ rather than to ethnic Israel, and he has already defined all those in Christ as being 'seed of Abraham' through their participation in Christ, in whom they are 'heirs according to the promise' (3:29 NRSV). Consequently, despite the unqualified covenant linearity of Gal. 4:1–7, there is nothing in that passage that testifies to an organic linearity. Instead, that passage seems suggestive that, for Paul, Jesus Christ is the pivot point from the story of ethnic Israel to another story altogether. The two 'stories' (to use the terminology of this project) are linked, associated, and intricately connected. But they are two stories nonetheless, not one.

Paul's allegory of Abraham's two 'women' and their offspring in 4:21–5:1 has much the same effect. In this passage a 'nonorganic' scenario is developed in explicit terms by means of a contrast between two forms of Abrahamic heritage: those born of the flesh for slavery and those born of the Spirit for freedom. What Paul's allegory affirms is that the line of Abrahamic heritage marked out by freedom and promise is the line of descent that traces itself back to Isaac, the child of promise. It is just as telling to notice that his allegory does not affirm an organic scheme. An organic version of this allegory would have traded heavily on the fact that Isaac was a patriarch of ethnic Israel and was the one through whom the Abrahamic blessing is to flow to all the nations who are free by faith. Belief in Christ is, in this envisaged allegory, the means of inclusion within the ranks of the children of promise along with Isaac, a patriarch of ethnic Israel. For gentiles, this form of inclusion may appear to be 'unnatural' since it does not involve circumcision, but since the circumcision

---

helpful. Nonetheless, since a full rejoinder to my critical friends is not possible here, I will leave them with the final word within the covers of this book. I transgress this rule only to say that nowhere did I suggest, as Hooker credits me with saying, that Paul's case in Galatians involves 'a denial of the importance of God's dealings with Israel' or that Israel's story is 'excluded' from Paul's theological consideration (see page 95). In fact, I attempted to illustrate precisely the opposite, even in Galatians. If some misunderstanding of my case has arisen, I regret any lack of clarity on my part.

of gentiles is a form of enslavement it therefore has no place in the lineage of the true Israel rooted in Abraham through Isaac. This envisaged allegory (above) would not have been difficult to construct and would have served Paul's purposes in Galatians fittingly. It would also indicate that Paul was willing to work with a scheme of organic linearity while at the same time reworking that scheme to remove the requirement of circumcision. But Paul did not take this path, preferring instead to set the two covenants out in oppositional juxtaposition through a reading of scripture that is surprisingly novel and idiosyncratic. In the allegory of Galatians 4, then, Paul is intent on avoiding a scheme of organic linearity, encouraging the Galatian Christians to 'cast out' those agitators whose story of ethnic Israel places gentile Christians within its eschatological unfolding. Paul makes no effort to redefine the agitators' pattern of organic complementarity; he finds it preferable simply to discard the pattern altogether.

It would not have taken much for Paul to argue something along these lines in Galatians:

1. Abraham, who demonstrated committed faith in God, was the patriarch of ethnic Israel, with whom God entered into covenant.
2. Messiah Jesus, as the seed of Abraham, redeemed Israel, inaugurating the eschatological age.
3. Gentile (along with Jewish) Christians who demonstrate committed faith in Israel's Messiah are thereby participating in the pinnacle of Israel's history (an age of faith) simply by means of their faith.

Except for the identification of Jesus as 'the seed of Abraham', all of these features appear in Romans, indicating that Paul's theological presentation *could* follow along lines such as these. But while the second point is evident in Galatians, Paul steered clear of the organic aspects of the first and third. No effort is made to recognise Abraham as the patriarch of ethnic Israel, and various attempts are made to avoid any such impression.[22] Similarly, Paul's handling of the 'story of Jesus' effectively ensures that Jesus serves as the 'pivot point' *from* one story (the story of Israel) *to* another one (the story of God's cosmic redemption in Christ) as the foundational story of the gospel. Paul could easily have laid out a universalistic version of Israel's story even in Galatians. But instead, he preferred to march out of the arena of organic linearity altogether.

What, then, of other features of Galatians, such as Paul's identification of cruciform love as the means whereby the law is fulfilled (5:14)? Does 'fulfil-

---

22. Paul's extensive concern throughout Galatians on Abrahamic descent clearly emerges from an interest in defining 'Israel', an interest that predates the letter itself (cf. J.L. Martyn, *Theological Issues in the Letters of Paul* [Edinburgh: T&T Clark, 1997] 162–63), whether it is to be attributed to the agitators' influence or to Paul himself.

ment' here equate to 'organic linearity' in the story of Israel? Clearly this is possible, in which case Paul would seem to be deconstructing the case that his earlier arguments had developed. More likely, then, Paul did not intend in 5:14 to sneak organic linearity in through the back door having already turned it away from the front door. Instead, he depicts self-giving love as having been upheld within the law as the pattern of life appropriate before God, even if it took a radically new 'narrative' of divine activity to enable that pattern of life to transpire. There is no need to invoke organic linearity to explain this verse. Paul envisaged scripture (γραφή) to have 'pre-preached the gospel' (προευηγγελίσατο, 3:8) to Abraham, a gospel that concerned not only Christ (e.g., 3:16) but also the people of Christ (e.g., 3:8). Self-giving within Christian communities is not used here to signal that gentiles have been inserted into Israel's story (nor is it taken to signal this in the comparable passage Rom. 13:8–10; cf. 8:2–4); instead, Paul understands it as the corporate sign that the pre-preached gospel of blessing is now actively engaging the world in communities of cruciform existence.

What then of the identification of the Christian community as 'the Israel of God' in 6:16?[23] The main interpretative alternatives are two: either (1) Paul permits late in the letter what earlier in the letter he had excluded, envisaging Christians as falling within Israel's larger story, or (2) Paul considers Christians to be 'the Israel of God' only in a linguistic sense, apart from the term's traditional narrative context. In the second case, 'Israel' would simply specify those who enjoy a special relationship with God in a pagan world, apart from tribal deities and 'elements of the world' (4:3, 8–10). This application of the phrase 'the Israel of God' would be wholly consistent with the way Paul has already in Galatians stripped the phrase 'the seed of Abraham' away from its most natural root in the narrative of ethnic Israel. In each case, Paul removes the traditional connotations of these terms so as to deconstruct an overarching organic narrative. This manner of regrounding controversial terminology in different linguistic and narrative soil is one of Paul's rhetorical strategies. By it, he appropriates key terms in the Galatian debate for himself by filling them with new content.

Paul's audience have already been prepared for redefinition of this kind not only in the redefinition of the term 'seed of Abraham' but also in his comments on 'Jerusalem' in 4:25–26. The two Jerusalems mentioned there are not associated favourably but are dissociated. In declaring 'the Jerusalem that is above' to be 'our mother', Paul means to reconstruct the identity of the Galatians in

---

23. That Paul has the Christian community in mind here is disputed but remains, in my mind, the most plausible interpretation. See J. Becker, *Paulus: Der Apostel der Völker* (Tübingen: Mohr Siebeck, 1989) 492–94.

such a way as to dislodge their attachment to the earthly Jerusalem and certain 'religious' phenomena associated with it (esp. in the Christian church
there). In effect, Paul has taken a key term, 'Jerusalem', and given it two bifur-
cated referents (the Jerusalem above and below), each with their own separate
and distinct 'narratives'. The same would seem to apply to the term 'the Israel
of God'. By applying the term 'the Israel of God' to Galatians who do not
envisage themselves as incorporated into the history of ethnic Israel, Paul
imagines himself to have ironically scored the fatal rhetorical blow against a
scheme of organic linearity.

## SYNTHESIS

In the introduction to this book, we noted Richard Hays' suggested procedures for discerning narrative contours within Paul's texts and thinking. He
proposed a two-step process: (1) a Pauline text can be scanned for narrative
features that indicate the existence of an underlying narrative substructure; (2)
an estimation should then be given regarding how a proposed narrative substructure has contributed to and imposed constraints on Paul's argument ('how
this story shapes the logic of argumentation in the discourse').[24] If the paragraphs above have completed the first step of the process, we can now turn
more considered attention to the second step: analysing how a 'story of Israel'
has imposed itself on Paul's theological reflections.

One problem immediately arises, however. As we have seen, not all the features of the story of Israel are stable and consistent within Galatians and
Romans. In order to determine the relevance of this observation, it might be
helpful to recall the map of human cognitive processing set out by N.T.
Wright, outlined in the introduction to this book. As was shown there, Wright
postulates a tripartite scheme of human epistemic processes, involving (1) a
precognitive worldview or symbolic universe (the lens through which one
views the world), (2) the stories that give expression to and embody that worldview ('worldview-by-means-of-story'), and (3) the beliefs that emerge from
and are given form by those worldview stories. In an assessment of stable and
unstable features in the narrative of Israel, the stable narrative features are
clearly the best candidates for belonging to the narrative that has shaped Paul's
discursive parameters; any unstable features would appear to have been shaped
one way or another by the rhetorical requirements of the situation. Articulating the manner in which unstable features relate to Paul's rhetorical 'prudence'

---

24. R.B. Hays, *The Faith of Jesus Christ* (Chico, Calif.: Scholars Press, 1983) 28; 2nd
edn, 29.

is not an easy matter, as will be shown. Initially, however, an inventory of the stable and unstable features is required.

## Stable Features in Paul's Story of Israel

Judging from Paul's use of the story of Israel in Galatians and Romans, certain features of this story seem relatively fixed and stable: (1) God entered into a relationship of election with Israel (e.g., Rom. 9:4–5; Gal. 3:23–25); (2) despite that special relationship, Israel is trapped 'under the cosmic power of Sin' (e.g., Rom. 3:9; Gal. 3:22) except for the salvation afforded in the Messiah; (3) God's eschatological act of salvation provides Israel with redemption (or the potential for redemption, at least) as the first outcome of God's eschatological activity (e.g., Rom. 15:8–9; Gal. 3:13; 4:5). Common to Galatians and Romans, these three features have a strong claim to be stable aspects of Paul's 'worldview-by-means-of-story', at least at the time of writing these letters late in his Christian ministry.[25] Distilled, these three stable features suggest that at any given point Paul's theologising is constrained by two main narrative currents: (1) Israel's position alongside gentiles 'under Sin' (apart from their inclusion in Christ), and (2) the character of God as faithful and committed to his covenant people.[26] For Paul, these seem to be more than ideological nuggets, detachable from a narrative context to exist as doctrinal maxims; their role as constraining features within Paul's theological processes is inseparable from a broader narrative framework.

## A Divergent Feature in Paul's Story of Israel

While Romans and Galatians reveal the existence of stable features in Paul's story of Israel, they also reveal divergences in his handling of Israel's story line.[27] One feature of Israel's story appears in two different versions: that is, the relation of gentile Christians to Israel's ongoing history as God's chosen

---

25. It would not be surprising if the first and third features (i.e., Israel's covenant relationship with God, and Israel's redemption as an eschatological phenomenon) were part of his 'worldview-by-means-of-story' even prior to his experience of the risen Christ. The second (i.e., Israel's position 'under Sin') has frequently been thought to have been foreign to Paul's cognitive processes prior to his encounter with the risen Christ (cf. E.P. Sanders (*Paul and Palestinian Judaism* [Philadelphia: Fortress Press, 1977] 443), although this is far from certain and is frequently challenged; e.g., F. Thielman, *From Plight to Solution: A Jewish Framework for Understanding Paul's View of the Law in Galatians and Romans* (Leiden: Brill, 1989); N.T. Wright, *The Climax of the Covenant: Christ and the Law in Pauline Theology* (Edinburgh: T&T Clark, 1991) 260–62.

26. This is not to deny that, for Paul, God's acts may include novelty and freedom as well.

27. Since the theme of ethnic Israel's future salvation appears only in Romans (11:26), it can be included in neither the 'stable features' category nor the 'divergent features' category.

people. In Romans, the relationship is occasionally depicted as organic, with the stories of Christ and of Christians as emerging naturally from within the ongoing story of Israel; gentiles who believe in the 'servant to the circumcised' are participating in the fulfilment of Israel's story (11:17–24; 15:8–10, 27).

Nonetheless, in his letter to the Galatians (written prior to Romans in any scholarly reconstruction), Paul attempted to sever an organic relationship between Israel's story and that of Christians. If Jesus' death offers redemption to Israel and to the world, it is not the case that the world's redemption is inserted into a larger narrative of Israel's redemption; if God's measures to deliver the world from 'the present evil age' necessarily involved, as a prerequisite, God's measures to deliver Israel, it does not necessarily follow that Israel's redemptive state is what gentile Christians are now participating in. Those within the 'new creation' might think of themselves as God's 'Israel' (6:16) but only in the sense of those specially related to God ('known by God') in a pagan world (4:8–9), not in the sense of those who have entered the boundaries of ethnic Israel's eschato-logical stage of development. This is not to suggest that the Galatian letter com-pletely decouples the story of Israel on the one hand and the stories of Jesus and his followers on the other, for the Christ event had initial effectiveness with regard to Israel's redemption (3:13; 4:4–5). Moreover, the consequent effects of the Christ event included the enlivening of a lifestyle that was already envisaged by the law given to Israel (5:13–14). But nonetheless, Galatians 3–4 releases a dev-astating flood against a scheme in which Christians are to envisage themselves as participating in an ongoing story of Israel's salvation history. What Paul pur-posefully avoided saying about Israel, along with what he avoids saying about Abraham and Christ, amounts to a rejection of the notion of organic linearity in which the gentiles participate in Israel's 'spiritual blessings'.[28]

## Assessing the Situation

How might this situation (i.e., the differences in Romans and Galatians) be explained? Presumably an explanation informed by a broader textual sampling would engender a greater degree of confidence about any proposed solution. Nonetheless, expanding the textual sample would only postpone dealing with a fundamental issue: the manner in which the organic narrative is advocated in one letter and undermined in another. In the methodological considerations that follow, I hold the assumption that the two postures demonstrated by Paul towards an organic narrative of Israel are not both reconcilable within a con-

---

28. It is often legitimate and revealing to ask what is omitted in order to construct a profile of something. For instance, what a particular newspaper regularly omits in its coverage is often as significant to its identity as what it includes.

struct called 'Pauline theology'; if one version of the story has rights to exist within that construct, the other does not.

Various options present themselves as alternatives to or modifications of this assumption. It might be argued that Paul's handling of the story of Israel in Romans and Galatians is not really all that different on the matter of organic relatedness. For instance, we might want to agree with the frequently expressed view that in every instance Paul maintains there to be 'one continuous people of God from Abraham through Moses to Christ and beyond',[29] thereby including Galatians within the scheme of organic linearity. Alternatively, we might prefer to argue that there is no real organic linearity in Romans, thereby accommodating it to the pattern laid out in Galatians.[30] In my estimate, these alternatives do not respect the differences between the letters when one is read in the light of the other.

An alternative might be to appeal to an implied narrative 'substructure' of Galatians, thereby permitting organic linearity to fill the 'theological space' between the lines of Paul's explicit discourse in that letter.[31] But the problem here is that the explicit discourse seems to run contrary to organic linearity. Reading organic linearity between the lines or appealing to a substructure of organic linearity merely moves the problem to different terrain; it does not solve the problem.

Another option is to suggest that both versions of the story of Israel are themselves the product of Paul's rhetorical needs within the respective situations and do not exist apart from those rhetorical contexts. As such, the two versions are not reconcilable within a construct called 'Pauline theology' but might simply be indicative of two moments of 'Pauline theologising'. One might easily argue, for instance, that the organic relationship depicted in Romans is targeted to meet situational needs. As he writes to the Roman Christians (the argument might go), Paul was mindful of his impending meeting with the Christian leaders in Jerusalem (cf. 15:25–33), who themselves seem to have construed the relevant stories organically.[32] In the light of previous tensions in his relationship with these leaders, and with the prospect of

---

29. B. Witherington III, *Paul's Narrative Thought World* (Louisville, Ky.: Westminster/John Knox Press, 1994) 38.

30. See the articles by John Barclay and Francis Watson in this volume. While in this volume Hooker and Dunn think 'organic linearity' animates not only Romans but also Galatians, Barclay and Watson think it absent even from Romans. I seek to maintain an intermediate position.

31. Morna Hooker makes use of this option in her reply (see page 92): 'To understand Paul's argument, we have to remember the assumptions underlying the dispute— assumptions that are not necessarily spelt out (though they are hinted at) in the letter.'

32. See R. Bauckham, 'James and the Jerusalem Church', in R. Bauckham (ed.), *The Book of Acts in Its Palestinian Setting* (Grand Rapids: Eerdmans, 1995) 415–80, 450–62.

his 'collection' for Jerusalem Christians being deemed unacceptable by significant parties in the Jerusalem church, Paul's thinking in the months prior to
the encounter might well have been affected by a determination to articulate
his theology in a manner more conducive to agreement. Or perhaps the argument could be marshalled that the organic version of the Israel story was used
by Paul in Romans to assuage the corporate tensions within the Christian communities in Rome, as gentile Christians were coming to imagine God to be
favouring them over and above the Jews (at least if this scholarly commonplace
is correct; cf. 11:13–24). The incorporation of gentile Christians into the story
of Israel would be the theological pill to heal corporate pains and ensure collective survival. With regard to Galatians, it is easy to see how a nonorganic
version (if accepted by the recipients) could help to undermine the allure of
the views of the agitators, whose story of Israel seems to have been organically
conceived.

So there is reason to wonder whether, in these instances at least, rhetorical
needs are generating theological pathways; rhetorical studies of Paul regularly
stress the need to identify 'the persuasive devices in the text in order to filter
out their effect on the theological ideas expressed'.[33] Nonetheless, in the case
under consideration here, this rhetorical explanation is not quite persuasive.
It seems to underplay two points that are scored large in the literature of earliest Christianity: (1) the 'story of Israel' was of grave significance in the self-
definition of many early Christians, and (2) the implications of that story were
fiercely disputed among many early Christians, among whom Paul figured
prominently. Consequently, I find it difficult to believe that *both* the organic
and nonorganic versions were generated solely by rhetorical requirements.
The larger historical context of early Christian self-definition suggests that
Paul must have held some definite views on this aspect of the story of Israel
prior to the writing of Galatians and Romans.[34] Although the versions represented in those letters are well suited to carry force in their respective situations, it would be overly hasty to conclude, simply on the basis of rhetorical
'fit', that *both* of those versions were generated merely by rhetorical urgency.
Although Paul may have made use of organic and nonorganic versions at dif-

---

33. L. Thurén, *Derhetorizing Paul: A Dynamic Perspective on Pauline Theology and the
Law* (WUNT 124; Tübingen: Mohr Siebeck, 2000) v. Cf. J.P. Sampley, 'From Text to
Thought World: The Route to Paul's Ways', in J.M. Bassler (ed.), *Pauline Theology, Volume 1: Thessalonians, Philippians, Galatians, Philemon* (Minneapolis: Augsburg Fortress,
1991) 3–14, 4.

34. Cf. also R. Scroggs, 'Salvation History: The Theological Structure of Paul's
Thought (1 Thessalonians, Philippians, and Galatians)', in Bassler (ed.), *Pauline Theology*, 212–26, 220.

ferent points, one version must have stronger claim to be emblematic of the undergirding configuration of Paul's theologising in general.[35]

If rhetorical factors are not ideally suited to provide a full explanation of the issue at hand, perhaps 'aesthetic' judgements might be conscripted for the task. For instance, if one were of the opinion that the organic relationship that appears occasionally in Romans is less prone to contortion and 'extravagance of argument' than Paul's case in Galatians, it might seem natural to conclude that the organic version is more indicative of Paul's narrative thought world. The ease with which Paul occasionally (but not uniformly) depicts the story of Israel unfolding to include gentile Christians might suggest that he naturally preferred lines of organic linearity. But such reasoning is vulnerable to a high level of subjectivity, since some interpreters consider Galatians to be indicative of Paul's most natural theological pathways on the matter of Israel's story. For them, the 'aesthetically appealing' organic relationship that appears in Romans is a later modifying spin on the 'brute Paulinism' of Galatians.[36] Moreover, Romans itself is not wholly devoid of problematic argument. Consequently, aesthetic appeals may be one basis for judging this matter, but they are weakly founded and can be used to support either possible conclusion.

It might be possible to prioritise the organic over the nonorganic version by highlighting Paul's state of mind when writing the two letters. So, it might be wise to concur with the following estimate:

> The apparent de-emphasis of Galatians on Israel's salvation history . . . may well have suited the polemical context in which Paul found himself having to justify his gentile mission apart from Jerusalem and Antioch. Even if this were true for Galatians, however, Romans shows that, *upon calmer reflection*, Paul's reaction did not last.[37]

Estimates of this kind have good merit but require further substantiation. First, it is not wholly obvious that moments of 'calmer reflection' (i.e., Romans) should be allowed to take precedence over moments of knee-jerk 'reaction' (i.e.,

---

35. For this reason also, solutions that envisage merely 'creative tension' in this matter (e.g., Sampley, 'Romans and Galatians', 335; also 'From Text to Thought World', 6) sit too lightly to important data. The 'creative tension' solution works well for features like 'freedom yet responsibility', 'present yet future', 'grace yet works' and the like, but not for 'organic yet nonorganic'.

36. This is the implication of Martyn's 'Romans as One of the Earliest Interpretations of Galatians', in his *Theological Issues*, 37–45.

37. M. Bockmuehl, 'Antioch and James the Just', in B. Chilton and C.A. Evans (eds), *James the Just and Christian Origins* (Leiden: Brill, 1999) 155–98, 184 n. 110, emphasis added. Cf. Sampley, 'Romans and Galatians', 319, 333; idem, 'From Text to Thought World', 7.

Galatians). Occasionally the knee-jerk impulse is far more indicative of one's convictions than any amount of subsequent calm reflection or posturing. Second, clearly Galatians and Romans both contain aspects of concerned 'reaction' and considered 'reflection'. The common tendency to characterise Galatians as 'reaction' and Romans as 'reflection' may result in an overpolarisation of the two letters, thereby skewing the issue at hand.[38] Third, although Paul is not 'calm' when writing Galatians, that fact alone is poorly suited to the task of determining the nature of the theological proclivities in that letter. Certainly the 'pathos' with which Paul writes to the Galatians has affected his presentation of 'logos'. But are we to conclude from this that a groundswell of hotheaded emotion has eroded Paul's ability to maintain his fundamental theological sensibilities? Paul's passion in Galatians is attributable to the fact that certain features fundamental to 'the truth of the gospel' have been compromised by communities that he thinks should know better. Consequently, it may be that Paul's invective in Galatians *did not contribute to a subsequent theological imprecision* but in fact *emerged from an entrenched theological position*.[39]

Other considerations might afford assistance in adjudicating between the organic and nonorganic versions. Closely related to the matter of Paul's state of mind is the matter of genre. Romans is frequently understood as a letter 'which is less caught in the flux and developing discourse of Paul with his churches than the others'.[40] At least part of Paul's motivation for writing Romans seems to have been to set the record straight about the kinds of things that he himself stood for; sending that record to Roman communities was an attempt to alleviate the suspicion about him held by some within those communities—communities that he hoped would send him on his way into a mission further west. Surely, if Paul needed to profile himself accurately to the Roman Christians, his letter to them should serve as the 'plumb line' within the extant Pauline corpus.[41] Consequently, in an attempt to tease out the version of Israel's story most indicative of Paul's thinking, it might be advisable to prioritise the organic relationship depicted in Romans over the nonorganic relationship depicted in Galatians.

---

38. What would happen to the formula, for instance, if Galatians were depicted not simply as 'reaction' but as an unguarded and candid defence of 'the truth of the gospel'?

39. Cf. Scroggs ('Salvation History', 214): 'Paul means what he says, even when angry or otherwise distubed.'

40. J.D.G. Dunn, *The Theology of Paul the Apostle* (Edinburgh: T&T Clark, 1998) 25. Cf. S. Westerholm, *Preface to the Study of Paul* (Grand Rapids: Eerdmans, 1997).

41. Dunn, *Theology*, 26. Rather differently, G. Hotze (*Paradoxien bei Paulus: Untersuchungen zu einer elementaren Denkform in Seiner Theologie* [NTAbh, N.F. 33; Münster: Aschendorff, 1997] 138, see n. 260) argues that Romans and Galatians are *both* letters offering a fundamental presentation ('grundlegende Darstellung') of Paul's theology.

On the other hand, Romans might be likened to an election manifesto of sorts, setting out in gloss and spin the merits of a candidate for those whose support is being sought (cf. Rom. 15:14–32). If traces of that genre have made their way into Romans, there is little reason to think that the packaging is wholly representative of the product. In any event, while Romans may be 'less caught in the flux' of situational discourse, the situational factors loom large over even that letter and have clearly influenced the presentation of his arguments from start to finish. Moreover, another letter stakes a claim to represent the Pauline product, and that is Galatians, where Paul presents his equivalent to 'the truth, the whole truth and nothing but the truth' (e.g., Gal. 1:6–12) and where a nonorganic version of the story is found.

Perhaps a developmental scheme can provide the explanatory scaffolding for the two versions of the story of Israel evident in Galatians and Romans.[42] Paul's thinking likely developed to some extent over the course of his twenty-five years or so of Christian ministry, and it might well be possible to trace developments on particular matters even within the extant Pauline corpus spanning some ten or so years. In this regard, we may be well advised to think of Romans as 'the most mature statement of [Paul's] theology'.[43] However, developmental schemes, at least on the matter at hand, fall short in my estimate for two reasons: (1) as indicated already, Paul must have reflected on the controversial 'story of Israel' at many points long before the writing of any of his letters, so his convictions on the matter must have been fairly well defined by the time of writing both Galatians and Romans;[44] (2) my best guess is that Galatians was written (to communities in south Galatia) in 54 C.E., leaving only a few years between the

---

42. A developmental scheme might be consistent with the 'state of mind' and 'genre' options considered above, but it is nonetheless distinct from them.

43. Dunn, *Theology*, 298.

44. J.C. Beker ('Recasting Pauline Theology: The Coherence-Contingency Scheme as Interpretive Model', in Bassler [ed.], *Pauline Theology, Volume 1*, 15–24, 22) argues that 'the concept "development" needs much more careful analysis' by differentiating between 'peripheral' and 'central thought structures': A possible shift in Paul's thought with respect to the interim state of the dead is clearly of quite different significance than would be, for instance, a shift with respect to the law or christology'. P. Achtemeier ('Finding the Way to Paul's Theology: A Response to J. Christian Beker and J. Paul Sampley', in Bassler [ed.], *Pauline Theology, Volume 1*, 25–36, 29) is right to question on what basis peripheral is distinguished from central, but those who would place 'Israel' within the category of 'peripheral' have the burden of proof on their shoulders.

Similarly C. Roetzel's claim ('The Grammar of Election in Four Pauline Letters', in D.M. Hay [ed.] *Pauline Theology, Volume 2: 1 & 2 Corinthians* [Minneapolis: Augsburg Fortress, 1993] 211–33, 226) that Galatians is 'the first time' that 'Paul thinks through how it is possible for gentiles to be incorporated into God's family' seems highly problematical, making 'peripheral' what certainly was far more 'central' than Roetzel's statement allows.

writing of Galatians and Romans (early 57 C.E.). These two factors reinforce each other, suggesting that, while there may be a 'maturing' form of development in some areas of Paul's thought within the fifties, it is overly optimistic to think that a developmental scheme can provide a solid foundation from which to assess the differences in Paul's stories of Israel in these two texts.[45] There is, of course, a sense in which Paul's presentation has developed from Galatians to Romans, since in Romans Paul had found a way to fit a version of organic linearity into his theological presentation. But this looks suspiciously like an unnatural theological branch that had been grafted into the root of Paul's theology rather than a form of development in which inchoate or undeveloped aspects of Paul's presentation in Galatians mature, ripen, and evolve into what we find in Romans.[46]

I have suggested, then, that Paul's two divergent 'stories of Israel' cannot be explained by appealing to (1) a 'narrative substructure', (2) the influence of the rhetorical situation, (3) aesthetic qualities of Paul's argumentation, (4) Paul's 'emotional' state, (5) differences in genre, or (6) a developmental 'maturation' in Paul's thought. The fundamental datum that still requires explanation is the following: Although the organic version of Israel's story appears in significant places in Paul's argument in Romans, he is intent on establishing in Galatians, one of his most profound and influential texts, the essentials of his gospel without compromise, and there the organic version is explicitly undermined in significant and sustained fashion. As I see it, only two explanatory options remain: either Paul compromised a fundamental theological component on at least one occasion in the defence of (other aspects of) his gospel (i.e., Galatians), or an organic salvation-historical linearity is not an essential feature in the articulation of his gospel. Stated in different terms, either Romans is characteristic of Paul's narratively configured theologising, in which case Galatians is an uncharacteristic text in which he has been thrown off his theological balance by the situation at hand; or Galatians is characteristic of Paul's narratively configured theologising, in which case Romans represents Paul's attempt to enunciate his theology in garb that would more likely be appealing to Christian leaders in Jerusalem and/or helpful to his Roman audience.

Of these two options, I find the second to be more compelling. Granted, it is not impossible for fundamental features of Paul's 'worldview' to have been

---

45. Cf. J.C. Beker, *Paul the Apostle* (Philadelphia: Fortress Press, 1980) 33; H. Räisänen, *Paul and the Law* (Tübingen: Mohr Siebeck, 1983) 8-9; M. Hengel and A.M. Schwemer, *Paul between Damascus and Antioch* (London: SCM Press, 1997) 11-15.

46. Envisaging how and why this 'development' came about involves reconstructing historical and theological issues that lie beyond the scope of this project, although I hope to elaborate a case in further publications.

compromised in order to preserve other crucial features.[47] But I find it hard to believe that, in his early work among the Galatian Christians, Paul could have peddled a gospel with a relentlessly invariable organic component, only to undermine that component in pronounced fashion in a letter later written to them. The fact that Paul could 'compromise' a full-bodied organic linearity in Galatians suggests that this was not an essential feature in his theological processes, and that the Galatians did not perceive it as such. Even Romans might offer some support for this view, since the organic linearity found there is not sustained throughout the whole letter. At times even in Romans, Paul writes in ways that indicate how the story of ethnic Israel fails to provide coherence throughout the course of salvation history (e.g., 4:9–25; 5:12–21).[48]

Since the organic feature of Israel's story is unstable in Paul's letters, it is unlikely to have operated at the level of 'worldview-by-means-of-story' or first-order cognition in Paul's epistemic processes. Consequently, it is unwise to envisage the organic relationship between the story of Israel and the story of Christ's followers as a stable generator of other aspects of Paul's thought. Although Paul held that 'whatever was written in former days was written for our instruction, that . . . by the encouragement of the scriptures we might have hope' (Rom. 15:4; cf. 4:23–24), this conviction seems not to have been intricately or essentially connected to an organic unfolding of Israel's narrative that engulfs gentile Christians.[49] Perhaps Paul's attitude towards the organic version of Israel's story was much like his practice of Jewish lifestyle as reflected in 1 Cor. 9:20–21: it was something to be adopted if required by the situation, but it was not essential, and it had the potential to obstruct the furtherance of the gospel in certain situations.

In the process of comparing two of Paul's letters on the matter of the 'story of Israel', we have found features that, due to their 'textual stability', are eligible to be considered as 'pre-textual ingredients' in the process of Paul's theologising. We have also found one feature that is unstable within the extant Pauline corpus and that thereby requires special consideration in relation to

---

47. Beker thinks this is what has happened in Galatians; cf. Beker, *Paul*, 57–58; idem, 'Recasting Pauline Theology', 19. Something similar has probably happened in Rom. 2:14–15; see my *Eschatology and the Covenant*, 186–89.

48. Cf. L.E. Keck ('Review of James D.G. Dunn's *The Theology of Paul the Apostle*', *SJT* 53 [2000]: 380–89, 387): In Romans 4 'Abraham's being the patriarch of uncircumcised believers and of circumcised believers is not a matter of [organic] continuity at all but of similarity. . . . The continuity is not between believers but in God'.

49. Compare, e.g., the author of the *Epistle of Barnabas*. For him, although there is no ongoing 'story of Israel', the law and the prophets are still 'scripture' that speaks to instruct Christians (e.g., 4:6–7). Scripture is simply 'a parable of the Lord' for the benefit of Christians, without sustained significance pertaining to the 'story of Israel' (cf. 6:10–14). Granted, Paul is more nuanced than this author, but on this point a likeness might be evident.

Pauline theologising and/or theology. Regarding the organic version of Israel's story, while it makes an appearance within the Pauline corpus, in at least one situation Paul considered it to jeopardise valid Christian identity. In that situation, he was content to polemicise against it altogether rather than redefine it or harness it to his own advantage in some other fashion. Consequently, organic linearity of the kind discussed here should not take pride of place in any scholarly abstraction of 'Pauline theology', nor should it be depicted as a stable generator in Paul's theologising. Whatever narrative of Israel Paul might have had, an organic version was not intrinsic to Paul's theological processes.

## REFLECTIONS ON NARRATIVE APPROACHES TO PAUL

As was indicated in the introduction of this book, the issue of enumerating the narrative ingredients remains unresolved among advocates of contemporary narrative approaches to Paul. Some prefer to speak of Paul's 'thought world' as involving one large story with smaller subnarratives within it. Others prefer to speak of a 'conglomerate' of stories working in relationship, the number of these independent stories ranging from three to five. In my view, various strengths attend to each scheme.

Approaching Paul's texts from a multistory scheme has the advantage of doing justice to the contingent nature of Paul's thinking at any given time. We have seen how a diversity of assemblage is evident in Galatians and Romans, at least on the matter of organic linearity. Articulating this diversity at any particular point seems eminently easier in a complex multistory scheme than a simple one-story scheme.

Nonetheless, the multistory scheme itself has two main weaknesses. First is the matter of narrative taxonomy. Although not addressed in this article, I suspect that, in a five-story scheme, Abraham is a figure who fits naturally into different stories: the 'story of God and creation',[50] the 'story of Christ', the stories of 'predecessors and inheritors' of faith,[51] and (at least in Romans 9–11) the 'story of Israel'. It is difficult, then, to place Abraham exclusively within one specific story. Perhaps, then, the narrative model needs to be enlarged so that the perceived number of stories increases from five to six, including now the 'story of Abraham' as well. But at some point the proliferation of stories will have the potential to weaken the methodological coherence of the approach. One can easily envisage other enumerations to emerge. To what extent, for example, should we imagine a 'story of Moses', a 'story of David', or (as a few might argue) a 'story of Noah', within Paul's thought world? And why stop

---

50. So also, see E. Adams, 'Paul's Story of God and Creation: The Story of How God Fulfils His Purposes in Creation', in chapter 2 above.

51. Since in Romans 4, for instance, Abraham cannot be contained within 'the story of Israel' exclusively.

there? With increasing interest in the influence of imperial cult and emperor mythology, why not supplement these scriptural narratives with others rooted in the Graeco-Roman world, starting with a 'story of the Roman emperor'? To what extent might the proliferation of proposals along these lines make the narrative enterprise suspect, explaining everything without the prospect of being falsified? Will the potential accumulation of narrative components ultimately leave the narrative project reduced to an unprofitable exercise?

Besides narrative enumeration, there is also the matter of the relations between narrative components. Proponents of the multistory scheme tend to envisage the various stories as 'superimposed' on each other, being 'on top of' one another and 'intertwining' with each other.[52] While these metaphors helpfully highlight the interaction between narrative elements, the narrative taxonomy remains somewhat vague, imprecise, and in need of further refinement if its interpretative potential is to come to fruition.

Finally, the 'narrative approach' itself requires consideration. In none of my exegetical work have I found it illegitimate to discuss Paul's texts in terms of narrative when analysing what he says about Israel. With regard to the simple process of exegesis, however, I am not aware of any significant way in which a heightened attentiveness to narrative dynamics has resulted in new exegetical insights or the profiling of certain textual features in unprecedented ways.[53]

Two qualifications are immediately in order, however. First, the attempt to reconstruct a stable narrative that animates both Romans and Galatians has itself been a fruitful exercise and falls in line with the methodological interests of certain advocates of a narrative approach (e.g., Hays, Wright). Working from textual indicators to 'pre-textual' (or 'extratextual') narrative has offered stimulating results, with significant implications for reconstructing Paul's theology and mission.

Second, even if a narrative approach does not necessarily *advance* textual exegesis, it nonetheless offers a necessary *exegetical control*. Any study that fails to take account of the narrative dimension of Paul's thinking is, I suspect, certain to move along rough terrain, at least when considering his depiction of Israel. To give just one example, J. Lambrecht's study of Rom. 15:8–9 is a careful exposition of the text within the mainstream tradition of exegesis. Of the five main exegetical issues that he deals with in that passage, the last is said to be so important that it 'must not escape our analysis'.[54] This issue concerns the relation of 15:8b ('in order that

---

52. Dunn, *Theology*, 18. Cf. Witherington, *Paul's Narrative Thought World*, 5.

53. The existence of narrative contours in Paul's theologising is likely to have fewer implications for exegesis than for Christian ethical, practical, and (awkwardly) 'systematic' theology. For a recent example of the latter, see G. Sauter and J. Barton (eds), *Revelation and Story: Narrative Theology and the Centrality of Story* (Aldershot, U.K.: Ashgate, 2000).

54. J. Lambrecht, 'Syntactical and Logical Remarks on Romans 15:8–9a', *NovT* 42 (2000): 257–61; all quotations are from 260–61.

he might confirm the promises given to the patriarchs' NRSV) to 15:9a ('in order
that the Gentiles might glorify God for his mercy' NRSV). In particular, Lambrecht sets himself the task of discovering which of these two phrases is to carry
more theological weight in Paul's case. It almost goes without saying that, when
a Christian exegete asks this kind of question of a Pauline text, the answer given
will almost inevitably favour 15:9a (divine mercy upon the nations) as 'the main
point of what the author wants to say'. Without a narrative framework, the
exegete will all too often be left with a frame of reference unnatural to the subject matter.[55] Had Lambrecht taken more account of the narrative dimension of
Paul's theologising, he might have been able to avoid characterising 15:8b as simply an 'interruptive addition' (his paraphrase omits the relevant phrase altogether)
and might have been able to do full justice to that phrase in accord with a narrative scheme concerning the unfolding processes of salvation history. In contrast
to Lambrecht, I would want to highlight 15:8b, not as 'more important' than
15:9a but as an essential component of a narrative in which God's mercy upon the
gentiles has as its necessary prerequisite the fulfilment of God's faithfulness to
Israel—a feature common to both Romans and Galatians.[56] Neither aspect of this
narrative should be detached from the other; they are held together in a dynamic
relationship that is best served within a narrative context.

In summary, we have seen from this survey and synthesis both the expected
and the unexpected: the expected, in that whenever Paul reflects on 'Israel' he
does so in a manner characterised by narrative; the unexpected, in that Paul han-
dles one narrative strand of that story in Romans in a such a way as to run against
the grain of his handling of it in Galatians. Paul's 'stories' of Israel in Romans and
Galatians, then, attest to the complexity of his narrative theologising.[57]

---

55. We might want to ask, for instance, whether the presidency of John F. Kennedy
on the one hand or the Viet Nam war on the other was more influential on the development of the national psyche of the U.S.A. in the 1960s. No doubt a case could be
made either way, depending on how one chose to prioritise the relevant evidence. Perhaps a better solution, however, would be to appreciate the place of each phenomenon
within its 'narrative' context—that is, within the ongoing processes of social definition
that characterised the various stages of that decade.

56. See further my *Triumph of Abraham's God*, 90–95.

57. My thanks to those who have commented on earlier drafts of this essay in personal correspondence (Markus Bockmuehl) and at various seminars (New Testament
seminars of St Andrews University, Aberdeen University, Hope University College
Liverpool, and the International Christian College of Glasgow, as well as the Inhalte
und Probleme einer neutestamentlichen Theologie seminar of SNTS, Montreal 2001),
and of course to Morna Hooker for her response, which follows.

# 5

# 'Heirs of Abraham': The Gentiles' Role in Israel's Story

*A Response to Bruce W. Longenecker*

MORNA D. HOOKER

## INTRODUCTION: THE UNDERLYING STORY

The importance of narrative for the great majority of our biblical writers seems to me to be self-evident. The 'historical' books of the Old Testament, together with the Gospels and Acts, consist largely of stories; the psalmists and prophets make constant reference to the story of God's dealing with his people, Israel; and Revelation attempts to unfold the story of the future. It is hardly surprising, then, that the Victorian hymn writer declared, 'God has given us a book full of stories'.[1] Even the Pauline letters, though concerned with the problems of his congregations and filled with theological statements and ethical advice, refer constantly to what Paul terms 'his' gospel—that is, the story of what God has done in Christ. And though Marcionite and anti-Semitic tendencies within the church have often tended to isolate the story of Jesus from its context, it is clear that for Paul it was part of an ongoing story about God's purpose for his creation and for his people Israel.

This underlying story was recognised by many twentieth-century biblical scholars—for example, by those who stressed the importance of *Heils-geschichte* for understanding the biblical text, and by those influenced by the so-called 'biblical theology' movement. The irony was that this cosmological story, based on 'myth', was seen by many as a barrier to twentieth-century Christian belief. In 'demythologizing' Paul's theology, Bultmann tore him out

---

1. Maria Matilda Penstone, 1859–1910.

85

of his context and tried to make sense of him in an alien setting. If we want to understand Paul's thought, we must seek also to understand the framework and assumptions of that thought.

The central role of narrative in the Bible should not surprise us, for all cultures use stories to express their 'worldview'—their beliefs about the world and about their gods. Since Jews believed that their God had an enduring concern for Israel and was involved in their history, their stories reflected their understanding of God's purpose for the world and for God's people.

So in what sense is the narrative approach to Paul doing anything essentially new? Is it not simply putting a welcome emphasis on the feature that underlies Paul's theology and reminding us that attempts to force Paul's thought into the patterns imposed by systematic theologians are doomed to failure? One particular emphasis in the narrative approach has been singled out for our consideration: the suggestion that the overarching story consists of five substories. The 'grand Story'[2] has thus been put under the microscope and pulled apart. I am puzzled by this, for in Paul's theology the individual substories make sense *only in relation to the others*: the story of Israel is part of the story of creation and humanity; the story of Christ belongs to the story of the world gone wrong and to the story of Israel; the story of Christians—of humanity restored—depends on the story of Christ. The analysis of the individual stories is akin to the form critics' examination of pericopae, each of which tells a 'story' that, in order to be understood fully, has to be seen in the context of the Christian story as a whole.

But was this 'grand Story' ever told as a unity? Certainly every aspect of it is touched on in Romans and seems to underlie Paul's argument. Paul's 'worldview' embraces God's creation, Adam's Fall, the call of Israel and her failure to obey God, the sending of God's Son, our reconciliation to God in him, the new life of those led by the Holy Spirit, and the final restoration of creation. Others before Paul had held similar views: the prophets who hoped that the *Endzeit* would be as the *Urzeit* clearly held together stories about the creation, about Israel, and about the End, though belief in a story about a messiah might or might not be part of that story.

If I am puzzled by the desire to analyse the 'grand Story' into substories, the notion that there is a 'story of God' puzzles me even more! A 'story' concerns something within history and describes events that change and affect the characters, but God is by definition *outside* history, and does not change (Mal. 3:6). God is 'Yahweh', the one who is who God is (Exod. 3:14), the first and the last (Isa. 44:6; 48:12), the everlasting God, whose purpose is sure, whose

---

2. The term is used by B. Witherington III, *Paul's Narrative Thought World* (Louisville, Ky.: Westminster/John Knox Press, 1994) 6 n. 7.

covenant love is steadfast, whose word is inevitably fulfilled (e.g., Isa. 14:24; 45:23; Mic. 7:20). Certainly one can talk about God *in relation to* the 'grand Story', for God is at work in all the so-called 'substories', and Paul clearly sees the *purpose* of God being worked out in the stories of creation; the Fall; the call and failure of Israel; the life, death, and resurrection of Christ; and the restoration of humanity and of creation. But it is surely better to speak of God as *behind* this story rather than as *having* a story.

The individual 'substories', I have suggested, make sense in Paul's thought only in relation to each other: they are 'chapters' in a book, 'episodes' in a long story, rather than short stories in a collection. But there are, of course, different ways of telling the parts of this story: the Bible is, indeed, 'full of stories'. Thus there are two different accounts of creation in Genesis and two different ways of interpreting the story of the Fall: while Paul himself attributes responsibility to Adam, the author of 1 Tim. 2:14 places the blame firmly on Eve. The 'story of Israel' is told many times, by historians, prophets, and poets. As for the story of Jesus, Paul refers to it in many different snippets, all different. His accounts of what will happen at 'the End' are notoriously difficult to reconcile. The various stories that are actually told, then, are merely attempts to express the way in which the inscrutable purpose of God is being worked out. It is that inscrutable purpose that explains the existence of the world and the course of events, and Paul's 'worldview' consists in his belief that it is this divine purpose that gives them meaning. Yet this belief in the divine purpose is itself inevitably expressed in a 'story', since it concerns the ways in which God's purpose for creation will finally be achieved.

These many stories, then, are ways of telling part of the bigger story that lies behind them—the 'grand Story' that maintains that the world is in God's hands—and behind that story is God.

It would seem, then, that there are dangers in concentrating on one episode in the 'grand Story', since that can easily distort our understanding of the whole. But this danger is no new one, for Paul's complaint against the Judaizers was precisely that they had succumbed to it. It would seem that at least some Jews tended to behave as though 'their' part of the story was the whole story: it was for Israel's sake that God had created the world, and God's purpose would be complete when Israel, under God, was given dominion. Paul's understanding of the story was broader: since all creation was to be restored, all humanity would be redeemed, and though this redemption would come through one who was 'born under the law' (Gal. 4:4) and 'of the seed of David' (Rom. 1:3), it would include 'those outside the law' (1 Cor. 9:21) also, for Christ is the 'Last Adam' (Rom. 5:18; 1 Cor. 15:22), who is 'the image of God' (2 Cor. 4:4), and so the pattern after whom all humanity is being recreated.

The Adam imagery points to the wider story: since the 'all' who die in Adam includes gentiles as well as Jews, the 'all' who are to be made alive in Christ will do the same; Adam's descendants are not confined to Jews.[3]

If there is danger in focusing attention exclusively on one part of the 'grand Story', there is danger also in assuming that when one *part* of this 'grand Story' is touched on, the 'whole' of that particular part will be told. It is obvious that Paul frequently touches on 'the story of Jesus', but rarely does he spell it out at length—and when he does, in Phil. 2:6–11, there is no clear reference to the resurrection![4] Paul touches on the particular aspect of the story that is relevant for the issue he is discussing. Thus when he refers to 'the story of Israel' in Romans and Galatians, he does not spell out the whole of that story but uses whatever is necessary in it for his purpose. And since the letters are written to deal with different circumstances, the story is used differently in each of them in order to make different theological points.


## THE STORY OF ISRAEL IN ROMANS AND GALATIANS

The recognition of the fact that Paul is not concerned to spell out the 'grand Story' (let alone one *part* of that Story) every time he commits his thoughts to written form provides the clue in any comparison of the way in which he deals with 'the story of Israel' in Romans and Galatians. If Paul deals at length with the story of Israel in Romans, it is because the question of God's faithfulness to his covenant is a major issue in that letter: his concern is to show that his understanding of God's faithfulness is in no way challenged by his mission to the gentiles. With what Bruce Longenecker says about Romans I have no real disagreement (apart from his references to 'the story of God'): he recognises the interrelatedness of what I have termed the various 'episodes' in the 'grand Story'. Remarkably, however, he says nothing here about Romans 4—a passage where, as we shall see, what he terms 'organic linearity' is far less in evidence than in the corresponding passage in Galatians 3.[5] In Romans 4, Paul—speaking as a Jew—introduces his discussion with a reference to 'Abraham, our ancestor *according to the flesh*'. He uses precisely the same phrase when

---

3. Contrast 4 Ezra 6:53–59, where the 'other nations', though descended from Adam, are said to be 'nothing' and behave like wild beasts.

4. Cf. the fragmentary 'summaries' in Rom. 1:3–4; 4:25; 1 Cor. 15:3–8; 2 Cor. 5:21; 8:9; Gal. 3:13; 4:4–5; 1 Thess. 5:10.

5. He does, however, acknowledge later that 'organic linearity' is missing from Romans 4 (see 'Sharing in their Spiritual Blessings? The Stories of Israel in Galatians and Romans', page 81).

referring to the fact that Jesus was 'of David's seed' (1:3) and when he speaks of him as Israel's Messiah (9:5). The phrase is a reminder that, however 'earthy' the images Paul uses, the 'organic linearity' between Israel and *gentile* Christians is never a matter of *flesh*: Christians—Jews and gentiles alike—are called to live according to the Spirit and not according to the flesh (8:4–9), and their place in the 'olive tree' depends on faith (11:20).

It is when Longenecker turns to Galatians that I find myself in stark disagreement with his views. He begins by summarising the views of the 'agitators': they 'envisaged Israel's story to embrace those gentiles for whom the story of Christ had salvific significance' (see page 65). But only, of course, those gentiles who were willing—by circumcision—to become Jews are embraced, and this view can hardly be fairly described as 'similar' to the view expressed by Paul in Romans (see page 65)! But Longenecker continues well enough, with the recognition that Paul and the agitators in Galatia had in common 'the certainty that Israel's story is one of special relationship with God' (see page 65). For Paul, this conviction is demonstrated in his likening of the law to a 'pedagogue until Christ came' (3:24). Gal. 3:13–14 and 4:4–5 'indicate a convergence of the stories of Israel and Jesus, with the story of Christian communities included in that convergence' (see page 66). The belief expressed in the phrase 'to the Jew first and also to the Greek' is, he argues, 'just as much a part of Paul's presentation in Galatians' as in Romans (see page 66). With this clear recognition of 'covenantal linearity' as his starting point, Longenecker nevertheless goes on to argue that the understanding reflected in Galatians of the relationship of the gentiles to the story of Israel is quite different from that which lies behind Romans: the essential difference is that whatever 'linearity' is present in Galatians, it is not *'organic* linearity' (see page 70; cf. page 74).

It is clear that Paul is arguing in Galatians against *one particular form* of 'organic linearity'—namely, the belief that Christians could not participate in the blessings promised to Abraham *unless they became Jews*, through circumcision and obedience to the Law. Paul argues his case with considerable passion and heat. But is it true to say that, in Galatians 3–4, he 'goes to great lengths to deconstruct strong organic ties between Israel's history and his gentile mission'? Or that 'Paul strains against all odds to depict Abraham in any possible way other than as the patriarch of ethnic Israel'? Or that 'Abraham and Christ are associated with each other in a manner that wholly bypasses Israel's constitution and constituents' (see page 67). I am puzzled by these statements, since it does not seem to me that Paul is interested in doing any of these things! God's dealings with Israel are not in question in this letter, and Paul has no reason to deny their importance; the issue that separates Paul from those who are agitating the Galatians is the way in which God's salvation comes to *gentile* Christians. On this point, Longenecker maintains that Paul *might* have argued that '[g]entile Christians who demonstrate committed faith in Israel's Messiah are thereby participating in the pinnacle of Israel's history (an age of faith) simply by means of their faith' (see page 70). He might indeed—and in fact, he does, in Gal. 3:1–5! There he appeals to the Galatians' own experience of the Spirit as evidence that they are already sharing in the blessings of the Last Days; they do not need to perform 'the works of the law'—to revert to the era dominated by 'flesh'—in order to enjoy the blessings that had been seen as 'the pinnacle' of Israel's hopes. The 'gospel' they received was 'the gospel of the Christ' (i.e., the Messiah, 1:7); the blessing they enjoyed had been promised to Abraham, the father of Israel (3:6–29). But that particular way of arguing was clearly not enough to persuade Paul's opponents, who were still living in the era of the flesh and thus demanded 'organic linearity' with Israel via *circumcision*. What he does, therefore, is to remind them that they enjoy a different kind of 'organic linearity'—or 'participationistic linearity', as Longenecker also terms it—namely, organic linearity with Abraham, the patriarch of Israel. The faith of believers unites them with Abraham not simply because they share the same faith but because that faith *incorporates believers into Christ*, who is the one true seed of Abraham. Paul is arguing for 'organic linearity' in terms of the *Spirit*, not the *flesh*, and in terms of *faith*, not the works of the *law*.

Longenecker rightly notes that Paul's argument in Galatians about Abraham's 'seed' is somewhat different from the one he uses in Romans. Surprisingly, however, he does not point out that the passage in Galatians *supports* the idea of 'organic linearity' in a way that the corresponding discussion in Romans does not! In Romans 4, Abraham's 'seed' (plural) are identified as all who share the faith of Abraham, gentiles as well as Jews: they are his seed because they are *like* him in having faith. The blessing was pronounced on Abraham *before* his circumcision and thus extends to all who have faith, not simply those who obey the law. In Gal. 3:16–17, the 'seed' is identified with Christ alone, but the promises made to Abraham and his 'seed' are now being poured out on gentile Christians—because they are 'in Christ' and hence Abraham's 'seed' (3:26–29). The covenant made with Abraham and his seed (3:16) was not annulled by the law, which came after the covenant was ratified. Because the link with Abraham in Galatians is by incorporation *into* Abraham's seed, it is much stronger than the link in Romans.

But has 'the story of Israel' perhaps been 'bypassed' in Galatians, as Longenecker suggests? The answer is 'No', since the link between Abraham and gentile Christians is *Christ*. It is noteworthy that it is not *Jesus* who is identified as 'the seed of Abraham',[6] but *Christ*, whose 'organic' relationship to Israel

---

6. *Pace* Longenecker, 'Spiritual Blessings', 70.

is obvious—though Paul underlines it by describing him as 'born under the law' (4:4). God has not 'bypassed' Israel's story, for God has used her promised Messiah to fulfil God's purposes. Abraham, therefore, is not portrayed here simply as 'a figure that permits organic linearity between Christians and Israel'[7] but a figure who *demands* this 'organic linearity' through his descendant, the Messiah.

Longenecker's statement that in Galatians 'Paul strains against all odds to depict Abraham in any possible way other than as the patriarch of ethnic Israel' thus seems to me a gross distortion of the evidence. What he 'strains against all odds' to establish is that Abraham is the 'patriarch' of those who, in Christ, are his 'seed', *even though* they are gentiles. If Abraham and Christ *appear* to be 'associated with each other in a manner that wholly bypasses the story of Israel', that is because the rest of Israel's story is not relevant to Paul's argument at this particular point: his concern is only to show how *gentiles* can inherit the promises. Nor is he concerned 'to deconstruct strong organic ties between Israelite history and his gentile mission'; what he is concerned to do is to *construct* strong organic ties between Abraham (and the promises made to him) and his own gentile converts, and to show how the promises made to Abraham had been fulfilled *without* circumcision. The 'organic tie' that Paul is anxious to sever is not the one between his gentile converts and Israel's history but the tie that his opponents are trying to establish between those converts and circumcision—the 'fleshly' organic tie that would bring them 'under the law'.

Turning to Paul's treatment of the law in Galatians, Longenecker argues that Paul 'plac[ed] the giving of the law beyond the salvific "covenant"' and that he made no attempt 'to yoke the story of Israel with [the stories] of Christ and the people of Christian faith' (page 67). The giving of the law was, indeed, regarded by all Jews as 'one of the most momentous events shaping Jewish history' (page 67), but however formative, it was only one event in that history and cannot be *equated* with that history. To reduce 'Israel's story' to the period of the law would be to accept the arguments of Paul's opponents. Although Paul may regard the giving of the law as 'a parenthesis between . . . God's promise to Abraham and the coming of Abraham's exclusive seed, Jesus Christ' (pages 67–68), that does not mean that he regards *Israel's history* as a 'parenthesis'. The law was, in Paul's view, a temporary measure, 'added' in order to deal with transgressions (3:19), but it was given by God and had a positive role as 'pedagogue' (3:24). Paul had no need to spell out the positive role of the law or the benefits of being a Jew—his opponents had emphasised these all too successfully! His concern was to oppose their argument that gentiles needed to become Jews in order to belong

---

7. Longenecker, 'Spiritual Blessings', 68. Longenecker denies even this much in Galatians.

to God's people and to be heirs of the promises made to Abraham. Of course, then, he emphasises the temporary role of the law!

Because gentile Christians are 'in Christ', they are not only 'Abraham's seed and heirs, according to the promise' (3:29) but also 'sons' of God (4:5–7). Longenecker admits that 4:1–7 is 'promising' to those looking for 'organic' linearity in Galatians (page 68), but he is unwilling to agree that it is to be found there. Yet Paul argues here that the coming of God's Son, born of a woman, born under the law, not only set Jews free from bondage to the law and enabled them to enjoy the benefits of sonship but also made gentiles participants in the same privileges. As proof of their new status, both have received the gift of the Spirit.

To understand Paul's argument, we have to remember the assumptions underlying the dispute—assumptions that are not necessarily spelt out (though they are hinted at) in the letter. Paul's opponents began from the belief that Israel (i.e., Israel according to the flesh) was God's Son, and that, at the end, the Spirit would be poured out on Israel. Paul, however, has insisted that 'the "blessing" of the Spirit would be given through Abraham's seed to "all the nations"' (Longenecker, page 69) because he believes that, in Christ, 'the nations' have been integrated into Israel's seed. Why, then, does Longenecker expect Paul to say that the Spirit was 'intended for Israel' (as opposed to the gentiles)?[8] For Paul, God's intention was not so limited! Similar assumptions underlie the discussion in Romans 9–11, where he explains why Israel was chosen by God. It is precisely because Paul is anxious to establish that the inclusion of the gentiles in the covenant promises was part of God's purpose that he traces the 'organic linearity' back to the very beginning of Israel's history.

'It would', suggests Longenecker, 'have been simple for Paul to state explicitly in 4:1–7 that gentile Christians were participating in Israel's maturity by their faith in the Messiah who had redeemed Israel' (page 68). But why *should* he have put it in that particular way? Moreover, the *elements* of that statement are either present or assumed. Paul's opponents had undoubtedly stressed that Jesus was *Israel's* Messiah, and Paul's own gospel is about 'the Christ' (i.e., the Messiah; 1:7). Israel's 'maturity' means enjoying the privileges of sonship (4:1–5)—privileges that gentiles now share (4:6–7). Their new status comes through faith in Jesus *Christ* (3:16)—the one through whom *Israel* had been redeemed (3:13; 4:5). The way in which Paul bewilders exegetes by switching between first and second person plurals is some indication of the way in which gentiles *are* now 'participating' in Israel's history.

Paul's use of the 'allegory' of Sarah and Hagar in 4:21–31 is clearly designed to undermine the arguments of his opponents. For them, the only true children of Abraham are those who are descended from Isaac: gentiles claiming a place

---

8. Longenecker, 'Spiritual Blessings', 69, my italics.

in God's kingdom are no better than illegitimate offspring. For Paul, too, it is essential that Abraham's seed should be identified as 'children of *promise*' (i.e., children of Isaac), not as those 'born according to the *flesh*' (as was Ishmael). He cannot, therefore, use here the kind of argument he uses in Rom. 11:13–24, where wild olive shoots are grafted into a cultivated tree. Longenecker suggests that Paul might have used an organic version of this allegory, but though he claims that it would not have been difficult to construct, he does not explain how it would have run! The 'organic' version was in fact spelt out in Gal. 3:6ff., but that necessarily concentrated on Abraham's offspring through Isaac. The version of the story used in Galatians 4, which contrasts Abraham's two sons, does not lend itself to 'organic' interpretation. The promise of blessing concerned the descendants of Isaac alone (Gen. 18:18); in stark contrast, Ishmael and his descendants are doomed to endure slavery and exile (Gen. 16:12). The antithesis between the two groups is built into the story: Jews, claiming to be Isaac's children, have excluded the gentiles from the inheritance; now Paul reverses the interpretation and *appears* to be excluding the Jews!

Remarkably, however, the antithesis is *not* as great as the story seems to demand, because Paul treats the story as though it were an 'apocalyptic' vision. The two women, Sarah and Hagar, are said to represent two covenants, and it becomes clear in the exposition that one of these was the covenant made between God and Israel on Sinai; the other was the covenant referred to in 3:15 between God and Abraham. Longenecker concludes that these two covenants stand 'in oppositional juxtaposition' (page 70), and Paul's conclusion in 4:30, quoting Gen. 21:10, might seem at first to confirm this understanding of the passage. This, however, ignores the fact that Paul is treating the story as an 'apocalyptic' text. At the earthly level, Hagar, the slave, is identified as Mount Sinai, but she also corresponds to the earthly Jerusalem, and her children are in slavery (i.e., under the law). At the heavenly level there is *another* Jerusalem (i.e., Sarah) who is free, and she is 'our mother'—that is, the mother of those who have faith in Christ.

It is noteworthy that Paul refers to 'the *Jerusalem* that is above'. Here is a clear link with Israel's history! The heavenly vision relates, in the manner of such heavenly visions, to God's purpose for the *earthly* Jerusalem, which is at present in slavery. The earthly is temporary; the heavenly, eternal. The apparent antithesis between the two covenants is less important than the link between them. Those who claim to be Abraham's descendants 'according to the flesh' are not precluded from becoming his children 'according to promise', as 3:23–29 demonstrated: indeed, that is God's intention for them. Those who accept what is offered in the covenant of promise are no longer fettered by the covenant that enslaves. Paul's exposition repeats the message of 3:6ff.: the law is not opposed to the promises of God (3:21) but points forward to it (3:24); and with the arrival of the promised blessing in Christ, the curse is annulled. In 4:21–31, also, it is not the heavenly vision alone that points forward to the fulfilment of God's purpose, but scripture itself. It is significant that this passage is introduced and concludes with appeals to 'the law'! 'Do you not hear the law?' (4:21). 'What does scripture say?' (4:30, quoting Gen. 21:10). The law itself witnesses to its own temporary nature. Once again, as in Galatians 3, Paul is not attempting to 'bypass' Israel's story, but simply to demonstrate the folly of going back in time to the era of the law: the present Jerusalem has to give way to the Jerusalem that is above.

Paul's reference to 'the law', here and elsewhere in Galatians, is significant, for it is the basis of his argument with his opponents. Like them, he accepts its authority, and he dismisses as absurd the notion that it might be contrary to God's promises (3:21–22). The law bears witness to God's covenant with Abraham and points forward to the *fulfilment* of God's promises. Even its negative effect (imprisoning all things under sin) had a positive purpose (that the promise might be given to those who have faith, 3:22); it was a 'pedagogue' to lead Jews to Christ (3:24). But that custodial role belongs to the past: to deny that the law is necessary for those who have now inherited the promises is not to deny its importance in the past or to ignore the history of Israel. Christ himself was 'born under the law' (4:4), and Paul's insistence on this fact emphasises the links between God's dealings with Israel and the fulfilment of God's promise to Abraham in Christ.

In Gal. 5:14, Paul points to the fact that the whole law is 'summed up' or 'fulfiled' in the command to love one another; Longenecker notes this passage but plays down its significance. Yet it is the law *given to Israel* that is spoken of here, and its essence is seen in Christ and lived out in the Christian community. The law might not have been able to give the life it promised (3:12), but it pointed clearly enough to what God required of God's people—the love for others that is now realised in the lives of those who 'live by the Spirit' (5:16).

What, finally, of Paul's remarkable evocation of blessing on 'the Israel of God' in 6:16? Longenecker dismisses the possibility that Paul is referring here to 'ethnic' Israel; certainly that would undermine his case! He suggests that the phrase implies *either* that Christians do, after all, fall 'within Israel's larger story'[9] *or* that 'Paul considers Christians to be "the Israel of God" *only in a linguistic sense*' (page 71). He opts for the latter. But this 'solution' totally ignores the problem! *However* we interpret the phrase—whether we take it as referring to 'ethnic' Israel, to Jews *and* Christians, or to Christians alone—we are confronted with the remarkable fact that Paul here uses the phrase 'the Israel of God', a phrase he uses nowhere else. *Why?* And why should he use it 'only in a linguistic sense'? If throughout his argument he has—as Longenecker suggests—been deliberately *avoiding* the notion of 'organic linearity' between Israel and Christians, it would

---

9. Longenecker, 'Spiritual Blessings', 71. It is not clear to me whether he is suggesting that Paul has *narrowed* the phrase to mean Christians *alone* or *broadened* it to mean 'Jews and Christians'.

be extraordinary if he chose this unusual term to refer to Christians here. Why employ this language? Longenecker argues that the term 'Israel' could 'simply specify those who enjoy a special relationship with God in a pagan world' (page 71). But *why use a term that evokes the notion of linearity with historical Israel?* Even if Paul meant that Christians had somehow 'displaced' Israel, the use of the name (like the references to Abraham and to Jerusalem) implies an ongoing link between God's dealings with Israel in the past and his dealings with this 'new' Israel. However we interpret this verse, therefore, this phrase alone points to an 'organic linearity' between Israel and the Church.

## CONCLUSION

There is no denying Paul's negative attitude throughout Galatians to those who claim privilege on the basis of circumcision and the law. This negative tone is very largely due to the circumstances that led to the letter's composition. If the benefits of belonging to Israel are not mentioned, that is because they were not the matters in dispute. If Paul said almost nothing about Israel's history subsequent to the call of Abraham, that was not because he 'attempted to sever an organic relationship between Israel's story and that of Christians' but because it was not relevant to his argument and because it, too—apart from the role of the law—was not in dispute. The matter in dispute was how (if at all) gentile Christians could inherit the promises made to Abraham, and thus become members of God's people. The obvious answer was 'by circumcision, and so by obedience to the law'. Paul's answer was 'by faith'. He would, I suggest, have been astonished to hear his argument interpreted as a denial of the importance of God's dealings with Israel. It is surely ironic if his emphasis on the *inclusion* of gentiles into Abraham's seed leads us to the conclusion that 'Israel's story' is therefore *excluded*. For the blessing of the gentiles through Christ is an essential part of that story. If there is any 'exclusion', it applies only to those Jews who do not believe and who, failing to understand the significance and role of the law, do not receive the promises.

The different ways in which Israel's story is handled in Romans and Galatians, therefore, are not due to 'unstable' elements in that story but are rather the result of the different circumstances underlying the letters. Paul's purpose in Romans is not only (as in Galatians) to show that both Jews and gentiles are brought into a right relationship with God through faith and not through the works of the law but to explain also that God remains faithful to God's promises to Israel. In other words, Paul is not telling *different* stories in the two letters but drawing on different elements in the one story: Longenecker's attempts to explain what he perceives to be radical differences are misguided, and the stark alternatives he poses to explain those differences are unnecessary. Of course, we do not have to imagine that Paul 'peddled a gospel' of *any* kind in preaching to the Galatians, only to 'undermine' it later in his letter! There is nothing in Galatians to undermine the belief that God's dealings with Israel and with the gentiles are parts of the same story. Nor are we forced to suppose that Romans is merely 'Paul's attempt to enunciate his theology in garb that would more likely be appealing to Christian leaders in Jerusalem and/or helpful to his Roman audience'. Paul's discussion of Israel's story in Romans 9–11 is introduced by 9:1–5, sufficient evidence that his theology is from the heart, not dressed up to make it appealing to others. The belief that gentiles have been incorporated into the people of God is an essential part of Paul's 'story' of how God's purpose for the world is being accomplished.

Ultimately, however, the problem with Longenecker's analysis stems from his attempt to distinguish a 'covenantal linearity' from one that is 'organic' (or 'participationistic'). The terms, as he acknowledges, are not Paul's, and the attempt to distinguish between these two forms of 'linearity' seems to distort Paul's intention. What Paul distinguishes are the *covenants* made with Abraham and with Moses (Gal. 5:24): the former embraces the gentiles; the latter does not. Gentiles participate in the promises to Abraham—and so in Israel's story—because they are Abraham's seed (whether because, as in Rom. 4:17, they share Abraham's faith, or because, in Gal. 3:16, 29, they are 'in Christ'); or, to use another image, they are grafted into the olive tree, whose roots are the patriarchs (Rom. 11:28). What they do *not* participate in is the covenant made with Moses, who was entrusted with the law. Christians' relationship with Abraham can be described as a 'linearity' that is both 'covenantal' and 'organic', but in both Romans and Galatians, Paul is adamant that they should have no such relationship with Moses.

Longenecker's conclusion is a negative one. He feels that a narrative approach has not added to his exegesis of the Pauline text. If by 'narrative approach' he means the 'multistory scheme' that has led him to believe that Paul's attitudes to Israel's role in history in Galatians and Romans are inconsistent, then I, too, find it unhelpful! Concentration on the way in which one episode of the 'grand Story' is handled in different epistles can lead to distortion. If, on the other hand, 'narrative approach' means simply the recognition that behind Paul's theological arguments there is a fundamental belief in God's purpose for the world, and that this is inevitably expressed in the form of narrative, then that recognition can, indeed, act as 'a necessary *exegetical control*', as Longenecker suggests (page 83). When seen against the background of the 'grand Story' of God's purpose in history, the emphasis given in particular circumstances to a particular detail in the story will be less likely to distort our understanding of the whole. Since Paul's theology is concerned with God's activity through history, it is clear that his interpreters should not ignore the role of 'narrative'.

# 6

# The Story of Jesus in Romans and Galatians

Douglas A. Campbell

## INTRODUCTION

This chapter is a brief beginning in an important but complicated issue, namely, the narrative dimension in Paul's christology (here limited to Romans and Galatians).[1] Furthermore, this issue—which is really generated by a particular methodological angle of approach—has been strangely neglected by Pauline interpreters, and this is the more surprising given the influence of Richard Hays' dissertation *The Faith of Jesus Christ: An Investigation of the Narrative Substructure of Galatians 3:1–4:11*, published in 1983.[2] Since the publication of that important

---

1. Constraints of space have led to the mere broaching of a number of important suggestions in what follows. For these to be fully plausible, I am well aware that much more thorough demonstration and treatment is required. Hence I hope to undertake shortly a book-length treatment that has long been in the planning. This will not focus on narrative christology per se but on Paul's argument and theology as it unfolds within and beyond Romans 8.

2. SBLDS 56; Chico, Calif.: Scholars Press (its importance is further reflected by its recent reprint; Grand Rapids: Eerdmans, 2001). Hays remains one of the major figures in this area, if not its leading protagonist, producing an impressive number of studies, especially *Echoes of Scripture in the Letters of Paul* (New Haven, Conn.: Yale University Press, 1989).

N.T. Wright's work is also very important—and likely to become more so—but as yet lacks a definitive treatment of Paul (that is, excepting his unpublished D.Phil. thesis on Romans [Oxford University, 1980], which remains rather inaccessible). See, however, his *The Climax of the Covenant: Christ and the Law in Pauline Theology* (Edinburgh: T&T Clark, 1991; Minneapolis: Fortress Press, 1992), which frequently presupposes

study, this type of analysis has been rarely undertaken[3] (and, when attempted, it has also tended to be somewhat disappointing[4]). Perhaps other scholars have, like me, been nervous about various exaggerated claims made on behalf of the method by some of its practitioners, and also about its possible abuses. However, I hope to show shortly that these concerns, while real, are not inherent in the method itself. Hence the correct response to such concerns is really 'right use' rather than 'abandonment'. Moreover, the realisation has emerged with special force for me during the course of this investigation that to abandon this type of analysis is ultimately to impoverish dramatically our understanding of Paul's thought. I would suggest that the story of Jesus, properly understood—and this also means detecting its connections with *other* important stories—is an *irreducible* element in Paul's theological description as it unfolds in these two letters, as well as a highly integrative approach that illuminates and strengthens connections in his thinking with other significant themes and issues. But before attempting to establish these claims in detail, various possible concerns with the method must be addressed.

## INITIAL METHODOLOGICAL CLARIFICATIONS

I would suggest that the nervousness felt by many scholars in relation to narrative methodology is ultimately unnecessary but that it does often represent

---

strong narrative concerns (chapters two, seven, eight, and ten through fourteen are relevant). Also important is his *The New Testament and the People of God* (London: SPCK; Minneapolis: Fortress Press, 1992), which traces narrative concerns in relation to late Second Temple Judaism, and his 'Romans and the Theology of Paul', in D.M. Hay and E.E. Johnson (eds), *Pauline Theology, Volume III: Romans* (Minneapolis: Fortress Press, 1995) 30–67. Wright's work is rigorous and highly methodologically integrated. It is, however, vulnerable in my opinion to the methodological problems associated with strong prior commitments to a metanarrative (see below).

3. The use of structuralism and related approaches was voguish in the seventies and early eighties (i.e., Russian formalism, Czech structuralism, and so on), hence Hays' use of well-known theorists of East European folk traditions (V. Propp, A. J. Greimas, etc.). This trajectory is also apparent in the concerns of *Semeia*, which devoted many issues to such methodological angles during this period, but almost none since. (Somewhat strangely, despite the devotion of an entire issue to him, E. Güttgemanns has not been influential to my knowledge in English-speaking scholarship.) This raises the question discussed briefly below, namely, whether it is wise to link the narrative analysis of Paul to a particular school of narrative theory (something Hays later wisely expresses flexibility in relation to, and this essay follows that decision).

4. For example, see B. Witherington III's rather diffuse *Paul's Narrative Thought World: The Tapestry of Tragedy and Triumph* (Louisville, Ky.: Westminster/John Knox Press, 1994). F. Matera's treatment of Paul is an improvement but necessarily brief given his treatment of New Testament christology as a whole in particular dialogue with narrative. See his *New Testament Christology* (Louisville, Ky.: Westminster John Knox Press, 1999).

valid concerns about excessive or false claims for the approach that ought rightly to be rejected. The first such potentially problematic claim probably concerns the nature of 'story' itself. Is the method linked inexorably to a particular definition of narrative? Must we sort out what narrative is before we can apply it to Paul's texts? It seems to me that there are a number of potential pitfalls here.

It is unlikely that we will be able to arrive at a precise, mutually agreed on, fully satisfactory definition of what a story is, for there is probably no absolute definitional centre to the notion of story. Stories are generally identified by readers through the recognition of a particular text's distinctive features, from which point interpretative expectations follow, especially in relation to genre. This suggests the presence of 'a family resemblance', to borrow Wittgenstein's useful notion, rather than the fulfilment of a particular absolute structure or formula. That is, stories are recognisable as such because they share a number of overlapping features, not because they all fulfil a given essential definition of 'storiness'. And those constellations of textual features will shift over time and space, as will readers' expectations—so an ancient story, although usually recognisable as such, does not usually read the same way as a modern one. Hence the quest for a detailed definition of what a story is will likely prove futile. Moreover, if particular characterisations of Paul's thinking are linked tightly to a given definition of story, then they are likely to date rapidly, as those definitions do. Consequently it seems wise to sit loosely to any notion of definition and to speak of various narrative features, the possession of a sufficient number of which allows us to recognise narrative elements, or even relatively complete stories, in the broader texture of Paul's thought as revealed in Romans and Galatians. Among those features that suggest narrative is a striking personal dimension conveyed largely by the activity of personal actors, who usually undertake actions, often in relation to one another, and to whom events occur. These actions and events often then unfold to create a plot, the latter often also exhibiting a problem-solution structure. Hence stories are especially useful types of texts for giving an account of the behaviour, actions, history, and/or accomplishments, *of people* (or, more strictly, of personal actors). This cluster of features can serve as a rough guide to us in what follows.

From this point it is important to recognise the issue of explanatory pressure or direction, for a story is just a particular interpretative perspective that readers may or may not feel is appropriate for the description of Paul's texts. Thus any a priori claims for the *necessity* of a narrative explanation, whether in whole or in part, are false. Paul *might* have an underlying narrative informing his theological reflection—or may even be dependent on a cultural metanarrative—but he might not. Such claims have to be demonstrated, not presupposed. Similarly, Paul's thinking might exhibit important narrative elements.

But evidence will still need to be marshalled cogently in support of that claim. In short, there is nothing inherently necessary about a narrative explanation; its utility must emerge from the material that it is being applied to.[5]

Having introduced some caveats, however, it is also important to grasp that this particular interpretative perspective is in many ways rather distinctive and, as such, offers interpreters certain advantages as they seek to explicate Paul's thinking.

## SOME EXPLANATORY ADVANTAGES

Stories seem to be highly integrative explanations in several important respects. As textual phenomena, like all texts, narratives tend to be significantly informed by *other* texts.[6] Hence all stories are, to a degree, reminiscences of other stories. That is, they tend to have a prominent and important intertextual dimension (which assists their correct recognition). But as such they are also almost invariably reworkings or transformations of those other texts. Thus there is usually a shifting, creative dimension to the intertextuality of stories—they seldom merely repeat but usually update, twist, vary, and comment. In what follows, we must try to be sensitive to this dimension of narrative and to its theological consequences.

But the integrative, even expansionist, tendencies in stories are not exhausted by their textual linkages, important though these are. We have already noted that stories tend to possess personal actors that are involved in some plot (although they do not have to have these). A particular story therefore tends to possess its own basic integrity and will consequently be recognisable in a variety of different ways. Its key events and/or actors will also probably be identifiable through a number of alternative formulations (viz., Saussurian paradigms are present here). Moreover, once an element has been recognised, the rest of the story—or at least part of it—will be implicit in this recognition.

These features allow stories to be recognised in superficially quite diverse material, to which they can thereby impart a narratively informed unity. They

---

5. Hence my inability to endorse fully the work of Wright and those echoing him—although numerous insights and strengths remain within his work.

6. Here I am ultimately dependent on a seminal insight of R. Barthes, 'Style and its Image', in S. Chapman (ed.), *Literary Style: A Symposium* (New York: Oxford University Press, 1971) 3–15. It is pursued especially masterfully in my view by M. Riffaterre, *Semiotics of Poetry* (Bloomington: Indiana University Press, 1978); idem, *Text Production*, trans. T. Lyons (New York: Columbia University Press, 1983).

possess, in short, an integrative explanatory potential. It goes without saying that such integration must not be imposed insensitively. The allusions to key narrative elements must be genuine, and the further implied elements plausible and relevant. But given the satisfaction of these methodological demands, a narrative method can potentially deliver an integrative and coherent sense to texts where many other New Testament techniques tend rather to atomise and to fragment data. The result can be a greater conceptual coherence in Paul's thinking as a whole, or at least in certain parts of it.

It is also important to recognise some of the approach's weaknesses. In particular, narratives, as the unfolding of events and plots in relation to personal actors, tend to presuppose a linear temporal framework, although narrative texts tend of course to be highly complex in their actual treatment of time. The world that narratives inhabit, like the worlds of their personalised actors, tend to unfold through time. Hence it will be important to identify when narrative explanations are being pushed into extratemporal areas (a not infrequent occurrence in theological discussions). Narrative texts *cannot supply cogent explanations at these points*—that is, beyond the borders of space-time reality—since they really have to presuppose those. Put slightly less dismissively, their suggestions at such points must be carefully reinterpreted.

With these preliminary methodological observations completed, we can turn to a detailed investigation of the story of Jesus in Paul's letters to the Christians[7] in Rome and in Galatia.

## PREAMBLE

There are clearly considerable methodological dangers involved in any demonstration of a story of Jesus in Romans and Galatians that is pursued synthetically, namely, by identifying various small units within this story throughout those two letters and then combining them into one overarching narrative. We would have few guarantees that this narrative was actually right, and we might also thereby be insensitive to multiple narrative elements and levels. In my view, then, it is best to proceed in the opposite direction, trying to find a reasonably complete and explicit rehearsal of a key story in one text, then tracing it through its more vestigial possible occurrences elsewhere. This approach offers far more controls for our investigation. And while Hays' classic analysis began with Galatians—in particular, with 3:13–14 and 4:4–5—I find that Paul's most comprehensive exposition of the story of Jesus in Romans

---

7. I use this anachronistic term deliberately to avoid the difficult questions that are begged when any one of Paul's terms for 'the saved' are selected (see n. 20 below).

and Galatians—if not in his corpus as a whole (including Phil. 2:5–11!)—is in Romans 8. The narrative investigation of that chapter, centred on its christology, will consequently be the foundation stone on which the rest of this analysis is raised.[8]

## NARRATIVE MOTIFS IN ROMANS 8

Few scholars seem to have been overly concerned with the narrative dimension in Romans 8, and those who have noted that dimension have tended not to pursue the christological material meticulously. (This seems curious in that it does emerge as fundamental to the section's argument. Is this perhaps further evidence of some of the difficulties that can be caused by metanarrative commitments?[9]). So we have to develop a slightly distinctive approach from this point. We will first identify a string of key motifs and sequences and will then consider if a single narrative binds them together. However, we must begin this process with some brief remarks concerning this discussion's setting or contingency.

I would suggest that there is a sense in which Paul is killing two (if not three) birds with one stone in this climactic, and very important, argument—and this text is primarily an argument. He wishes to articulate the vigorous ethical state of Christians even though they are no longer governed by the written Torah. They are to act rightly and, indeed, *can* act rightly (cf. 3:8; 6:1; 7:5–6) because they are now free from the cosmic influences of Sin and Death. However, he also seems concerned to defuse any sense of eschatological anxiety—that God

---

8. L.E. Keck's important analysis ('"Jesus" in Romans', *JBL* 108 [1989]: 443–60) overlooks the relevance of this chapter because of its explicit focus on 'Jesus', but it should still be consulted. Disquiet might also be expressed by those concerned with my beginning with Romans, and the consequent possibility that a much earlier Galatians may be significantly different. In relation to any such concerns I would first suggest that Galatians must have its own argumentative integrity respected—irrespective of its placement vis-a-vis Romans—but I have tried to do this. Second, I would not place these two letters far apart in any case; space clearly precludes arguing this position in any detail here, so it must suffice to say that, in my view, these two letters were composed close together in time (viz., separated only by some months) and reflect similiar provenances. Third, the starting point is in any case methodological, taking the most complete narrative discussion as its beginning. Any narrative claims in other letters from such a starting point must of course also negotiate any relevant issues of contingency en route.

9. See, e.g., Wright, *Climax*, 193–225; F. Thielman, 'The Story of Israel and the Theology of Romans 5–8', in Hay and Johnson (eds), *Pauline Theology, Volume III*, 169–95; and S.C. Keesmaat, *Paul and His Story: (Re)interpreting the Exodus Tradition* (JSNTSup 181; Sheffield: Sheffield Academic Press, 1999).

will punish Christians on the Day of Judgement (cf. 2:5–16; 5:2–11). (The third possible element here is the suggestion that present suffering is a sign of God's displeasure, and so current lack of social status and/or hardship would contribute to the eschatological anxiety just noted; see esp. 8:33.[10])

Paul seems to address these concerns in Romans 8 by articulating the state of the Christian as he understands it in some detail. The same dynamic construction that moves us beyond a sinful and enslaved past, enabling us to act rightly but independently of written Torah (8:1–13), *also* guarantees our future inheritance and glorification (8:14–39). That is, we move out of the complex of Death, where Flesh and Sin are also involved, into a present existence free from the past, and one also assured in relation to the future (where the continuation of that past state of Death would have issued in condemnation)—and this despite any present appearances to the contrary (see esp. 8:33–35). So, essentially, two complementary arguments are played out of the same structure by Paul in Romans 8 to address these two concerns, that underlying structure being, of course, the nature of Christian salvation.

Within his powerful articulations in relation to these concerns are Paul's most concentrated narrative statements about Jesus (so his narrative statements here are part of an unfolding argument). They occur explicitly in two short sections where God is the subject that also speak compactly of 'his' Son in the context of a brief exposition of eternal, otherwise hidden, strategies (8:3–4a and 8:28–30 and 32, taking these last verses in close relation to one another). But these two brief subsections are coordinated with the rest of the chapter's argument by means of a pneumatological discussion, Paul's longest such analysis. The motif of the Spirit is introduced from 8:2 and continues to feature in an important argument that dominates Paul's discussion through to 8:17. (The motif of the Spirit also reappears in 8:26–27; *prior* to 8:2 and 4b, however, see only 1:4; 5:5; and 7:6.) And this more extended 'bridging' discussion also contains a considerable amount of important material about the Son and his story, although clearly it is present more indirectly (a point we will return to). We must now focus on these specific texts in a little more detail.

---

10. A thesis espoused by R. Jewett in relation to the verb ἐγκαλέω in 8:33; a full treatment can be expected in his commentary (forthcoming in the Hermeneia series [Fortress Press]). Jewett draws heavily on M. Reasoner's work as the background for this reading (*The Strong and the Weak: Romans 14:1–15:13 in Context* [SNTSM 103; Cambridge: Cambridge University Press, 1999]). Reasoner's important thesis would, in my view, be further strengthened if it accommodated the thrust of this essay's final section, which discusses the role of πίστις in Paul's story of Jesus.

## PAUL'S STRATEGIC CHRISTOLOGICAL STATEMENTS (8:3, 29, 32)

In 8:3 Paul states, 'God, having sent his own Son in the precise likeness of sinful flesh, and to atone for sin'[11] (ὁ θεὸς τὸν ἑαυτοῦ υἱὸν πέμψας ἐν ὁμοιώματι σαρκὸς ἁμαρτίας καὶ περὶ ἁμαρτίας). The phrase περὶ ἁμαρτίας (translated here 'to atone for sin') has attracted much attention as a supposed clue to Paul's atonement theology. Elsewhere in Romans, such cultic imagery occurs in relation to the atonement unambiguously only in 3:25 (although cf. 12:1 and 15:16). This phrase in 8:3 is the standard Septuagintal locution for the sin offering. It also occurs in the context of the instructions for the feast of Yom Kippur, signifying there atonement more generally (see Leviticus 17), and it occurs, in addition, in Isaiah 53 (although perhaps not especially strategically; see 53:10). Consequently, some generalised sacrificial connotation is hard (and probably pointless) to deny. But the phrase is so isolated that it is also extremely difficult to claim more than this. Hence I would suggest the foregoing rendering simply in terms of atonement, leaving the exact mechanics of that atonement as yet unspecified but able to be articulated more fully by the ensuing argument (which does not disappoint us). Our particular concern here will of course be to explore if a narrative explanation is ultimately required.

Similarly, we ought not rush to render the terminology of divine sending (viz., attempting to resolve the issue of preexistence). The object of the divine despatch is, however, clear—namely, that God's Son should assume a precise likeness of sinful flesh (the use of ὁμοίωμα ['likeness'] by Paul generally emphasises similarity[12]). This identification with the highly problematic condition of humanity (see esp. 7:7–25) is a critical element in the atonement effected for us. And it is achieved by God's own Son, the motif of 'son' being, rather significantly, present in the letter prior to this only in Romans 1 (specifically as the Son of David in 1:2 and the resurrected Son of God in 1:3; see also 1:9) and in 5:10. Romans 8 contains the only other three instances in the letter (viz. here in 8:3, and in 8:29 and 32).

We have not learned a great deal from this very compact statement, but important issues are being tabled: the mission of God's Son, clearly at the divine behest, and the atoning effects of his assumption of sinful flesh.

Romans 8:29 signals a return to the compact terminology of 8:3: 'because those whom he knew beforehand he also chose beforehand to be conformed

---

11. Here my own translation; where translations are not my own, NRSV or other Bible versions are indicated.

12. See elsewhere in Rom. 1:23; 5:14; and 6:5, as well as Phil. 2:7.

to the image of his Son, so that he might be the firstborn among many brothers'. This is an important statement because, while not perhaps greatly illuminating either the precise identity of the Son or his mission in detail, it again places him at the very centre of the divine plan to redeem humanity and also links that plan explicitly to the terminology of brotherhood. Indeed, this is the only explicit statement in Paul's letters that links the ubiquitous term 'brother' to a theological explanation, here a christological one. To bear the image of the Son is to be his brother, although this image is only completed eschatologically (see 8:30). His story—whatever that might be—is 'our' story.

In 8:32, the third christological statement in the chapter and also the third instance of 'son', Paul quotes part of Gen. 22:12/16 (although without signalling that quotation with an introductory formula). The God who is for us 'did not withhold his own Son but gave him up for all of us'. And again, this is a brief but important statement. It alludes fairly directly to the famous story of Abraham's near-sacrifice of Isaac (although most commentators fail to see much significance in this allusion). It then emphasises that, unlike Abraham, God did not hold back the knife, so to speak, but slaughtered his only Son on our behalf. And this powerful claim functions within a broader a fortiori argument premised on divine benevolence. The God who is prepared to sacrifice his only Son for 'us' is not going to fail to support us in the present, despite possible extremities, and in the future, irrespective of what dark powers threaten us (so principally 8:32b–39, but this train of thought begins in 8:18). It is an action that speaks fundamentally of an unshakeable divine love for humanity—a love experienced by those called to it. So the atonement is linked directly with divine love.

The view at this point is intriguing and at times powerful, but hardly clear. Fortunately, rather more information about Christ is implicit in the chapter's argument although, unlike the foregoing, this is not tabled in direct relation to him.

## PAUL'S BRIDGING STATEMENTS
### (8:2, 4b-6, 9–17; esp. 8:14–17)

In 8:2 Paul signals the introduction of a vital element in the following argument, namely, 'the Spirit of life'. This motif dominates the discussion from 8:4b (where Paul's first direct christological statement finishes) up to 8:17. This particular passage is largely focussed on the ethical concerns that have dominated the letter from 6:1 (and perhaps as far back as 5:12), but it also has a future eschatological dimension that is signalled in 8:11 and then becomes explicit and more detailed from 8:14. Most important, in 8:14–17 Paul attributes a number of distinctive qualities and features to Christians as they wait for their destiny to unfold. More specifically, those who are led by the Spirit are 'sons of God' (8:14b, 19) and 'children of God' (8:16, 21). They have been 'adopted' (8:15) and thus no longer possess the fearful minds of slaves but, rather, minds that cry 'Abba Father'. Furthermore, to be a son or child is also to be an heir and to be destined for glory (so 8:17; cf. also 8:30), provided a period of suffering also takes place (8:17, but also 8:18–26; that is, shortly this becomes a sustained theme).

Implicit throughout this argument—whether in its ethical emphasis or its concern with assurance—is the notion that the Spirit is creating Christians at the behest of the Father but using the template (literally 'image') of the Son (see 8:29). What the Son has done, and where he has been, is what Christians are currently being 'mapped onto' by the activity of the Spirit. This process is by no means complete; however, it is decisively inaugurated—it is this inauguration that delivers a greater ethical capacity, free from slavery to Sin and Flesh, and that also provides an unshakeable assurance concerning the future that is grounded ultimately in God's love. It follows directly from this that the qualities now attributed by Paul to the Christian originate in the Son, something that should occasion little surprise given their overt semantic similarity as well. Hence we may quite legitimately reverse the contingent flow of Paul's argument and add to the unfolding picture of the Son as it is given to us directly by Paul, the qualities given indirectly in relation to Christians and the Spirit (something that considerably broadens our data).

In sum, Romans 8 supplies—both directly and indirectly—a series of important motifs concerning Christ and his role in salvation. He is 'his' (i.e., God's) 'own' 'Son'. God is not designated 'Father' by Paul in Romans 8, but the point is still made fairly directly. God the Father 'sends' his Son Jesus, or 'delivers him up', or 'does not spare him' (clearly an action with a focus on Easter). This involves suffering and eventually death. (It may well also involve a degree of prior call and appointment: cf. 8:30 and 1:2, 4.) This is all intimately related to love, so that its effecting reveals a fundamental and unshakeable benevolence.

After this despatch to suffering and death, however, a countervailing upward trajectory seems to take place. The Son is resurrected and glorified and now sits at the right hand of God, from which point he can pray for those still embroiled in struggles. This upward movement is, on the one hand, a freedom from a condition of slavery (one doubtless rooted ultimately in 'sinful flesh') and, on the other, an entering into a glorious inheritance. Within it one can cry a cry of adoption, 'Abba, Father', which is also the call of a child or son as against a craven and fearful cry of slavery.

Hence clearly one story of Christ is involved here but it contains two distinctive internal movements or trajectories; one from 'sending', through suffering, to death; and the other from death, through resurrection, to heavenly glorification (cf. Phil. 2:5–11). We need now to investigate this story's structure in a little more detail.

Ironically, the way Paul presents this story in the argument of Romans 8 makes it quite clear that it is not a story of Christ alone, and can never be. First, we must note the role of the Father, who seems to plan the entire drama. He sends, probably also having appointed and called, Jesus; a painful sending because it is also a surrendering up of something precious, his own Son. It is an act of, and hence also a story about, his love. Hence the story *must* speak of both these actors simultaneously. The Father will not be the Father without a Son to send and to sacrifice; the Son not a Son without a Father who has sent and surrendered (and whom presumably he also obeys). Moreover, Christ is not resurrected merely at the behest of the Father but by the Spirit. Indeed, the Spirit is consistently in this story a Spirit *of life* who creates life (so 8:2, 6, 10, 11, 13b, and 16–17; cf. esp. 4:17, 19). Hence the story is also incomplete without him.[13] To speak of the Father's relationship to the Son or vice versa is to speak of the Spirit's role in reestablishing that (so that, perhaps, we can therefore speak easily of a Spirit associated both with the Father, God, and with the Son, Christ, as in 8:9 and 11). But the proliferation of narrative motifs in relation to the Christian also makes it plainly apparent that the Spirit is, in addition, incorporating *other* people, selected long ago, into this principal set of trajectories. The Spirit's life-giving activity, although centred on Christ, is not limited to Christ. Hence the readers of the letter, and Paul himself, are clearly actors that are, to a degree, implicit in this story. Paul is claiming that this story is *constitutive* of their stories (whatever they may be). Hence it is a salvific story (as long as it is true).

For these reasons, in speaking of a story of Jesus in Paul's theology in Romans 8, it is imperative in my view not to limit the story to that specific actor, important as he is, but to grasp that any such story is simultaneously a story of God the Father, of the Spirit of God, and of the incorporation of people into that story.[14] *To lose sight of any one of these aspects is to falsify our account of this story as Paul articulates it.*

---

13. In using this pronoun, I am following convention here (and elsewhere) and not implying anything about the Spirit's gender. In fact, it is important to sustain the gender-based allusions within the narrative, and English unfortunately provides few resources for doing this in a non-gender-discriminatory way.

14. The question of its interaction with any putative story of Israel is important but far from simple. In essence, although this is clearly a Jewish story, in that it uses Jewish motifs and subelements (see more below), and is even arguably the fulfilment of one particular element within Judaism, it is clearly retrospectively constructed in order to give an account of the Christ event. Hence any previous stories have been *radically* reformulated.

The most obvious step to take next within our analysis is to ask if this story appears elsewhere in Romans, and then in Galatians. And if our further investigation suggests a reasonably widespread use, we would also expect our basic account of this story to receive greater articulation, from which point we can pose intertextual and interthematic questions with more hope of success. Hence it might be helpful to schematise the key narrative at this point.

### Trajectory One: Descent[15]

(1) God the Father (2) sends, delivers up, and does not spare,[16] (3) his own (4) Son, Jesus. (5) Jesus suffers (6) and dies, (7) in an act of identification. (8) This act also atones, or (in the most general terms) deals with humanity's problems, especially in relation to Sin. (9) This is also an act that speaks of the love of both the Father and the Son.

### Trajectory Two: Ascent

(10) The Spirit of God and Christ, (11) also the Spirit of life, (12) resurrects Jesus, that is, creates new life in and for him, (13) and glorifies him, (14) to the right hand of the Father, (15) from which point he reigns, (16) and also intercedes.[17] (17) This is a glorious inheritance. (18) He cries 'Abba, Father'. (19) As such he is 'the firstborn' (20) among many other 'brothers', (21) for whom he is also an 'image'.

---

15. I am of course cheating a little bit here by drawing essentially on the terminology of Phil. 2:5–11. But it had to be introduced at some point and nothing in Romans or Galatians gainsays the framework. I would be quite happy for those methodologically more pure than myself to use alternative terms.

16. As my respondent notes fairly, this element, especially in terms of 'sending', creates important resonances with other New Testament texts and hence suggests a high degree of narrative interweaving in these (and immediately surrounding?) terms, and at those points.

17. I do not see any direct attestation in Romans or Galatians to the notion that Jesus returns in glory to judge the living and the dead, etc. However, I am open to correction on this point, and, besides, the introduction of Paul's other letters clearly and quickly introduces this element. Similarly, Romans and Galatians provide us with little information with which to fill out the earthly part of Jesus' story. Space precludes a detailed discussion of the possible use of Jesus sayings in these letters (I am rather a 'minimalist'). Once again, however, the introduction of other letters, and especially of 1 Corinthians, would allow us to point to a reasonably extended account of the Passion in Paul that probably begins with the Thursday night (i.e., the Last Supper), extending through the betrayal and subsequent events to the crucifixion. This fascinating but difficult issue cannot be resolved here in relation only to Romans and Galatians. In a sense it also concerns the *next* question: Having established what story of Jesus Paul uses, we can then turn to ask why he has left out what he seems to have omitted.

## ELSEWHERE

If, taking our cue from 8:29, we take this story that emerges from Romans 8 as something of a template, then it is possible to discern its operation in other parts of that letter, and also in Galatians. It remains important not to become overly enthusiastic at this point; our story's significance should not be exaggerated. But neither should it be underemphasised.

In my view, the following texts in Romans may well contain utilisations of this basic story: Rom. 1:3–4; 2:16b; 3:24b–25a; 4:24b–25; 5:5–10, 17b, 19b; 6:4, 7, 9; 9:5b; 10:6b–7 [cf. Deut. 30:12–14]; 11:26–27 [cf. Isa. 59:20–21/Psa.14:7]; 15:3, 7–8a. Space does not permit the citation of these texts here, but the reader is encouraged to consider them. These texts do not add anything substantial to our fundamental outline, although many, if not all, of its elements are reinforced at some point. But some interesting new emphases from them should be noted:

1. The earthly life of Jesus is said explicitly to be Jewish and, more specifically, Davidic, hence also explicitly messianic (1:3; 9:5).
2. The story of the Son's abasement to death (often denoted in Romans by 'blood') also involves his obedience (see 5:19), as well as an explicit burden-bearing (15:3).
3. Conversely, his exaltation explicitly involves his rule and his role in future judgement (see esp. 2:16b; 5:17; and possibly 6:9).
4. The terminology of 'Son of God' is explicitly explained by 1:4 with reference to the resurrection, which, through the Spirit of sanctification, declared Jesus to be the Son of God 'with power', and so also appropriately receiving the name 'Lord'.
5. The love of the Spirit is also involved in this process (so explicitly 15:30).

When we turn to consider Galatians, we should note especially the following passages: 1:3b–4, 6a; 2:19b, 20b; 3:1b, 13, 16b/19b; 4:4–7; 6:2, 12b, and 14. Once more, many of the elements in our principal story are clearly reinforced by these texts. And a few new nuances are also discernible:

1. Galatians has a strong emphasis on the rather more offensive notion of the cross of Christ, as against merely his death or blood. There is no doubt in Galatians—whereas one would not necessarily know it from Romans—that Jesus died the shameful death of crucifixion.
2. There is also arguably a notion of deliverance from curse, in addition to deliverance from Sin, Flesh, and Death, as Jesus 'is laid on wood' (3:13; cf. Deut. 21:23; see also Deut. 3:10 and 27:26).
3. Jesus is identified—somehow—as the 'seed' of Abraham in fulfilment of the promises in Genesis concerning Isaac and the further descendants of Israel as

a whole. That is, Galatians emphasises the sense in which this central story supposedly connects directly and specifically to the Jewish patriarchs, and especially with Abraham (cf. also 4:21–31; cf. in addition Rom. 9:4; 15:8).

4. Gal. 4:4 emphasises that when God sends 'his Son', he is born 'of women [and] *under* law so that he might purchase those under law; in order [also] that we might receive adoption' (4:4b–5).

These texts also raise directly the issue of contingency, that is, the question of whether the story suggested by Romans 8 modulates significantly, or even changes, between Romans and Galatians.

## THE QUESTION OF CONTINGENT DIFFERENCES

Clearly there are important differences of emphasis and articulation between the two letters' attestations to the story found in Romans 8. In large measure, however, this can be explained by the Galatians' firsthand knowledge of Paul and his teaching. He does not need to spell out his programme in full to them since he has taught them personally—a luxury the Romans (fortunately for us) did not enjoy. But do the four new emphases in Galatians deliver a different story?

I suspect that the motif of curse is heavily contingent in Galatia—that is, it is motivated by specific circumstances there as Paul perceives them. The motif is absent in its entirety from Romans, yet it is emphasised at various points in Galatians (see esp. 1:8–9; 3:10). The perceived use of Deuteronomic language by his opponents may well explain Paul's twisting of this motif in relation to Christ and his own gospel. Hence it should not be viewed as a substantial modification of the basic story—it is evidence, however, of Galatians' rather more aggressive tone.

The emphasis of Galatians on the cross will also hardly be taken as significantly divergent, although it does point to an apparently contingent dimension in Romans. Paul seems in his later letter to be trying to avoid an overly scandalous or offensive portrayal of Christ's death, preferring simple references to it in terms of death and, beyond this, of biblically—if not cultically—resonant notions (evidence no doubt of some of the Jewish sensibilities among his audience).[18]

We will postpone for the moment consideration of our final two Galatian nuances—Christ as the singular seed of Abraham and his entry into a state

---

18. In our corporate consultation, this claim was disputed, and with some justification. While Romans never has the noun 'cross', it does have the cognate verb 'to be crucified with'—although only once (6:6). I continue to detect a subtle shift in expression but am not strongly committed to the point. Indeed, it is also entirely fair to point to other quite offensive notions in Romans, hence the argument that Paul is avoiding offence is clearly false. Perhaps one can still claim, however, that he is trying to avoid *unnecessary* offence. And other texts seem to support a degree of political carefulness on Paul's part in relation to the Roman context (esp. 13:1–7, but also perhaps implicitly in 2:17–24)—something not at all evident in Galatians.

'under law'—since they lead us into a consideration of intertextual matters. Suffice it to say that there are clear differences in contingent emphasis between the two letters. However, these are also largely standard. Galatians is more abbreviated, less concerned with offending Jewish sensibilities, and rather more shocking if not aggressive in its use of this story. Romans is more fulsome and less scandalously phrased. It is also far more concerned to engage the story of Jesus with royal messianic themes (three of the five nuances outside Romans 8, noted previously). In Romans, Jesus is descended from David, is declared the Messiah by his resurrection, and prays and reigns on high, from whence he will come to judge the world (an observation we will also explore in more detail momentarily in relation to intertextual matters).

We need to consider one last basic matter in relation to this narrative, however, before passing on to consider its more disputed aspects, namely, its allusory deployment. This will also allow us to address briefly one of the most important rejoinders to the importance of the foregoing schema.

## SUMMARY PHRASES

It is important to appreciate that the story of Jesus just described explains both the terminology of the fatherhood of God and of the brotherhood of Christians in Paul.[19] Both these data can be overlooked or underemphasised by interpreters, perhaps because of their familiarity, but they are distinctive theological emphases on Paul's part that appear throughout his writings (especially the latter).[20] And in the absence of cogent alternative explanations for

---

19. M. Mitchell also points to the importance of shorthand references to the story itself that have not been emphasised here, namely, 'the gospel', 'the preaching', and 'the word', in her 'Rhetorical Shorthand in Pauline Argumentation', in L.A. Jervis and P. Richardson (eds), *Gospel in Paul: Studies on Corinthians, Galatians and Romans for Richard N. Longenecker* (JSNTSup 108; Sheffield: Sheffield Academic Press, 1994) 63–88. This essay also elucidates, with help from ancient rhetorical practice, the methodological issue of shorthand and/or allusory references *to* the underlying narrative. (My thanks to Troy Martin for reminding me of the importance of this study.)

20. The phrase 'God the Father' (or its equivalent) enjoys a solid distribution through all Paul's undisputed letters with twenty-three (or perhaps twenty-four) instances: Rom. 1:7; 6:4; 8:15; 15:6; 1 Cor. 1:3; 8:6; 15:24; 2 Cor. 1:2, 3 (2 times); 6:18 (?); 11:31 (note: 'the father *of* the Lord Jesus Christ'); Gal. 1:1, 3, 4; 4:6; Phil. 1:2; 2:11; 4:20; 1 Thess. 1:1, 3; 3:11, 13; Phlm. 3.

Paul's most favoured designation for Christians is 'brothers'—*not*, contrary to popular belief, 'believers' or even 'saints'. The instances and ratios in a seven-letter canon are 127/23/42 or 6.1.2. Brothers occurs in relation to Christians in Romans 18 times; 1 Corinthians 38 times; 2 Corinthians 12 times; Galatians 11 times; Philippians 9 times; 1 Thessalonians 19 times; Philemon 4 times; here a total of 111 times.

these two important motifs, it seems fair to suggest that their presence indicates the almost ubiquitous function of this story (not as a whole, but doubtless presuppositionally), since that story explains them completely.

These observations also effectively counterbalance the negative contention that Jesus is seldom spoken of as 'Son' (or some such) by Paul, suggesting in turn that any story centred on Jesus' sonship (or sonship *per se*) is presumably of little interest to him (so Werner Kramer's widely influential thesis[21]). This suggestion seems to involve a narrative misunderstanding. Although the atoning function of Jesus seems to be spoken of by Paul in terms of his sonship, his present situation, as dictated by the second trajectory of ascent, is one of lordship. Hence if he is to be designated rightly in terms of the narrative, he ought to be referred to as 'Lord', Paul's preferred title for him.[22] Only when Jesus' past atoning function comes into view would we expect Paul to revert to the notion of sonship, something that will therefore also depend to a degree on contingent circumstances. So when Paul is prompted to address the atonement in detail, notably in Romans 8, although also with strong anticipations in Romans 5 and at various points in Galatians, we *do* seem to have an explicit emphasis on sonship. Hence this essentially statistical objection would, it seems, be greatly assisted by a better understanding of the actual narrative underlying much of Paul's terminology in relation to Jesus, and its force can safely be repudiated. The paucity of references to Jesus in terms of sonship is a product merely of narrative and contingent factors.

We have also seen that this story contains for Paul an important incorporative aspect as the Spirit of life conforms people to the template of Christ's ascent and descent. And this aspect of the story is almost certainly alluded to through 'in Christ' phraseology (or its equivalent). That phrase will not be exhausted by such allusions since it often seems innocuous and/or merely a designation for Christians. But it occurs frequently enough in the settings of Paul's most important narrative discussions of incorporation to seem to carry this summary content on occasion (see Rom. 6:11, 23; 8:1, 9–11, 39 [possibly also 3:24]; and Gal. 2:19, 20; 3:26, 28; 5:6).[23] Moreover, symbolism drawn from baptism seems also to be Paul's preferred way of describing the actual incorporation of Christians into Christ in more detail (cf. Rom. 6:1–11; Gal. 3:27), with its suggestions of complete involvement, of descent and ascent (into and out of the water), and of reclothing.

---

21. See his *Christ, Lord, Son of God* (London: SCM Press; Naperville, Ill.: Allenson, 1966).

22. The data is usefully assembled and commented on by Keck, 'Jesus', esp. 446 (nn. 10 and 11).

23. See again Keck's apposite remarks in 'Jesus', 447–48.

In short, the probable summary elements for this story in Paul suggest its very substantial importance for much of his thinking (and this against any countervailing suggestions based narrowly on the actual incidence of sonship material). The story of a Father and his Son, who brings many (if not all) to sonship and to brotherhood, so that they can then also be referred to as being 'in Christ', seems to be a *very* fundamental notion for Paul.

We turn now to the fascinating question of its possible intertextual dimension. That is, although we have isolated an important story that exhibits a clear narrative structure in two complementary parts, we have yet to identify the origin of the shape of, and specific material within, this story.

## THE NARRATIVE POSSIBILITIES

Much past analysis of this question has, in my view, suffered from a degree of narrative myopia. Instead of asking what intertext(s) or distinctive symbolic reservoirs might explain the constellation of motifs that we have already isolated (which is a much easier question to pursue), scholars have tended to focus on individual motifs. And this procedure of focussing on individual motifs has tended not to impart either decisive answers or conceptual and/or argumentative unity to Paul's discussions. (Paul's discussion in the key text has also tended to be segmented into smaller, somewhat discrete, units.)

We must ask at this point simply this: What story (if any) best accounts for the motifs that we have already isolated in their two distinctive sequences? And it can be seen almost at a glance that none of the usual candidates can do so. These fall into three basic categories: (1) nonnarrative analogues drawn from surrounding society, (2) Graeco-Roman narrative analogues, and (3) Jewish narrative analogues. We can narrow these options almost immediately, however. It is doubtful that we need to appeal to fundamentally sociological and/or legal notions in order to explain Paul's basal story (images drawn from these quarters do not seem able to explain the entire sequence), especially in view of Rom. 8:29, perhaps supported by Gal. 4:28, where a narrative grounding is explicit. (This does not exclude a supporting role for such notions.) Similarly, Graeco-Roman narrative notions will struggle to account for various, more Jewish, emphases in the sequences (e.g., resurrection, the Spirit of life, and messianic lineage), although some aspects of the story are certainly potentially explained by such stories. (Such narratives could therefore usefully serve a contextualising strategy on Paul's part; see *perhaps* Phil. 2:5–11.) That is, it seems almost immediately apparent that Paul's story is primarily dependent on *Jewish* narrative material. But within this broad category, there are many specific possibilities. Scholars have appealed at various times to narratives about the following: Wisdom (or its close equivalent); Adam (or a counter-Adam notion); 'the binding of Isaac' (i.e., Genesis 22); Israel, both historical (e.g., the exodus) and eschatological (e.g., future glorified sonship); Davidic notions; and even priestly motifs. A careful comparison of the narrative resources in each of these possibilities reveals, however, (although this is where I feel the limitations of space especially acutely), that only *two* possibilities match our two narrative sequences perfectly.

I would suggest that the two distinctive (although not separate) trajectories in Paul's basal story are informed by two distinctive Jewish intertexts. The first story, a story of descent by a Father's own Son through obedience to suffering and death, a story that also speaks of love, is informed in my view by the story of Abraham and Isaac in Genesis 22.[24] Only this much-neglected story can account for all the motifs that Paul deploys here, and yet it does so exactly.[25] The presence of the

---

24. The story has been neglected for two main reasons. First, scholars have been preoccupied with its possible attestation to a penal substitutionary theology of the atonement, that is, to the atoning function of Christ as that is conceived by traditional contractual Lutherans and their like, and they have consequently overlooked its other possible contributions. However, my use of the story is rather different. Although still interested in the atonement in more general terms, I am interested primarily in whether the narrative present in Genesis 22 informs Paul's narrative argument. My interests, then, lie with a broader and more basic comparison—and the question of its possible role in any atonement theory should only arise from this basis. Second, scholars have accepted poor arguments (largely from B. Chilton and P. Davies) for the developed tradition's late date and have overlooked the concrete evidence for its pre-Christian date— in its relatively highly developed form—that has become available, relatively recently, from Qumran (as noted by Vermes). See esp. B. Chilton and P. Davies, 'The Aqedah: A Revised Tradition History', *CBQ* 40 (1978): 514–46; and G. Vermes, 'New Light on the Sacrifice of Isaac from 4Q225', *JJS* 47 (1996): 140–46. The studies of Vermes' student, R. Hayward, are excellent: 'The Present State of Research into the Targumic Account of the Sacrifice of Isaac', *JJS* 32 (1981): 127–50; idem, 'The Sacrifice of Isaac and Jewish Polemic Against Christianity', *CBQ* 52 (1990): 292–306. Most secondary discussions of this motif's use in Paul are in fact not especially useful. Notable exceptions, however, are A.F. Segal, 'He Who Did Not Spare His Own Son: Jesus, Paul and the Akedah', in J.C. Hurd and G.P. Richardson (eds), *From Jesus to Paul: Studies in Honour of Francis Wright Beare* (Waterloo, Ontario: Wilfred Laurier Press, 1984) 169–84; and R. Penna, 'The Motif of the '*Aqedah* against the Background of Romans 8:32', in *Paul the Apostle, 1: Jew and Greek Alike*, trans. T.P. Wahl (Collegeville, Minn.: Liturgical Press/Glazier, 1996) 142–68. See also J. Levenson's rather neglected but insightful *Death and Resurrection of the Beloved Son* (New Haven, Conn.: Yale University Press, 1993).

25. It has the added virtue of explaining some of the allusions elsewhere in Paul's letters, notably in 1 Corinthians, where paschal connections are important. Paul also speaks of Jesus rising '*on the third day* in accordance with the Scriptures' (1 Cor. 15:3–4; cf. Gen. 22:4). Gal. 3:13 may also become more resonant: 'Cursed is everyone who is laid on wood.'

patriarchs in some relation to the basal story of Jesus has already been mentioned.[26] And Paul does quote a text from this story in the middle of his critical analysis—a clue that most commentators seem studiously to overlook (it is one of only two such quotations in Romans 8). Most important, the story explains Paul's *argument* in the critical chapter.[27]

From 8:18 to 8:39 (and reprising the concerns of 5:2–11), as we have already seen briefly, Paul is concerned largely with assuring Christians in the face of struggle and suffering that God's love is unshakeable and will eventually conquer all on their behalf. The proof that he tables in primary support for this is the a fortiori argument that a God who does not spare his only Son but offers him up for a hostile humanity must be trustworthy and will therefore also assuredly deliver the further security and support that struggling Christians need, irrespective of the opposition they face (that is, secular or cosmic)—something that will issue ultimately in eschatological glorification. His love is demonstrated and assured in the interim by this definitive proof, that is, by the sacrifice of his only Son that has already taken place. The presuppositions for this proof are in turn that God loves his only Son (and that he *is* his Son!) and that God nevertheless delivers him up for 'us' (something that the argument assumes is effective).[28] But what lies behind this love of God for his Son, and his painful delivery up to death, on which the whole argument turns? I would suggest that it is the story of Abraham's offering up of his only son, Isaac, except that in this instance the knife is not stayed and the Son is duly slaughtered in order to reconcile a hostile humanity (hence small wonder that an allusion to this story takes place at the height of the argument). In short, it is this story that explains Paul's dependence in this setting on the definitive evidence

---

26. Indeed, much that Paul argues rather cryptically in Galatians becomes clear if it is grasped that Jesus' death was patterned in a direct way on Abraham's offering up of Isaac—i.e., why Jesus can be baldly identified with the singular seed promised to Abraham from 3:16 (in historical terms, Isaac) and also why Paul can allegorise so extensively and pertinently in relation to Hagar, Ishmael, Sarah, and Isaac, in 4:21–31.

27. The main competitor to this suggestion is probably Keesmaat's graceful, and at times highly persuasive, study (*Paul and His Story*). Genesis 22, however, in my judgement, gives a better account than the Exodus account of the sustained terminology of Father and Son, of the descent of the Son into redemptive suffering (which has an atonement phrase attached to it in 8:3), and of the function of Jesus as a template (literally 'image') for the new humanity, as well as lending a rather stronger force to Paul's argument. (The enthronement account then copes better with the important datum of 'Abba Father' in my view.)

28. Notice that this shifts the moral framework of the story, resolving many of the potentially problematic dimensions in the original narrative (that so exercised Kierkegaard).

of the *love* of God the Father for his Son—love that is now also clearly displayed towards humanity through the death of his Son on their behalf.

The second story, a story of ascent through resurrection to glorification and heavenly enthronement, is in my view explained by royal messianic theology, and in particular by the Old Testament's enthronement texts, among which Psalm 89 is outstanding. Only that story explains all this trajectory's motifs, and it explains them perfectly—namely, how a chosen Son can be exalted, anointed, and enthroned by God, and so rightfully receive the titles of Messiah, Lord, and Son, thereby also entering onto a glorious inheritance (interpreted here also eschatologically). This state includes sovereign, priestly, and forensic powers (that is, rule, intercession, and judgement). And at the centre of this ceremony, as explicated especially by Psalm 89, the newly designated son cries to his God, 'Father'[29] (see LXX 88:27 [= 89:26]: αὐτὸς ἐπικαλέσεταί με πατήρ μου εἶ σύ, although other royal enthronement texts support this; see esp. 2 Sam. 7:14–16; Psa. 2:7–8; and Psalm 110).[30] This cry—doubtless a real event of acclamation in the actual ritual, which also would have involved anointing and enthronement—encapsulates the powerful covenantal relationship now established between the new king and the God of the nation that is expressed in terms of immediate kinship. In short, I would suggest that the second sequence in this story resonates with an interpretation of Jesus' resurrection in terms of a heavenly enthronement by God of a chosen royal son, along with his glorification, which also included (it should not be forgotten) the receipt of a title 'that is above every other name' and the ongoing exercise of royal and priestly powers (something with a potentially adoptionist dimension, but the early church probably had such a dimension at times). Paul's contingent use of this story is, however, radically inclusive (on the basis of his pneumatology).

---

29. I am assuming here J. Barr's repudiation of J. Jeremias' popular reading of Abba in terms of 'daddy', Barr simply suggesting 'Father'. See his '"Abba, Father" and the Familiarity of Jesus' Speech', *Theology* 91 (1988): 173–79; idem, '"Abbâ" Isn't "Daddy"', *JTS* 39 (1988): 28–47. Intriguingly, commentators have generally been loath to abandon Jeremias' charming reading completely (two of the less sentimental being Käsemann and Fitzmyer). Indeed, there does not seem to have been a confident alternative interpretative move beyond Jeremias' suggestion.

In order to avoid some of the foregoing discussion's impasses, I would suggest using the phrase's *Aramaism* as a more profitable clue to its interpretation. The immediate setting of the phrase in both Pauline texts, next to heirship and inheritance, and also its distinctive first-person-plural conjugation also suggest to me that Paul's point may be the simple one of *inclusion*—that is, the inclusion of his audience within the royal cry of Jesus himself (something he explicitly attributes to the work of the Spirit). Such inclusion would be a guarantee of eschatological blessing.

30. I suspect that the Jewish dynasties that ruled Judaea during late Second Temple Judaism also appealed to much of this imagery, viz., the Hasmoneans and Herodians.

I am especially encouraged in the foregoing identifications by their strong contingent plausibility, particularly in relation to Romans, where the second sequence's thematology is especially in evidence (and the first not absent).[31] The original Christian influence on the Roman community was doubtless both early and Judaean. That community's theological traditions therefore go back to the earliest post-Easter period, probably in a special relation to the apostolic couple Junia and Andronicus (Rom. 16:7), who had been Christians and leaders for a longer period even than Paul and hence almost certainly came from Judaea. And at this point the Aramaic element in the adoptionist resurrection tradition becomes especially understandable, namely, 'Abba Father'. This terminology reflects a *Judaean* provenance[32] (cf. elsewhere in Paul only 1 Cor. 16:22, where Judaean influence is also apparent).[33] Moreover, complementing this primitive resurrection theology, which is influenced by certain Old Testament texts much beloved of the early church, is a primitive martyrological tradition (not necessarily atoning) that views Jesus' death as the execution of a godly, righteous, and innocent person who dies in loyalty and obedience to God at the hand of a tyrant and who is vindicated through resurrection (cf. intriguingly Acts 2:23–28, 36; 3:13–15, 17–26; 4:10–12, 25–28; 5:28–32; 7:52, 56).[34] That is, we seem to find here a quite restricted interpretation of the significance of Jesus' death (in a sense, it has *no* real significance beyond the normal martyrological one of faithfulness in trial to the ultimate point, on analogy to the early Jewish view of Isaac and the other martyrs). The primitiveness of these interpretations, coupled with their close scriptural connections, seems to me to support further our overarching hypothesis.

It remains, then, only to note that Paul's deployment of these two sequences is both integrated and radically soteriological. By merging the two sequences together—as Easter demands—the adoptionist connotations of the second sequence are erased. It is God's *only Son* who dies and is resurrected, which also thereby casts God principally in the role of Father and the Spirit in the role of life-giver. Moreover, this sequence transforms those who are integrated into it by the Spirit, as baptism symbolises. Consequently, ethical

---

31. So, most obviously, Rom. 1:2–4, but see also 9:4. Martyrological concerns are apparent, in my view, esp. in 1:17; 3:25; 5:1–11, and 5:19.

32. A provenance also plausibly posited, of course, in relation to the disruptions in Galatia.

33. This all predates the composition of Mark; hence I have not referred to his use of this tradition, which may in any case be a spurious overlap (see Mark 14:36 and context).

34. Levenson (*Death*) emphasises the association between the Passover, the Aqedah, and the death of the first-born son—something with clear connections to the Exodus tradition as well.

transformation will be real and apparent, and eschatological assurance can also be sure; the God who does not spare his only beloved Son but delivers him up for the world can be relied on to defeat any countervailing powers of darkness, and can also be trusted fundamentally in and of himself—as can his Son and his Spirit.

Hence (to point out the obvious), under the pressure of the Easter events, these traditional Jewish narratives have clearly also been transformed—immediately indicating the perils of approaching Paul's thought in terms of a *prior* conception of salvation history, and of any enlistment of narrative in that cause, although important salvation-historical consequences do immediately and necessarily follow from all this. These stories no longer speak precisely of what they used to speak of; neither do they refer in exactly the same way to God. In the very process of supplying further sense to Paul's explanation, they have had their own content subtly altered. Under the pressure of the Christ event, which these stories are being utilised to explain, Paul's Jewish narrative resources have been reshaped in accordance with his new, quite particular explanatory needs. In essence, in the process of supplying meaning to that event, their own configuration of meaning has been altered as it has been brought under the influence *of* that event (and this process therefore needs to be our descriptive starting point).

This leads us to the brink of two final controversial questions. First, we must ask how this story begins. And, second, we must reflect on what role the term πίστις ('faith' or 'faithfulness') plays in this story's subsequent influence in other Pauline texts (if any).

## THE BEGINNING OF THE STORY

Especially since a well-known study by J.D.G. Dunn,[35] the question of how this story begins has been regarded as more difficult than perhaps hitherto suspected. And one of the reasons for ambiguity is probably by now largely apparent. Paul is not especially interested in the beginning of this story—and certainly not in Romans or Galatians (that emphasis is more apparent in 1 Corinthians, and perhaps also in Colossians). He focuses here on the *transformational* point, namely, the progress of Jesus through death to resurrection, since it is at this point that the Christian is reconstituted (and one suspects that this point is the critical one for him). Paul's contingent focal point in Romans and Galatians is often on the atoning significance of what God has done in

---

35. *Christology in the Making* (London: SCM Press, 1980).

Christ. Indeed, to spend time on Christ's status and entry into the story would be to distract the reader from the real object of that entry, which was transformational. Consequently it is sometimes difficult to tell how the story begins. Perhaps it begins as God the Father calls his 'Son' and sends him from within human history, much as a prophet of old might be commissioned and then sent to challenge the people of Israel. Or perhaps the Son possesses some higher status than this, being sent *into* this entire sinful situation from outside it, as it were, thereby suggesting his heavenly, or even divine, status.

The logic of the story creates the suspicion that Paul is really committed to the latter option. Christ deals with a state of dreadful bondage and oppression, one of slavery in the Flesh under the powers of Sin and Death, themselves assisted by the law, and he does so by 'entering' it. That is, Christ seems to appropriate that state of bondage, only then to carry it on to a point of utter extinction or termination on the cross. His resurrection then creates in effect an exit point for those who have recapitulated this journey to execution, and it is this that inaugurates the liberation and glorification promised by the model. Now, there is something rather curious about supposing that Christ begins this story of identification and liberation *from within that state*. Those within this state are under its sway. Is this then ultimately a story of self-help? Did Christ always carry this burden and never at any point *assume* it? Against this, Paul seems to suggest at times that God has deigned to send his Son *into* this state from outside it—an extraordinarily benevolent act—in order to rescue and liberate those trapped within it. It is ultimately the story of a divine rescue mission (as against a prison breakout). This narrative logic explains the language of entry and assumption that we find occasionally in Paul (see esp. Gal. 4:4–5 and also Phil. 2:6–7). It is also supported to my mind by the fundamental equality in the designation of God and Christ as Father and Son, respectively. (If we favour the immanent reading, we have to qualify these terms heavily, and especially the latter one, and then go on to explain the Father's peculiar affection for his 'own', but nevertheless merely metaphorical, Son.) Indeed, at the heart of the story rests the claim *that God himself* is intimately involved in this transformation of the plight of humanity, and in a benevolent and highly costly fashion. And it is difficult if not impossible to limit this involvement to the Father's initial command to someone to do something (the immanent reading of 'send'). In this story the Father, his Spirit, and his Son are all involved in the transformation of humanity, from within a matrix of loving relationships, at which point really we have to affirm a starting point in God himself and a consequent incarnational dimension to the entire process for Jesus. And with these regrettably brief comments, we turn to consider the question of the possible role of πίστις in this story.

# FAITH IN OR OF CHRIST:
## THE πίστις Χριστοῦ DEBATE

I have left my consideration of this debate to the end of this analysis deliberately.[36] This is partly to make it plainly apparent that the preceding discoveries and conclusions concerning the story of Jesus in Romans and Galatians stand independently of our conclusions here (that is, we can still derive much of value from the narrative perspective irrespective of our stance on this particular issue). But the implications of the πίστις Χριστοῦ debate should also be especially clear when they are treated from this late point.

The debate concerns initially (in this context) the interpretation of a handful of genitive constructions involving the substantive πίστις. The Greek phrase πίστις Χριστοῦ (or its close equivalent) in Rom. 3:22 and 26 and in Gal. 2:16 (twice), 20, and 3:22 can be translated either as 'faith *in* Christ' (an objective reading of the genitive) or as 'the faith *of* Christ' (a subjective reading of the genitive)—and the translation of several isolated occurrences of πίστις in the vicinity of these phrases will probably also be influenced by our decision here. We can now address these two options, along with their implications for our current discussion, in turn.

An objective construal (i.e., 'faith in Christ') will add nothing to the foregoing picture. This is because it construes the data associated with πίστις in an anthropocentric fashion—that data refers to what *the individual* must do in order to be saved, denoting activity by the Christian. It consequently has nothing to do with the actual mechanics of that salvation as it is effected by God in relation to Christ. In essence, then, to read these data objectively is to eliminate their significance in relation to the narrative construal of Jesus by Paul in Romans and Galatians. Hence this decision creates what we might dub the 'minimalist' construal of the narrative portrait of Jesus in Paul, that is, one reliant on evidence not involving πίστις (viz., the foregoing picture or some similar one).

Things are very different, however, with a subjective construal (i.e., 'faith of Christ'). This option is best treated in terms of three of its aspects. First, the subjective reading of these genitives, and of various other instances of πίστις in their immediate setting, clearly expands the presence of the story of Jesus in Romans and Galatians—and possibly quite considerably, since that signifier is such a key word in parts of those letters (see esp. Rom. 1:16–17;

---

36. A useful entry point to this debate—in addition to Hays' seminal study *The Faith of Jesus Christ*—is the brace of studies by Hays, Dunn, and P. Achtemeier that debate the issue in Part II of E.E. Johnson and D.M. Hay (eds), *Pauline Theology, Volume IV: Looking Back, Pressing On* (Minneapolis: Fortress Press, 1997) 35–92.

3:21–5:1; 9:30–10:17; Gal. 1:23; 2:16, 20; 3:2–26; 5:5–6; 6:10).[37] This decision will therefore generate a larger 'maximalist' position in relation to the story's influence in Paul.

Second, the subjective reading, which introduces this greater degree of distribution and influence, *introduces nothing new in terms of the story itself*, and this is a most important point. The story *already* contains an explicit element in terms of Jesus' obedience—the obedience and submission of the Son to the loving will of his Father—as well as a pronounced emphasis on the culmination of that process in his death by crucifixion. But the event of the crucifixion does not refer merely to Jesus' death, that is, to the precise moment when he expired. It refers to the entire event of his execution that culminated in his death—an event we might designate 'Easter Friday' (hence Paul's reference to Jesus' 'obedience' is almost certainly an abbreviated reference to the entire event;[38] cf. also Phil. 2:5–8). And the subjective construal of the disputed πίστις Χριστοῦ genitives sees these phrases (reading them largely martyrologically) merely as further references to Easter Friday; they are simply an alternative locution—technically a synecdoche[39]—for the whole event of the cross. Hence, clearly nothing startlingly new is being affirmed by the interpreter who reads these genitives as 'the faithfulness of Christ' (and this despite the asseverations of many of the reading's critics). The reading merely widens the influence of the narrative about Jesus through Romans and Galatians in terms of a sense or meaning that many scholars would concede already exists. It is a reference to Jesus' death that extends to his obedient delivery up to the point of death.

Third, it should also be appreciated that if we pursue the christological nuancing of Paul's πίστις terminology, then the relevance of the story of Jesus can be broadened in a surprisingly extensive and constructive fashion. In particular, its influence can now be detected in those ethical sections in Romans and Galatians that have often proved troublesome to scholars in the past

---

37. I would explain this in terms of Paul's well-attested desire in these two letters to cite scriptural texts throughout these discussions, probably because he is also here in something of a 'battle for the Bible'. *Pistis* terminology is supplied especially by Gen. 15:6, Hab. 2:4, and Isa. 28:16—all of which are critical texts for Paul in Romans, and the first two also in Galatians. The Habakkuk text, moreover, is susceptible to a messianic reading, and hence to a christological nuance in Paul's argument; or alternatively, Paul's christological argument is, when framed in these terms, susceptible to a scriptural, prophetic, nuancing. This was a tentative suggestion of Hays' (see his *The Faith of Jesus Christ*), and I endorse it firmly; see my 'False Presuppositions in the ΠΙΣΤΙΣ ΧΡΙΣΤΟΥ Debate (A Response to Brian Dodd)', *JBL* 116 (1997): 713–19.

38. So also Keck, 'Jesus', 457.

39. See Mitchell, 'Rhetorical Shorthand', esp. 66–67. This suggestion is developed more fully by her in relation to 1 and 2 Corinthians.

because of their possible discontinuity with preceding material. In Romans, we can note in particular the possible christological rationale now lying behind the transformation of the mind of the Christian (see 12:3 in its immediate participatory or transformational setting of 12:2–5). This motif frames much of what follows, especially the attitude of the strong towards the weak, an issue that greatly concerns Paul in this last major section of the letter (see esp. 14:1, 22–23; also 15:5, 13). That Paul can develop a powerful narrative role for πίστις is also already apparent in the much-avoided 4:17b–22. But Paul's argument in 1:16–17 and 3:21–5:1 also becomes rather more christocentric and 'staurocentric', as do his treatments of Abraham as a forerunner of the gospel and Israel's repudiation of it (see 9:30–10:17).

Similarly, in Galatians the construction in 5:6 is much more understandable with the 'love' mentioned there being *God's* and *Christ's* (cf. 2:20; note, 5:5 is also thereby illuminated). And in the letter's concluding phase of argument (often dubbed, rather unhappily, 'ethical'), a story of Jesus can plausibly be seen informing much of Paul's advice (see esp. 5:22–25; I would also argue for the interrelationship of 5:14 with 6:2 and see both as informed by the story of Christ; cf. at this point, in addition, Rom. 13:8 and also 12:9, 12–14). Indeed, much of Galatians receives a christocentric nuance if πίστις is read in relation to the narrative of Jesus (cf. 1:23; 2:16, 20; 3:2, 5, 11, 14b, 22–26; and 6:10).

In both these letters, it is also now possible to discern a greater degree of concern with assurance as against appropriation (something that can again iron out some past difficulties in interpretation). Whereas previously it has seemed a little opaque why Paul would recapitulate to Christians (and especially to those he has taught in Galatia) what the criterion for becoming a Christian is (i.e., 'faith in Christ'), the subjective reading ('faith of Christ') suggests rather that Paul is more occupied with assurance, that is, with the encouragement of those already Christians to maintain that commitment in difficult circumstances. And in doing so a narrative appeal to the life of Christ is both appropriate and empowering. Just as Jesus faithfully endured suffering to the point of death and then received a triumphant and glorious resurrection, so too Christians who maintain their loyalty to God and to Christ until the end will receive a resurrection. Moreover, in so doing, God is not asking them to imitate Christ (perhaps an impossible task) so much as to inhabit or to indwell him. That is, any such endurance through duress is evidence that the Spirit of God is actively reshaping Christians into the likeness of Christ, and that they are therefore already part of the story—a story that will result in eschatological salvation! Consequently such enduring fidelity is critical evidence that God is at work, incorporating the believer into the prototypical story of Christ. In essence, to be part of this first sequence, despite its difficulties, is to be guaranteed being part of its second—this is no mere *imitatio Christi*!

In short, some powerful theological applications can be seen to follow from the subjective reading of Paul's πίστις Χριστοῦ genitives—a reading that does not so much innovate as integrate and explain. It draws some of Paul's discussions together, focussing them more strongly on the critical moment that stands at the centre of the model of salvation that he preaches—'Christ crucified!' And as a result of this, the maximalist position has, I would suggest, much to recommend it (as well as less to be said against it than might otherwise be thought), although this is perhaps fully apparent only with a broader narrative perspective in view.

## CONCLUSION

In closing, it is important to appreciate the powerfully integrative force of the narrative methodology, here focussed on the story of Jesus in Romans and Galatians. It draws together Paul's arguments and links them in turn with important Jewish intertexts. Paul has clearly employed these earlier stories not just because they were traditional but because at the heart of his gospel and its claimed transformations of Christians, whether Jew or non-Jewish Greek, is an interplay between personal actors: the Father, his Son, and their Spirit. Hence these earlier sequences combine into a supremely appropriate narrative account or explanation of what he holds to be happening at the behest of these essentially divine actors in relation to the Christian experience of salvation. And in view of all this, it would seem that a degree of narrative explanation is *essential* and hence *unavoidable* if an accurate account of Paul's thinking at these vital points is to be given. Narrative is, then, far more than a merely useful methodological perspective. (It ought not, however, to be pressed too far beyond its natural temporal boundaries.) This story does receive discernible contingent emphases in Romans and Galatians; its deployment in the former is more restrained and messianic, but in the latter, rather more scandalous, and even offensive. Such emphases do not, however, seem in any way to alter the underlying story, merely to nuance it.

In addition, it is arguable that at least two specific Jewish stories can be identified in relation to Paul's narrative: (1) the story of Abraham and Isaac, drawn originally from Genesis 22, in relation to the Pauline story's emphasis on Jesus' descent into suffering and death; and (2) the story of the Israelite king's anointing, acclamation, and enthronement, in relation to the Pauline story's emphasis on Jesus' resurrection and ascent to heavenly dominion, inheritance, messiahship, and lordship. As Paul reshapes and deploys them, however, these traditional stories now comprise a startling account of human involvement in, and transformation by, the divine drama being played out between its central figures.[40] It is a startlingly original and powerful Christian vision, one whose significance is only further enhanced if the faithfulness of Christ is perceived to be one of its integral parts (but one that loses little, at least in the first instance, if it is not).

---

40. This drama arguably anticipates many of the theological discussions of later Orthodoxy concerning the trinity and the *theosis* of Christians. Ironically, it arguably anticipates many of the central themes in *Luther's* work as well. See C.E. Braaten and R.W. Jenson (eds), *Union with Christ: The New Finnish Interpretation of Luther* (Grand Rapids: Eerdmans, 1998).

# 7

# 'I Think, When I Read That Sweet Story of Old'

## A Response to Douglas Campbell

### GRAHAM N. STANTON

For some time now I have known about the interest in the narrative dimensions of Paul's theology that has arisen in the past fifteen years or so, though I cannot claim to have participated in the discussions myself. From the sidelines, so to speak, I have often wondered whether the trendy terminology of 'metanarrative' and 'story world' was being used to labour the obvious. For who would want to deny that a cluster of basic theological convictions concerning Jesus lie at the heart of Paul's thinking and that those convictions tell a story—or a series of related stories?

With the theme of this symposium in mind, I found two other stories buzzing in my ears even before I read Douglas Campbell's stimulating essay. First, a tale of nineteenth- and twentieth-century hymnody: 'Hymns are the folk-song of the church militant', one of the finest hymn writers of the twentieth century, Eric Routley, wrote in 1952. Hymns encapsulate, frequently in story form, the church's theology and often reflect, belatedly, swings in the theological pendulum. The phrase 'the story of Jesus' (or similar) was popular with nineteenth-century hymn writers. Perhaps the most widely used of those hymns was Jemima Luke's 'I Think, When I Read That Sweet Story of Old', the opening line of which I have used as the title of this response.

I had no difficulty in assembling from *The Church Hymnary* (rev. ed., 1929) seven hymns that use the phrase 'story of Jesus'; there are probably more. This hymn book was used for decades all over the English-speaking world in Presbyterian and Reformed churches and beyond. Several of its 'story of Jesus' hymns bear a striking resemblance in folk-song form to Campbell's outline of Paul's 'story of Jesus'. However, by the time the third edition of *The Church Hymnary* appeared in 1973, some of the 'story of Jesus' hymns had disappeared. By 1991 they had *all* been banished from one of the heirs of this tradition of hymnody, the highly acclaimed *Rejoice and Sing* (OUP, for the United Reformed Church).

There is a curious irony here. At a time when many Christians are being discouraged from singing, 'I think, when I read that sweet story of old' and ' I will sing the wondrous story of the Christ who died for me', Pauline theologians are suddenly talking about 'the story of Jesus'! I do not want to see those Victorian 'story of Jesus' hymns reinstated in future hymn books, for the theological and musical inadequacies of most of them are obvious. But it is worth asking whether the recent turn in Pauline scholarship resonates with a need Christians who sing 'the folk-song of the church militant' have been aware of for ages. Perhaps Christian theology does need to recall that at its heart there is a 'gospel *story*'? Is there a challenge here to contemporary hymn writers to follow the lead of their nineteenth-century predecessors and retell that *story* in modern idiom?

The second story buzzing in my ears as I prepared for this symposium is this: Talk of 'the story element' and of 'the narrative substructure' in Paul's thought seemed to me to be, in part, a curious and not wholly appropriate extension of narrative critical approaches to the Gospels. Is it mere coincidence that David Rhoads and Donald Michie published their pioneering book *Mark as Story: An Introduction to the Narrative of a Gospel* (Philadelphia: Fortress Press) in 1982, and that R. Alan Culpepper's *Anatomy of the Fourth Gospel: A Study in Literary Design* (Philadelphia: Fortress Press) was published in 1983? For it was in 1983 that the groundbreaking 'narrative' approach to Paul's theology was published, Richard Hays' *The Faith of Jesus Christ: an Investigation of the Narrative Substructure of Galatians 3:1–4:11* (Chico, Calif.: Scholars Press). For a decade or so after 1982 nearly every respectable book on the Gospels had 'story' in its title or subtitle. While 'story' and 'narrative' have not peppered books on Paul to quite the same extent as books on the Gospels, we seem to be dealing with a related story that needs to be teased out fully elsewhere.

And so to Campbell's fine essay. This is apple pie and motherhood, was my initial reaction. Who is to spurn or condemn these things? The exposition of the christology of Romans 8 is crisp, clear, and in places deeply moving to anyone personally committed to the story told here. I particularly welcome the strong insistence that 'the story of Jesus' told in Romans 8 is 'simultaneously a story of God the Father, of the Spirit of God, and of the incorporation of people into that story. *To lose sight of any one of these aspects is to falsify our account of this story as Paul articulates it*' (see page 107).

Once I had regained my critical faculties, however, questions began to crowd in. I shall set them out under six headings, well aware that it is much easier to raise questions than to offer answers.

# WHY ROMANS 8?

Why should the exegete of Paul's writings give a privileged position to Romans, and to Romans 8 in particular? Given the decision to concentrate on Galatians and Romans in this symposium, it is easy to defend the decision to give prominence to Romans 8, for this chapter does set out 'the story of Jesus' very fully. But it is not the only passage in the undisputed Pauline letters to do so. Whether we construe Phil. 2:6–11 as a hymn or as a story, as pre-Pauline or Pauline, this passage focuses even more sharply on 'the story of Jesus' than does Romans 8, as is conceded in the important note 15.

At times Campbell seems to fall into the old trap of reading Paul's letters wearing his favourite Romans spectacles. The phraseology of the essay's title, 'Romans and Galatians' is echoed in several places. This title rang an initial alarm bell: I would have preferred the reverse, even though it would have complicated the strategy somewhat. For example, Campbell wonders whether the story suggested by Romans 8 modulates significantly, or even changes, 'between Romans and Galatians' (page 110, as if Romans were the earlier letter! And there is a hint that one might open discussion of the disputed phrase πίστις Χριστοῦ with Rom. 3:22 and 3:26 rather than with Paul's earliest use of the phrase in Gal. 2:16.

This may sound like nit-picking, and so it is. But there is a related and more fundamental question. There is a clear implication that Romans 8 can and should be used as a template in reconstructions of the central strands of Paul's christological thinking. But as Campbell himself shows, if we are concerned to uncover Paul's *full* story of Jesus, we need to go beyond Galatians and Romans. And he would surely acknowledge that the other letters fill out the narrative substructure of Paul's christology still further.

If so, are we to assume that all the elements in the story are present all the time? If we approach Paul's letters from a narrative perspective, does the 'method' (the term used by Campbell) imply that we should first reconstruct Paul's full story of Jesus from *all* the undisputed letters before we start our exegesis? Did Paul's christological thinking not develop? Would it not be prudent to sort out the christological convictions that are shared by *all* the Pauline letters, and assume no more than that *minimalist* story of Jesus as we approach the exegesis of the individual letters?

## BEGINNINGS AND ENDINGS

This set of questions leads directly to my second point. Where does Paul's story of Jesus begin and where does it end? Beginnings and endings are fundamental to every story. The four Gospels serve as a reminder of this truism.

Even if (with Campbell) we sit loosely to the notion of a definition and prefer to speak of various features of narrative, a story must have 'actions and events' that 'unfold through the narrative's time to create a plot' (p. 99). And a plot must have a beginning and an ending!

Campbell postpones consideration of the beginning of Paul's story of Jesus until near the end of his paper and then skates around the issues. The 'beginning' is fuzzy: 'Paul is not especially interested in the beginning of this story—and certainly not in Romans and Galatians (sic!) (that emphasis is more apparent in 1 Corinthians, and perhaps also Colossians)' (page 118). No doubt it is fair to claim that in Galatians and Romans Paul is more interested in 'the *transformational* point, namely, the progress of Jesus through death to resurrection' (page 118). But what about the other letters, and Phil. 2:6–11 in particular? If we consider all the undisputed letters, then Campbell's point regarding the beginning of the story needs to be modified—unless, of course, we are fully persuaded that the preexistence of Jesus is no part of Paul's story of Jesus.

Where does the story of Jesus end? Next to nothing is said. Campbell notes from Romans 8 that Paul's Jesus is glorified 'to the right hand of the Father' (8:34) from which point he reigns and also intercedes. Galatians does not supplement the end of the story, as given in Romans 8. But, we may ask, is the *sessio ad dexteram* the end of the story? Romans 8 is full of eschatology. Surely for the Paul of Romans 8 the future cannot be considered apart from Christ, either for individuals or for the whole creation. So the 'story of Jesus' must go beyond the *sessio*.

And what about 1 Thess. 1:9–10 and related passages? In his striking initial thanksgiving Paul commends the Thessalonians for waiting 'for God's Son from heaven, whom he raised from the dead—Jesus, who rescues us from the wrath that is coming'. Does Paul drop the 'parousia' part of the story once he reaches Galatians and Romans? Surely not.

I recognise that the concentration for pragmatic reasons on Galatians and Romans in this symposium means that it is difficult to say more about the beginning and ending of the story than is said in Campbell's paper. Nonetheless it is worth asking whether we are to read Galatians and Romans with a clear beginning and ending to the story of Jesus in mind. Or is 'story' a coat that fits rather awkwardly?

## JESUS' EARTHLY LIFE

On Campbell's reconstruction, Paul's story of Jesus in Romans 8 moves directly from God's sending of his Son to the suffering and death of Jesus. We are told by Campbell that this is filled out slightly by the reference to the earthly life of Jesus as Davidic and messianic (Rom. 1:3; 9:5) and by the reference in Gal. 4:4 (NRSV) to the sending of the Son, 'born of a woman, born under the law'. But little more is said about the earthly life of Jesus as part of the 'story of Jesus'. That is certainly not what those nineteenth-century hymn writers had in mind when they referred to 'that sweet story of old'.

Since we are dealing primarily with 'the narrative dimension in Paul's christology', this is a surprising omission. When Paul first taught the Galatians, did he say nothing about 'the story of Jesus' between the sending and the suffering? In Gal. 3:1 Paul reminds the Galatians that in his initial proclamation he had painted a vivid verbal picture of the crucifixion of Jesus as a common criminal. Did none of the Galatians ask how that had come to pass? Are there not hints of a still fuller story of the last days in 1 Cor. 11: 22–26?

Is it not at least arguable that Paul fills out the story of Jesus as set out in Romans 8 with allusions to the teaching of Jesus in Romans 12–15? My list of such allusions would be minimalist, but it would include Rom. 14:14: 'I am persuaded on the authority of the Lord Jesus that nothing is unclean in itself'.

I am raising an issue that has been a bone of contention for a long time. Our editor suggests that 'the narrative features in Paul's texts are the tip of a narrative iceberg' (Longenecker, 'Introduction', page 11). If so, then Paul's initial proclamation may well have included rather more of the story of Jesus between sending and suffering than is hidden beneath the surface of the letters written for very different purposes. At the least, there is an issue here that merits discussion.

## A DIVINE RESCUE MISSON

Campbell rightly emphasises that the Father's sending of the Son for redemption in Gal. 4:4 and Rom. 8:3 is a central theme in Paul's story of Jesus. 'It is ultimately the story of a divine rescue mission (as against a prison breakout)' he astutely notes (page 119).

Even more might have been made of this 'sending' motif. For it is also fundamental to the fourth evangelist's story of Jesus at John 3:16–17 (and cf. 1 John 4:9). It is no coincidence that Campbell's lengthy paragraph in the exposition of Romans 8 has a Johannine ring. For in the 'sending' motif John and Paul are drawing independently on an early christological formula. So we are in touch here with a widely shared narrative substructure of the 'story of Jesus'.

But that is not all. The same theme (though without explicit reference to redemption) is prominent in Mark's allegorical reshaping of Jesus' parable of the tenants (12:6), which is echoed by Matthew (21:37) and by Luke (20:13).

The servants sent to collect from the tenants the owner's share of the produce are the rejected prophets and the one who is finally sent is God's own dear Son Jesus. The sending of Jesus to God's people is related to the sending of the prophets, but the evangelists take pains to distinguish Jesus from the prophets: Jesus is not merely the final messenger; he is sent as God's Son. The story of Jesus is part of the story of Israel: there is both continuity and discontinuity.

So my question is this: Should we not go much further and consider the aspects of the story of Jesus shared by several New Testament writers? Is there not a narrative substructure to New Testament theology?

## FIRST LISTENERS/OTHER STORIES

I turn now to still wider issues. Campbell's stimulating paper seems to me to be 'top heavy', as does the general narrative approach to Paul's theology. This 'angle of approach' (Campbell's term) reconstructs an underlying metanarrative that may inform most of Paul's theological reflection but with minimal concern for the reception of that story by the original listeners to Paul's letters in house churches.

We are reminded that narratives tend to be significantly informed by *other* texts. I welcome the insistence that 'Paul's basal story' is informed by two distinctive Jewish intertexts: the story of Abraham and Isaac in Genesis 22 and royal messianic theology. However, with the exception of the intriguing brief comment that the Roman community's traditions may go back to the earliest post-Easter period, perhaps even to the arrival of Junia and Andronicus from Judaea, we hardly catch a glimpse of 'on the ground' concerns in the Pauline churches.

Early narrative critical approaches to the Gospels tended to seal the text hermetically and thus isolate it from its original reception by 'on the ground' first-century communities. Narrative approaches to Paul's theology seem to me to be open to the same line of criticism.

Campbell does refer to Graeco-Roman analogues in his search for stories that are able 'to explain the entire sequence' of Paul's basal story, but he rightly rejects the possibility (page 113). The phraseology used in this quotation and in several paragraphs in pages 113–18 is unfortunate. I do not think we need to search for stories that *explain* or *best account for* Paul's story of Jesus. Much preferable terminology does appear: 'In the very process of supplying further sense to Paul's explanation, they [i.e., Genesis 22 and royal messianic theology] have had their own content subtly altered' (page 118). In short, it is a question of listening to Paul's story against the backdrop of the appropriate passages of scripture.

How was Paul's story of Jesus heard 'on the ground'? We need not look for analogues but rather for stories that would have resonated with or supplied further sense to Paul's story. Just down the street from the Pauline house church communities, plenty of stories were being told of 'many gods and many lords' (1 Cor. 8:6). In particular was the story of the Roman emperor. We now have increasing evidence for the pervasive influence of the imperial cult in the cities in which Christianity first flourished.

Here is one strand of that evidence:

> Providence has filled Augustus with divine power for the benefit of humanity, and in her beneficence has granted us and those who come after us [a Saviour] who has made wars to cease . . . And Caesar, when he was manifest, transcended the expectations of [all who had antici- pated the good news] . . . the birthday of our god signalled the begin- ning of good news (εὐαγγέλια, plural) for the world because of him.[1]

There is an unmistakable whiff of eschatology and of soteriology in this Cal- endar inscription, of which we now have fragments from five cities. This inscription was displayed prominently in Greek and in Latin in many more places in Asia Minor, and not only in the larger cities. Paul's story of Jesus was shaped and heard 'on the ground' not only in the light of Genesis 22 and royal messianic theology but also in the light of 'stories of the Roman emperors'.

In one of the many important observations in Campbell's paper, we are reminded that narratives tend to be informed by *other* stories; they are 'also almost invariably reworkings or transformations of those other texts' (page 100). My point is that those 'other stories' were both scriptural and nonscrip- tural. Narrative approaches to Paul's theology have so far given far more atten- tion to the former than to the latter.

## IS 'MYTH' A FOUR-LETTER WORD?

Finally, and briefly, has 'myth' become a four-letter word that should not be used in theologically correct circles? A cluster of issues is wrapped up in this question. They are relevant to most of the papers in this symposium, for most contributors seem to avoid studiously the term 'myth'. 'Myth' comes to mind at several points in Campbell's paper but particularly in the way he summarises the story of Jesus in Romans 8 in terms of 'descent' and 'ascent' trajectories.

---

1. The translation of part of the First Decree of the Asian Assembly from the so- called Priene inscription is adapted slightly from F.W. Danker, *Benefactor* (St. Louis: Clayton, 1982) 216–17.

'Story' can include myth, history, and legend. Perhaps that is partly why 'story' has become so popular in recent theological discussion. But the underlying questions must not be evaded by using 'catch-all' terms such as 'story' and 'narrative'. What is the relationship of 'story' to 'myth'? May not mythological language be as meaningful and unavoidable in christological discussion as metaphorical and symbolic language? How much 'history' does the Christian story of Jesus need to retain if it is to be plausible and credible as 'Gospel truth'? And why does Paul's powerful and compelling story of Jesus contain (on most definitions) more 'myth' than 'history'?

I suppose I am one of the scholars described as 'nervous' in relation to 'narrative methodology' (page 98). Although my previous questions betray my continuing nervousness, I have been persuaded that 'right use' is more appropriate than 'abandonment'. However, I remain much happier with terms such as 'angle of approach' than with reference to 'the method'. A narrative 'angle of approach' can help us to rethink fundamental issues in Pauline theology and to read Paul's letters more sensitively. But this approach needs to be supplemented from other angles if it is to avoid the sterility that is afflicting narrative critical approaches to the Gospels. I have learned a great deal from Campbell's paper. If I may subvert the opening line of Jemima Luke's hymn quoted as the title of this response, I have read a 'sweet story', and I have been forced to think.

# 8

# Paul's Story

## *Theology as Testimony*

JOHN M.G. BARCLAY

The emergence of 'narrative theology' over the last quarter century is part of a larger complex of trends within the humanities (for instance, in literary, moral-philosophical, and psychological theory), in which the category of 'narrative' has gained new analytical significance.[1] Among its attractions for theology has been its offer of apparently secure ground for Christian discourse while the postmodern flood sweeps away 'timeless truths' and 'positionless perspectives'.[2] The vagueness of the category 'narrative' (or 'story') has, in fact, enabled quite diverse parties to unite under this banner. But the centrality of the story of Jesus within the New Testament, and its significance within Christian theology as a whole, has the potential to forge fresh links between theology and New Testament studies.

For obvious reasons, narrative analysis of the New Testament has proved easier to apply to the Gospels than to the letters of Paul. Even Paul, however, sometimes tells stories, or parts of stories, and it has proved possible to argue that these are not incidental to Paul's theologising but are in some senses constitutive of it. In *The Faith of Jesus Christ*,[3] the pioneering work in this field, Richard Hays argued that the narrative elements within even such an apparently 'propositional'

---

1. See the collection of essays and introduction in S. Hauerwas and L.G. Jones (eds), *Why Narrative? Readings in Narrative Theology* (Grand Rapids: Eerdmans, 1989).

2. Among the plethora of works in this vein, see, e.g., G. Loughlin, *Telling God's Story: Bible, Church and Narrative Theology* (Cambridge: Cambridge University Press, 1996).

3. Subtitled *An Investigation of the Narrative Substructure of Galatians 3:1–4:11* (Chico, Calif.: Scholars Press, 1983).

text as Galatians 3–4 do not merely illustrate Paul's 'ideas' but constitute the irreducible and indispensable 'substance' of his gospel.[4] In particular, Hays proposed that Paul's theology in Galatians has as its 'narrative substructure' the story of Jesus Christ (including the story of his obedience and faith), and he suggested that study of Romans would indicate how this is part of a 'larger story' stretching from Adam to the eschaton.[5] The sophistication with which this highly fertile proposal was presented has ensured its broad influence in Pauline studies although, for many scholars, critical questions arise concerning, for instance, the degree to which Paul's text *alludes* to an implicit and partly hidden story and the relationship between the 'narrative substructure' of Paul's theology and the message that he proclaims as 'the truth of the gospel'.[6]

In other hands, claims for the significance of 'story' within Pauline theology have become both conceptually more diffuse and materially more specific. N.T. Wright, for instance, employs the category 'story' in an enormous variety of ways while simultaneously making the highly specific claim that the narrative structure of the New Testament, including Pauline theology, is *essentially* the Jewish story, now 'redrawn' around Jesus.[7] The construction of a generalised 'Jewish story' thus becomes the 'grid' within which the Pauline letters are read, and the church is positioned as the key player in the 'fifth act' of the

---

4. *The Faith of Jesus Christ*, 47.

5. *The Faith of Jesus Christ*, 263–64. He has himself developed this proposal in subsequent publications, including 'Crucified with Christ: A Synthesis of the Theology of 1 and 2 Thessalonians, Philemon, Philippians, and Galatians', in J.M. Bassler (ed.), *Pauline Theology, Volume I: Thessalonians, Philippians, Galatians, Philemon* (Minneapolis: Fortress Press, 1991) 227–46; cf. the related concerns of his *Echoes of Scripture in the Letters of Paul* (New Haven, Conn.: Yale University Press, 1989).

6. Hays (*The Faith of Jesus Christ*, 234) admits as 'crucial' his claim that the Pauline text is 'strongly allusive. Its [narrative] foundation and framework are for the most part hidden from view, implicit rather than explicit'. Hays explicates the relationship between the 'narrative substructure' and Paul's reflective discourse with the aid of the Aristotelian categories of *mythos* and *dianoia* (21–23, and passim). This suggests that the *mythos* embodies its own *dianoia*, yet the admission that 'the gospel story' is capable of alternative interpretations (6, 255) suggests an additional step of 'interpretation' beyond the mere telling of the story. I shall suggest below that the notion of 'pattern' (the distinctive shape in which Paul tells 'the gospel story') helps resolve this ambiguity in Hays' proposal.

7. N.T. Wright, *The New Testament and the People of God* (London: SPCK, 1992). At times (e.g., 43), Wright's use of the term 'story' becomes so all-encompassing that it is hard to know what would *not* qualify for this category. Wright's claim that the New Testament depends on an 'essentially Jewish story' (79) applies even to Paul (403–409), though Paul adds 'a subversive twist at almost every point' (405). See also B. Witherington III, *Paul's Narrative Thought World: The Tapestry of Tragedy and Triumph* (Louisville, Ky.: Westminster/John Knox Press, 1994).

cosmic drama.[8] There are multiple echoes here of the emphasis in an earlier generation on 'salvation history', and it is not surprising that the contemporary debate also echoes earlier objections to such a reading of Paul, particularly if this 'redrawn' *Heilsgeschichte* seems to threaten the centrality of christology and the critical message of the cross.[9]

Whatever other 'stories' Paul may, or may not, relate in his letters, my brief here is, in one respect, relatively uncontroversial: Paul manifestly tells some stories about himself in the course of his letters, not least in Galatians and Romans. In fact, Galatians 1–2 is a quintessential narrative, containing sequential episodes of a single story, complete with time indicators. What is less immediately obvious is how this story of himself relates to Paul's theology, and in particular, what connection it might bear to 'the story of Jesus'. I will argue that Paul recounts his life story precisely because it has theological significance; that he weaves his story into that of his churches (Gal. 4:12–19) and into the story of Israel (Rom. 9–11); but also that, more fundamentally, he moulds this 'I' saga, together with the others, into the shape of the crucified Christ (Gal. 2:17–21; 3:1; 6:14). Thus our investigation, while focusing on Paul's story of himself, will inevitably trespass into others' territory and will force us to raise many of the questions that arise more generally in relation to 'narrative' in Pauline theology. We may summarise our lead questions as follows:

1. What is the relationship in Pauline theology between 'story' and 'the truth of the gospel'? Do Paul's stories merely illustrate this 'truth', which could be adequately expressed in other terms, or are they its indispensable vehicles? If the latter, in what way do they convey that truth?

---

8. *The New Testament and the People of God*, 215–23, summarises the generalised 'Jewish story' that 'gives us a grid against we can measure the alternative stories told, implicitly and explicitly, by Jesus, Paul and the evangelists, and to see their points of convergence and divergence' (223). But this presupposes that there is a common Jewish story (despite the huge variety of perspective in Judaism) and that Paul is working within the same story framework. For the church's position in the 'fifth act', see 141–43.

9. Both Bultmann and Käsemann reacted, though in different ways, against O. Cullmann's focus on 'salvation history'; Käsemann's reaction is given notable expression in 'Justification and Salvation History in the Epistle to the Romans', in his *Perspectives on Paul* (Philadelphia: Fortress Press, 1971) 60–78. See also the rich analysis by U. Luz, *Das Geschichtsverständnis des Paulus* (Munich: Kaiser, 1968). J.L. Martyn has voiced comparable concerns about the revival of linear *Heilsgeschichte* as a framework for reading Paul; see his 'Events in Galatia: Modified Covenantal Nomism versus God's Cosmic Invasion of the Cosmos in the Singular Gospel', in Bassler (ed.), *Pauline Theology, Volume 1*, 160–79; cf. his *Galatians* (Anchor Bible; New York: Doubleday, 1997), esp. 347–52, where he also notes the partial difference between Galatians and Romans on this score.

2. What interconnections link Paul's various 'stories' (or story fragments)? Do they 'nest' within one another, the smaller 'subplots' within a larger, over-arching narrative? Or does some different principle, for instance some common 'pattern', connect otherwise disparate, and inherently nonlinear, stories?

3. In what respects is Paul's own story of theological significance? Is it, indeed, essentially a story about himself, or a story about the grace of God? And if the latter, what characteristics of grace does he emphasise within his story, and in what fashion (indeed, with what understanding of time) can Paul claim that he shares the story of Jesus?

If it is to go any way towards addressing such questions, our analysis of Paul's autobiography (or, better, testimony)[10] in Galatians and Romans will have to circumvent almost every issue of historical reference although these have generally absorbed the interests of scholars. With each letter, after an initial mapping of the terrain, we will attend to the way Paul tells his story (and to the extent to which it is, indeed, 'his' story) and then to the patterns by which this story is linked with that of Christ, the church, the people of Israel, and even the world.[11]

## PAUL'S TESTIMONY IN GALATIANS

### Mapping the 'I' in Galatians

We are alerted to the theological significance of Paul's story in Galatians by the protrusion of this self-description in the very first verse and by the extent of the narrative in which he plays the central role (Gal. 1:11–2:14). In particular, we cannot fail to notice that this narrative is introduced by the programmatic statements of 1:10–12 and is concluded and condensed in the paradigmatic narratives of 'we' (2:15–17) and 'I' (2:18–21). These signal, as clearly as one could wish, that Paul tells his story because it contributes cru-

---

10. See Martyn, *Galatians*, 157 n. 191; attentive readers will find the influence of Martyn's work throughout this essay, even where it is not explicitly acknowledged.

11. David Horrell rightly asks if my project, which starts from a story on the surface of Paul's text, is comparable to Hays' analysis of a narrative 'substructure' (see Horrell's 'Response', below). The question rightly identifies an important difference in focus, though I share with Hays a conviction that Paul's stories are integral to his theologising. At the corporate consultation it was observed that my essay could look out of place in this volume if Paul's story was no more than an appendix to a (putative) single, over-arching narrative from creation to eschaton. The thrust of my argument is that Paul's telling of his own story encapsulates how he understands the gospel and is thus integrally linked to the others by a common 'pattern'. I think I still belong in this company!

cially to the message of the letter as a whole. Recent research has rightly questioned whether Paul's purposes here are primarily 'apologetic'.[12] But if we prefer to label Paul's story 'paradigmatic', we must still decide what it is a paradigm of and how this relates to Paul's addressees. Lyons proposes that Paul's 'ethos' argument functions, like ancient 'autobiography', to provide a model for imitation. But this seems to fit the text poorly, since nothing in Galatians indicates that Paul wishes to use his life as a character model for the Galatians; indeed, it is hard to see how they could find the narratives of Galatians 1–2 instructive as a *moral* paradigm.[13] More promising is Schütz' contention that Paul's first-person narrative, and especially his 'biography of reversal', encapsulates the character of the gospel.[14] If Paul is using his story to talk about the gospel and the revolutionary effect of God's grace, then this could certainly apply to the Galatians as they too respond to God's call (both were called through grace; 1:6, 16). In this way, Paul's 'I' in Gal. 2:18–21 could both condense and generalise the previous narrative: it is both a 'personal I' and a personification of the 'we' experience of Christian believers in general.[15] This should alert us to the fact that Paul reads his own story not simply as that of a unique, and uniquely called, individual: precisely *in* his individuality and uniqueness is played out a common story of grace. We should expect, then, that Paul recounts his previous experiences in Galatia in 4:12–19 not for their historical interest, or simply to recall happier times, but because in his

12. G. Lyons, *Pauline Autobiography: Toward a New Understanding* (Atlanta: Scholars Press, 1985) and, in the same vein, B. Dodd, *Paul's Paradigmatic 'I': Personal Example as Literary Strategy* (Sheffield: Sheffield Academic Press, 1999). Both counter the 'apologetic' reading of Galatians 1–2 developed by H.-D. Betz. At the corporate consultation, some voices pressed for analysis of the 'alternative' version of Paul's story that was probably being peddled in Galatia. I would not deny the currency of a different account of Paul's life (Paul's oath in Gal. 1:20 surely suggests this), but I will retain the focus on Paul's own account, since our concern is his theology.

13. Lyons (*Pauline Autobiography*, 136) argues that 'Paul's autobiographical narrative serves as the paradigm of the behaviour he persuades his readers to imitate'; his thesis is overinfluenced by the canons of ancient autobiography that typically used self-portraits to depict ideal character types. On Gal. 4:12, which might seem to support Lyons' case, see below.

14. J.H. Schütz, *Paul and the Anatomy of Apostolic Authority* (Cambridge: Cambridge University Press, 1975) 114–58. See further the suggestive essays of B. Gaventa, 'Galatians 1 and 2: Autobiography as Paradigm', *NovT* 28 (1986): 309–326 and B. Lategan, 'Is Paul Defending his Apostleship in Galatians?', *NTS* 34 (1988): 411–30.

15. Note how Paul's personal 'who loved me and gave himself for me' in Gal. 2:20 matches the general statement of 1:4 ('who gave himself for our sins to free us from the present evil age'). However, the reference of the 'we' statements in Galatians 3–4 is not always clear, and these are not necessarily matched in each case by a personal 'I' claim for Paul.

encounter with the Galatian recipients of the gospel was enacted something significant about the character and reception of that gospel. Not surprisingly, 4:19 (Paul's desire that 'Christ be formed in/among you') echoes the paradigmatic statement about the 'I' in 2:19–20 ('Christ lives in me'). In the same way, he tells the Galatians of his persecution for the cross (5:11; cf. 6:17) not as one item in his autobiography, nor to elicit sympathy or admiration, but because his identification with the cross is the instantiation of that grace that also claims them and subverts their commitment to 'the world' (6:12–16). Paul's 'I' in Galatians is, therefore, not a purely rhetorical expression for 'every believer'. But what he says about his individual 'I' expresses the 'canon' (κανών, 6:16) that governs the existence of every person in Christ.

## Autobiography as Testimony: Galatians 1:11–17

There is good reason to believe that the contrast Paul paints between his 'former life in Judaism' (1:13–14) and his new life consequent on 'the revelation of [God's] Son in me' (1:16) is structured by the antithesis in the 'headline' statements of 1:11–12: these set in antithetical contrast the reception or teaching of material along human channels (κατὰ ἄνθρωπον or παρὰ ἀνθρώπου) and 'the gospel' or 'the revelation of Jesus Christ'.[16] Thus, although the term ἄνθρωπος does not occur in 1:13–14, we should read these statements about Paul's former life as first-person history in human terms. Indeed, what strikes us about these statements is their resonance with our standard expectations of historical discourse. Here Paul is placed within a familial and ethnic context (his race [γένος] and life course within 'Judaism' ['Ιουδαϊσμός]); his development is described in comparison with others ('I advanced in Judaism beyond many of my people of the same age'); and his progress is measured by reference to the systems of socialisation and tradition described as 'the traditions of my fathers' (αἱ πατρικαί μου παραδόσεις, 1:14). Birth, upbringing, social environment, cultural inheritance—these are the elements with which 'history' is made and told, even if individuals may adapt and partially transcend these human constraints. Strikingly, there is no reference to God in this very human account of history (even though it is explicitly a Jewish history!)—or rather, the only reference to God is in connection with 'the church of God' (1:13) to which Paul was vehemently *opposed* out of commitment to 'the traditions of my ancestors'!

What Paul next recounts in this narrative is categorically *not* another stage in his development within Judaism, a further step in his progress of zeal. Rather, with an abrupt change of subject from 'I' to 'God', Paul describes an

---

16. See Lategan, 'Is Paul Defending?', 422–26; and Martyn, *Galatians*, 146–51, 163–64.

event that owes absolutely nothing to upbringing, human development, or cultural tradition: 'God set me apart before I was born, called me through his grace, and was pleased to reveal his Son to/in me, so that I might proclaim him among the gentiles' (1:15–16).[17] The reference to being 'set apart from my mother's womb' (to give the literal translation), echoes, of course, prophetic call narratives,[18] but it also expresses, in the most dramatic form possible, the conviction that God's fashioning of history is independent of the normal channels of human causation. This 'setting apart' happens before birth, before human nurturing, before cultural socialisation, and before Paul himself became a human agent. The only agency here can be that of God.

Hence Paul's story becomes, in effect, a testimony, since its starting point and climax are fundamentally beyond his control and dependent on the grace of God's call. A little later, Paul confirms that this is how his narrative is to be read, for when he reports that the churches of Judaea recount his about-turn ('[he] is now proclaiming the faith he once tried to destroy'), he finishes with the statement 'and they glorified God because of me' (1:24 NRSV). If they do not so much admire Paul as glorify God, they recognise whose story they are recounting: this story is ultimately, and most importantly, the story of the grace of God.[19]

It is, of course, with this new, grace-accorded identity that Paul here tells 'his' story. If he had told his life history as a zealous persecutor of the church, it would have been a wholly different narrative. Paul's new narrative is not, therefore, the same human story that has merely undergone certain vicissitudes due to the 'intervention' of God. The change Paul experiences is an epistemological revolution that transforms his understanding of himself from before birth onwards. A typical human narrative is here bent into a wholly peculiar shape, not just by strange events but by a historiography that breaks the pattern of human tellings. Paul makes it as clear as possible that he no longer regards himself as living within 'Judaism'.[20] But this is not because he

---

17. Admittedly this change of subject takes place in a long subordinate clause, in a sentence that finishes with further 'I' statements (1:16–17), but that syntax linguistically dramatises the interruption of the 'I' story by a story set in motion by God.

18. Specifically Jer. 1:4–5 and Isa. 49:1–6; see K.O. Sandnes, *Paul—One of the Prophets? A Contribution to the Apostle's Self-Understanding* (Tübingen: Mohr Siebeck, 1991).

19. See Schütz, *Apostolic Authority*, 136–37.

20. J.D.G. Dunn's equivocation on this point (*The Epistle to the Galatians* [London: A. & C. Black, 1993] 55–59) characteristically trumps Paul's self-understanding and self-description with another, derived from *our own* definition of 'Judaism': Could the Paul who wrote this passage recognise himself as converting 'from one Jewish movement, the Pharisees, to another, the Christians' (57, following A. Segal)? Although Paul can continue to describe himself and Peter as 'Jews by nature' (φύσει Ἰουδαῖοι, 2:15), this by no means involves a continuing commitment to live as a Jew (cf. 2:14) and can only be spoken with the detachment from ethnic identity brought about by baptism into Christ (3:28).

has entered some other cultural medium, with its own rules of human traditioning, but because he now sees with utterly different eyes, from a perspective that radically relativises, if it does not wholly obliterate, all social and historical categories (cf. 3:28; 6:15).[21]

Before we leave this seminal narrative, we should attend to the following paradox: As Paul now recognises, there was never a time in his life when he was not already 'set apart and called by grace'.[22] However, the realisation of this reality, and its life-changing effect, was a specific event in his life, when God 'was pleased to reveal his Son in me'. In each case, we can say, the grace of God was present in Paul's history, but only in the second case was it present as a historical 'event' that changed the course of Paul's life. Between these two poles—between his existence before birth and the revelation of the Son— Paul's life in accordance with the traditions of his ancestors was something of an interlude.[23] Although he thought at the time that he was making 'progress' (προέκοπτον, 1:14), he now sees that he was going nowhere that counted before God. This interlude was not, however, an irrelevance: as his allusion to the prophetic calling indicates, it at least provided him with the language in which to express the meaning of the revelation he received. In truth, the gracious call of God undergirds Paul's whole story and provides the continuity between 'start' and 'finish'. But that grace was not manifest, and that continuity could not have been traced, in the human stories of ethnicity, heritage, tradition, and culture. It needed a revelation to put Paul's life together, joined, as he now saw, by the thread of God's gracious initiative.[24]

---

21. For Paul's understanding of Christian 'tradition' and its relationship to the gospel, see M. Winger, 'Tradition, Revelation and Gospel: A Study in Galatians', *JSNT* 53 (1994): 65–86.

22. Scholars (not least Stendahl!) generally take this 'call' to have taken place at the same time as the 'revelation of God's Son'. But the aorist participles ἀφορίσας and καλέσας, and the time notice 'from my mother's womb' that qualifies the former, leave open the possibility that Paul understands his calling to have been operative antecedent to the revelation, even antecedent to his birth.

23. So, rightly, Dunn, *Galatians*, 63, though we should note the negativity implied by the conjunction of 1:13–14: Paul's 'advance' in Judaism only produced opposition to God's church!

24. Horrell's 'Response' (below) properly insists that *we* can see continuities in heritage and tradition that Paul himself does not concede. This is an important addition to my analysis that highlights the fact that I am operating here largely from *within* Paul's discourse rather than analysing it, historically or theologically, *from outside*. I am aware of the risk involved in this procedure (not least its potential for self-deception) but find it necessary to give primary and full attention to the narrative contours as Paul portrays them.

## The Propulsion of Grace: Galatians 1:10–2:14

Paul's call narrative suggests that his life has an entirely new focus: however we read the ἐν ἐμοί in 1:16 (probably better as 'in me', from the hindsight of 2:20 and 4:19), the revelation becomes the new organising centre of Paul's existence that drives him to preach God's Son among the gentiles. He is answerable now not to his ancestors or to his contemporaries and compatriots (1:14) but to God (or Christ) alone: hence the wedge now driven between 'pleasing human beings' and fulfilling his duties as 'the slave of Christ' (1:10). Thus, as John Schütz demonstrated, the thread of narrative continuity in Galatians 1–2 is not Paul as such (his experiences and crises) but Paul's story insofar as it represents the experiences and crises of the gospel.[25] As 1:8–9 makes clear, Paul himself is subordinated to the authority of the gospel. Thus any first-person narrative can be only secondarily about Paul himself: it will be primarily about the gospel of which he is the instrument and witness.

Hence, the narrative of the Jerusalem meeting (2:1–10), whatever information it may yield historians about power struggles in the early church, is not simply *about* these struggles but about the triumph of the gospel. Paul's admission that he might have run in vain (2:2) is not a momentary slip that admits his political inferiority to Jerusalem but an indication that what matters most is the gospel that he proclaims (under the commission of 1:16), not his honour as an equal to the Jerusalem apostles. He here celebrates resistance to the 'false brothers', not because it vindicates him but because it ensures that 'the truth of the gospel might always remain with [or, for] you' (2:5 NRSV). Indeed, as 2:6 makes clear, human reputation based on performance (whether 'honourable' or 'dishonourable') is irrelevant: the slaves of Christ cannot pay attention to merely human opinion (1:10). Thus what the 'pillars' recognised was not that Paul was an apostle equal to them but that they had all been 'entrusted with the gospel' (although for different addressees), and that the crucial agent in this matter was not Peter, or Paul, but 'the one [God] who worked' in each of them (2:8). One can hardly fail to notice the three-fold repetition of this motif in 2:7–9, climaxing in the pillars' recognition of 'the grace given to me' (2:9, echoing 1:16). Here the history of the church is propelled by its recognition of an event whose origins lie beyond human agency. If it is not judged by this measure, the Jerusalem council is as insignificant as the human reputation of its participants.

By the same token, the crisis in Antioch is not fundamentally about the split between Paul and Peter but about the failure of the dominant parties to 'walk

---

25. Schütz, *Apostolic Authority*, 136–50; Martyn (*Galatians*, 159–61) speaks of 'the history created by the gospel'.

in line with the truth of the gospel' (2:14). This is the basis on which Peter is 'condemned', his failure characterised by his attending to the opinions of 'the people from James' and 'the circumcision people' (2:12; contrast 1:10). That Paul finishes his narrative with this sorry incident indicates that he is not chiefly concerned to demonstrate *his own* triumphant progress (he does *not* claim to have 'won'). His is now a life propelled by grace and, whether he wins or not, he will bear witness to that truth. If he is prepared to court the hostility of all at Antioch, he will do it again, if necessary, in Galatia (4:16). In both cases it is the truth of the gospel that is at stake and to which he is ultimately answerable. In this sense, Paul would not recognise his own story as a topic of importance within his theology: his story is, more importantly, the story of the gospel for which he lives (or, in other terms, the story of the Christ who lives in him).

## The Reconstitution of the Self: Galatians 2:15–21

Because the story of Paul is really about something larger than himself, he is able to condense it in general terms at the close of his narrative. In 2:15ff. Paul begins his closure in the first-person plural of Jewish believers who now take an ironic stance towards their Jewishness: recognising that justification is by πίστις Ἰησοῦ Χριστοῦ ('faith in [or the faithfulness of] Jesus Christ'), they know that 'the works of the law', or 'living like a Jew' (2:14), cannot be the limiting framework in which the grace of God takes effect. Because Peter and the other Jewish believers at Antioch had failed to be true to this realisation, Paul uses the counterfactual 'I' of 2:18 to sum up their disastrous option. The factual 'I' of 2:19–20 is then simultaneously Paul's own story (2:19 echoes 1:13–16) and the true experience of anyone who believes in Christ.[26] Galatians 2:19–20 thus brings to expression both what Paul's 'revelation' meant for him and what faith in Christ means for every believer: not some new piece of information, or some widening of the intellectual horizon, but a total reconstitution of the self.

The clauses of 2:19–20 may be analysed as a three-part, A–B–A, structure, according to the subject said to 'live':

A           I (through the law) died (to the law) that *I might live* to God;

   B       I have been crucified with Christ; it is *no longer I who live* but *Christ who lives* in me;

---

26. Perhaps 'dying to the law through the law' (2:19) is unique to Paul, or at least to Jewish converts. However, Paul sees a structural parallel (to put it no higher) between gentile slavery to 'the elements' and Jewish slavery to the law, so even this aspect of his 'death' has (partial) parallels. But the obscurity of Paul's 'through the law' makes it impossible to determine this matter fully.

A          The life *I now live* in the flesh, *I live* by faith in [or, by the faithfulness of] the Son of God, who loved me and gave himself
for me.

Since the 'I' is said to live even beyond 'death' in both A-statements, it has
been suggested that the central statement (B) is hyperbole, or, alternatively,
concerns a particular (fleshly) 'I' rather than the essential 'I' that persists
through this partial death.[27] Both these interpretations seem to me mistaken.
While the language of being crucified with Christ is clearly metaphorical,
there is no reason to doubt that Paul refers to the real and total demolition of
the self, as previously constituted. Our current awareness of the social and psychological 'construction of the self' should make us question the apparently
natural notion of an essential, stable, core to our being; we are thus, perhaps,
rendered more receptive to Paul's radical conceptuality in this statement. Paul
means it when he says that the whole self—in its perceptions, motivations, self-
understanding, and drives—is fundamentally reconstituted when it shares the
crucifixion of Christ. And then both the statements of subjectivity—both that
'Christ lives in me' and that 'I live'—can be taken as true, in a dialectical fashion.[28] The reconstruction of identity fashions in the believer a self that is both
one's own self and, at the same time, the expression of the person of Christ.
Thus, if believers in baptism 'put on Christ' (3:28), this reclothing is not the
acquisition of merely external trappings (by which the self is left essentially
unchanged) nor an obliteration of the self (rendering the believer some life-
less tailor's dummy). Rather, the agency of a 'new creature' in Christ is simultaneously the agency of a believer *and* the agency of Christ (or as Paul will put
this later: it is walking in, and walking by, the Spirit; 5:13–25; 4:6). Thus, to

---

27. Dunn (*Galatians*, 145–46) considers 2:20a ('[I]t is no longer I who live') 'of course
exaggerated' and 'overdrawn for effect'; 2:20b then states the matter 'in more sober
terms'. But this is to confuse the excess created by metaphor with that created by exag-
geration: Paul's 'I' has truly died, though not literally so (cf. 6:14). Older commentators compared this text with the split 'I' in Rom. 7:14–25 and took the dead 'I' here to
be 'the flesh' or 'the natural man': e.g., E. de Witt Burton, *A Critical and Exegetical Commentary on the Epistle to the Galatians* (ICC; Edinburgh: T&T Clark, 1921) 137. M.
Volf's stimulating discussion of this passage (*Exclusion and Embrace* [Nashville: Abingdon Press, 1996] 69–71) uses metaphors of centering and decentering the self, but
strains the text to have Paul make 'the same self' 'recentred', even 'reinforced'.

28. Discussions of this text reflect the concern neither to domesticate the radicality
of Paul's statements nor to have him propose the obliteration or erasure of the human
self. In my reading, the self is not obliterated (otherwise why would Christ have 'given
himself for *me*'?), but is the product of a recreative divine love; now structured by the
presence and agency of Christ, it is secure enough to be itself an agent that is radically
self-giving in love.

live 'by faith in [or, by the faithfulness of] Christ, who loved me and gave himself for me' is to enact the Christ life of self-giving love, which is the product of faith (5:6) and the fruit of the Spirit (5:22). No wonder this love can be described as 'the law of Christ' (6:2): mutual burden bearing is precisely to *be Christ* to one another (cf. Rom. 15:1-6).[29]

Paul's story is paradigmatic, therefore, not in the particulars of his individual life journey, nor in his achievements, but in the sense—and to the degree—that his encounter with Christ crucified has refashioned his existence.

## Paul's Story and Other Stories in Galatians

There is an evident structural symmetry between Paul's story (as a Jew) and the story of his 'people' (fellow Jews), as outlined in this letter. In both cases there is a proleptic grace: Paul was set apart from his mother's womb (1:15), and the gospel was pre-preached to Abraham (3:8). But this acquires meaning, or takes effect, in a specific revelatory 'event': the revelation to Paul, in one case (1:16), and the revelation of faith in the coming of Christ, in the other (3:23). Between these poles, the observance of the Mosaic law (keeping the traditions of the ancestors) was something of an interlude, which was not meaningless within a wider perspective but also not the bearer of grace. In each case, the decisive event is the revelation of Jesus Christ, by which the whole story is recast and the past reevaluated: just as Paul now recognises his previous life as opposition to God, so Paul sees Israel's past as slavery to the law and enclosure within sin (3:22-25). Now Israel is to recognise that her foundational charter, the covenant promises to Abraham, concerned the single seed, Christ (3:16), just as Paul now saw that his highest ambition, to live to God, was possible only through crucifixion with Christ (2:19). Thus the Christ event is the organising centre of both stories, which are reconstituted around it. Neither the Israel of God (6:16) nor Paul can be the same again, for to put on Christ is so to refashion identity that to be a Jew (or a gentile) is no longer of constitutive significance (2:15-16; 3:28). In this way, Paul's story is a microcosm of the story of his people: precisely because he was the paradigm Jew in observing the law (1:13-14), he is the paradigm of Jews who are reconstituted in Christ.

---

29. Note especially R.B. Hays, 'Christology and Ethics in Galatians: The Law of Christ', *CBQ* 49 (1987): 268-90. Cf. B.W. Longenecker, *The Triumph of Abraham's God: The Transformation of Identity in Galatians* (Edinburgh: T&T Clark, 1998) 69-89 and 147-72. He neatly sums up this reading of Galatians 1-2: '[W]hen Paul paints his own self-portrait, it is Christ who appears on the canvas' (150). And if the dialectic suggested above is true, one might also say that when Paul portrays the crucified Christ to the Galatians, it is his own life in which he finds this portrait displayed (4:14; 6:17).

There is also a striking, though subtle, homology between Paul's story and the narrative of the Galatian churches in 4:12–19. When Paul preached the gospel to them in weakness (4:13), they welcomed him, he says, 'as Christ Jesus' (4:14 NRSV). We would be tempted to dismiss this as hyperbole had Paul not talked earlier of Christ living in him (2:20). The enfeebled Paul was, for them, a representative, even a personification, of the crucified Christ whom he placarded (3:1).[30] Here, then, was *their* 'revelation of Jesus Christ' (cf. 1:16). And the effect of this revelation was quite as dramatic. In this encounter with Christ in Paul, they did not despise or spit on this 'trial', as normal cultural conventions would dictate (4:14). Rather, their honour system was as revolutionised as their religious commitments (4:8–9); they were severed from the values embraced by their compatriots quite as radically as was Paul. They were, we might say, crucified with Christ in order to live to God, and their extreme generosity (they would have given their very eyes, 4:15) was a sign of their reconstruction by the one who loved and gave himself. This was their (paradoxical) 'blessing' (4:15):[31] to be dishonoured in the world but refashioned by Christ. Their present change of policy suggests that they are rebuilding what they once destroyed (cf. 2:18), and Paul must therefore groan in longing that 'Christ be formed' in them (4:19; cf. 2:19). The truth they must encounter again (4:16) is the truth of the gospel that will transform them, as it transformed Paul, into the shape of Christ. The appeal that they become like Paul (4:12) is precisely to that end.[32]

Thus both Paul's story and the story of his churches are moulded by the event of Christ, and only so long as they are so moulded do they have significance

---

30. E. Güttgemanns, *Der leidende Apostel und sein Herr: Studien zur paulinischen Christologie* (Göttingen: Vandenhoeck & Ruprecht, 1966) speaks of Paul here as the epiphany of the crucified one (185).

31. Although μακαρισμός ὑμῶν could be translated 'your self-congratulation' (i.e., your joy or elation), the context and the parallel use of the term in Rom. 4:6–8 suggest 'being blessed' (by God), as the foil to their 'trial' (πειρασμός, 4:14).

32. Galatians 4:12 is notoriously difficult: the missing verb in the clause ὅτι κἀγὼ ὡς ὑμεῖς makes it hard to know in what sense, or at what point, Paul may be said to be, or to have been, 'like them'. However, that they should be like Paul is relatively transparent: I take it here to allude to 2:19–20, an allusion reinforced by Paul's hope (the only wish for the Galatians expressed in this paragraph) that 'Christ be formed in/among you' (4:19). At the corporate consultation, Francis Watson urged that Paul was a example to the Galatians also in his faithful adherence to the gospel, in contrast to their wavering from it (1:6; 3:1–5, passages that frame 1:10–2:21). This idea adds a welcome further dimension to the role of Paul as exemplar. Morna Hooker noted the rich parallels in Philippians to the notion of transformation into the shape of Christ, in passages that sadly cannot be explored further here. I would concur that Gal. 4:19 is closely parallel to Phil. 3:10–11.

before God. 'Churches of Galatia' they might be, but being the church will be of no value unless Christ crucified be formed within them. Paul's brutal insistence on this point is emphasised one last time in 6:11–17, where his paradigmatic 'I' forces the Galatians to consider a stark alternative: one can boast in the flesh, or one can boast in the cross. The former will proceed as if the history of the world is unchanged and will secure one's place within it; the latter will fracture every story, both the story of 'me' and the story of 'the world in relation to me'.[33] Without this caesura, the story of the new creation cannot be told at all; and the significance of any story will be measured by how much it turns precisely here.

## Conclusion

Through its interconnections with other stories, Paul's story of himself in Galatians reveals much about 'Paul and narrative' in general. In the first place, it has become clear that his own story is of significance only insofar as it is really the story of grace or the story of the gospel—that is, only insofar as it is moulded by the story of the crucified Christ. Neither Paul, nor Israel, nor the church have any stories of significance before God except those that are fractured by the cross of Christ. Inevitably, then, these will be stories where the common rules of agency, causation, continuity, and development will be broken, and not just in the occurrence of 'freak' events but in the framework and sense making of the story itself.

Second, because the connection and coherence between these stories is Christ crucified, they do not cohere by the normal criterion that the smaller plot fits within the larger, on a timescale congruent with human historiography. Although the crucifixion of Christ was indeed an event in history, it punctures other times and other stories not just as a past event recalled but as a present event that, in an important sense, happens anew for its hearers (Paul and the Galatian Christians) in 'the revelation of Jesus Christ'. In the preaching of the gospel, time becomes, as it were, concertinaed, and the past becomes existentially present. Without this constant present time, of gift and demand, the church becomes merely the bearer of a new tradition, playing out her part in a narrative whose turning point is long in the past. But for Paul the decisive event is always also now: Will Christ be formed in you (4:19)?

---

33. On the apocalyptic sense of κόσμος here, see Martyn, *Galatians*, 570–74; and E. Adams, *Constructing the World: A Study in Paul's Cosmological Language* (Edinburgh: T&T Clark, 2000) 225–28. But even if the context evokes an apocalyptic change of aeons, the ἐμοί suggests that this apocalyptic event has to become existentially true in the case of each believer.

# PAUL AS APOSTLE AND ISRAELITE IN ROMANS

## Mapping the 'I' in Romans

Although Romans, like Galatians, begins with reference to Paul's apostleship (Rom. 1:1–7), it lacks the extended focus on Paul's life story and sums up the drama of Gal. 1:13–17 with no more than two words: 'called' (κλητός) and 'set apart' (ἀφωρισμένος, 1:1, cf. 1:5). Although Paul comments in this letter on his apostolic mission and his desire to extend this to Rome (1:7–15) and Spain (15:14–33), he does not reach back behind this point to the 'revelation of Jesus Christ' that transformed his life, nor does he present that transformation as a paradigm of cocrucifixion with Christ. Instead, he presents this paradigm pattern—of judgement and grace, sin and justification, death and life—on a universal scale, in the world's slavery to sin (1:18–3:20), in the revelation of the righteousness of God (1:16; 3:21–26), and in the believers' cocrucifixion with Christ in baptism (6:1–11). This should not surprise us. In Galatians we found Paul's first-person narrative to be of significance for Paul not because it was about him but because it signalled the pattern of God's grace in Christ. In this sense his personal testimony is relatively dispensable, and he can paint the same grace story on a different canvas in Romans.[34] If the apostle's life is a paradigm of his message, there is no reason that he has to offer both at once.

Of course, Romans does offer a striking 'I' text in 7:7–25, which at least begins with some quasinarrative elements (7:7–13). With almost all Pauline scholars, I do not take these to be 'autobiographical' except in the most attenuated sense. Here (as also in 3:7) Paul's rhetorical 'I' dramatises his analysis of the paradoxical relationship of law and sin, and probes its personal dimensions, but nothing in the context or content of this passage indicates that it concerns, specifically, his own story. Of course, this does not mean that his own life under the law could have been *exempt* from the sort of crisis that he here portrays (with Christian hindsight). In that sense, Paul himself is undoubtedly *included* in the 'I' figure of these verses, but they cannot be said to be *about him* in any more direct sense than that. For this reason (and with some relief!), I will not include them here in my analysis of Paul's story in Romans.

Romans does, however, recount two aspects of Paul's life story that are of theological significance. First, in presenting his aims and progress as an apostle (1:7–15; 15:14–33), Paul demonstrates how his life has been fashioned by

---

34. There are no doubt also historical reasons, due to the exigences of each letter, for this difference of presentation (for instance, the extent to which the churches in Galatia and in Rome were previously acquainted with Paul). But our focus here is on the theological uses to which Paul puts his first-person narratives.

the gospel and is now committed to the birth and spread of gentile churches. Second, in discussing the faithfulness of God to Israel (Romans 9–11), Paul presents himself as an example of the 'remnant' saved by grace (11:1–6) and finds, even in his apostleship to the gentiles, some positive role in Israel's future (11:13–16).[35] Thus, Paul's story is presented in Romans as entangled with the story of the church and the story of Israel; the nature of this entanglement is what we must study here.

## Paul as Apostle: Fashioned by the Gospel

Although he does not recount a life story in Romans parallel to that in Galatians 1–2, Paul is as conscious here, as there, that his life has been shaped by grace, fashioned both by and for the gospel. Introducing himself as one who has been 'called' and 'set apart' (1:1), Paul signals that the most important feature of his life is the agency of God: his identity is formed not by a human tale of social environment and personal achievement but by the receipt of grace and apostleship (1:5; 15:15). If Paul does not set this portrait here in contrast to a former, or alternative, life pattern, he nonetheless makes clear that 'the gospel' has become the organising centre of his life. He has been 'set apart' for the gospel (1:1; cf. Gal. 1:16) and now regards himself as serving God specifically 'in the gospel of his Son' (1:9): there is no way in which he could 'live for God' (Gal. 2:19) otherwise. His immediate aim is thus 'to preach the gospel' (εὐαγγελίσασθαι) in Rome (1:15), just as his life's work is as 'a priest in service of the gospel' (ἱερουργοῦντα τὸ εὐαγγέλιον, 15:16); his travel plans are determined by the extent to which he has 'completed' that task (πεπληρωκέναι τὸ εὐαγγέλιον, 15:19) or has yet to fulfil it (15:20).

That this task does not just give direction to his life but also reshapes his very self is indicated by two features of his self-description in these passages. In the first place, Paul is careful to describe himself here not only as a 'slave' (1:1) or 'minister' of Christ (15:16) but also as the medium through whom *Christ* works for the obedience of the nations (15:18). The significance of this is underlined by the emphasis with which his boast is placed *in Christ Jesus* (15:17) and by his refusal to speak of 'signs and wonders' except as that which '*Christ* has worked through me' (κατειργάσατο Χριστὸς δι' ἐμοῦ, 15:18).

---

35. In the first, Paul's discourse displays some classic story features (the depiction of events, in sequence, with some sense of trajectory), although not arranged in their historical order. In the second, one might say Paul presents less his own story than his place within Israel's story (her calling, her stumbling, and her destiny); but his prominent placement of himself within that story justifies our attention to this passage within the remit of this essay.

Although Paul does not specifically name the *cross* of Christ in this boast, as he does in Gal. 6:14, the effect is structurally the same: precisely where he might claim human honour, in the performance of signs and wonders, the story is emphatically christomorphic. It is clear, then, that being 'called' by God in Christ is not just a 'vocation'. It involves a complete reconception of the self, in which even one's own agency is redefined.[36]

But Paul's life is reshaped by the gospel in another way, too. At several points in chapters 1 and 15 he emphasises that his calling is as an apostle *to the gentiles*. It is for their obedience of faith that he has received grace and apostleship (1:5; cf. 1:13–15), and his priestly task is to bring an acceptable offering of the gentiles, sanctified by the Holy Spirit (15:16). This drive for the sanctification of the gentiles arises from Paul's radical sense of the 'power of the gospel': in it is released 'God's power for the salvation of *everyone* who believes, both Jew (first) and Greek' (Rom. 1:16, my translation). Paul does not set this understanding of the power and grace of God specifically in contrast to *his own* former life or comprehension, but he says enough about 'the Jew' in Romans 2 to indicate how this gospel destabilises the category 'Jew' ('Ιουδαῖος, 2:25–29), and he makes no attempt to hide that this is his heritage as well (9:1–5). It is only because the 'power of the gospel' has reshaped his own identity as an heir to the 'promises of God' (9:4) that he can commit his life to bringing about gentile participation in those promises, and on terms in which 'there is no distinction between Jew and Greek' (3:19–30; 10:12 NRSV). In other words, his role as apostle to the gentiles presupposes that his theological categories have been changed at the most fundamental level, and changed by a 'power' that has redefined his own position before God.

One outworking of this revolution is the way in which new patterns of reciprocity between Jew and gentile have been formed within the church, of which Paul's own life is an example. With regard to the Romans (who are located 'among the gentiles'; 1:13), Paul, an Israelite reconstituted in Christ, has an obligation to bring the gospel (1:15) and to share some spiritual gift (χάρισμα, 1:11) for their benefit. But he also expects to *receive* something from their faith (1:12), to gain some 'fruit' (1:13); he asks that they wrestle with him, and for him, in prayer (15:30–31), and hopes for their hospitality and financial support for his mission to Spain (15:24). This pattern of mutual support and obligation is reproduced on a larger scale in the relationship between Jerusalem and the gentile churches. The saints in Jerusalem initially gave 'spiritual blessings' and are now to receive a 'fruit' (15:28) from the hands of gentiles; conversely, the gentiles, having once received, are now obliged to give

---

36. Hence, presumably, his confidence that he will come 'in the fulness of the blessing of Christ' (15:29); cf. Gal. 4:13–15.

(15:25–29). In both cases Paul's task is to enable the creation of a 'fellowship' (κοινωνία, 15:26) that, being drawn from both Jews and gentiles, transcends geographical and ethnic boundaries because what counts now is the common 'naming' of Christ (15:20; cf. 10:9–13). In this sense, Paul's work is a paradigm of what he expects within the Roman churches (14:1–15:13), but only because both he and they have had their minds remoulded to think 'in accord with Christ Jesus' (κατὰ Χριστὸν Ἰησοῦν, 15:3–5).

## Paul as Israelite: The Mystery of Grace

If the opening verses of Galatians signal that Paul will focus on the macro-antithesis of 'humanity' and 'God', the beginning of Romans shows that this letter will revolve around the history and destiny of Israel. The gospel for which Paul is set apart is immediately introduced as 'promised beforehand through [God's] prophets in the holy scriptures' (NRSV), and it concerns 'the seed of David' who was designated God's Son (1:2–4). Thus, although Paul does not develop this theme immediately, or introduce himself at once as an Israelite, it is no surprise to find him agonising over the question of God's faithfulness to Israel in Romans 9–11 and identifying in grief with his 'brothers according to the flesh' (9:1–3; 10:1–2). Paul thus identifies himself with Israel's crisis, and not just from the distance of the rhetorical 'I' of 3:7 but with total existential involvement. More than that, he also introduces himself at a crucial point in the development of these chapters, at which the lead question ('Has God's word failed?', 9:6) is repeated in pointed terms: 'Has God rejected his people?' (11:1 NRSV). Paul's reply, 'By no means!', is supported by the statement that 'I myself am an Israelite, a descendant of Abraham, a member of the tribe of Benjamin' (11:1 NRSV). With the analogy of Elijah and the seven thousand who did not worship Baal (11:2–4) Paul concludes, 'So too at the present time there is a remnant, chosen by grace [λεῖμμα κατ᾽ ἐκλογὴν χάριτος]. But if it is by grace, it is no longer on the basis of works, otherwise grace would no longer be grace' (11:5–6 NRSV).

Paul thus regards his story as relevant to the reading of God's purposes for Israel as a whole, but the question is how. In particular, how does he see his membership of this 'remnant' as demonstrating that God has not 'rejected his people' (11:2)?[37] At first sight, one might construe his argument as follows.

---

37. I follow here the majority reading of this passage that interprets Paul to be presenting himself as a Jewish believer in order to demonstrate that God has not rejected his people (so e.g., E. Käsemann, *Commentary on Romans* [London: SCM Press, 1980] 299). Although it is also true that Paul here establishes that he speaks from 'an authentically Jewish viewpoint' (J.D.G. Dunn, *Romans 9–16* [Dallas: Word, 1988] 635), the γάρ with which he begins this statement of his identity shows that he here provides some logical basis for the strong denial ('By no means') of 11:1a.

God has always made his selection (by grace) within Israel, right from the very beginning (9:6). As warned (or promised) in the prophets, God has left only a remnant for Israel (9:27–29), and that line of continuity, thin though it may be, has been maintained through Jewish believers like Paul. Thus he and fellow Jewish believers are like Elijah and those seven thousand in that they have not fallen into disobedience ('bowed the knee to Baal') or stumbled on the rock of offence (9:33). While the elect have obtained salvation, the rest of Israel has been hardened (11:7). While 'they' (the rest) have stumbled and been cut off from the olive tree (11:11–24), and while 'you' (gentiles) have been (by definition) disobedient to God (part of the wild olive), 'we' (the remnant) have remained on our feet (or, in the terms of the other metaphor, still joined to the tree) and thus provide that physical, genealogical guarantee that God's purposes for his people have not entirely failed.

However, closer study of the passage, and of Romans as a whole, shows that this first reading of the passage is badly mistaken. The fatal flaw in this reading is its requirement that the remnant have remained, as it were, steady on their feet, whereas everything in Romans in general, and in Romans 9–11 in particular, shows that all, without exception, have stumbled. If appeal to Romans 3 (or the implied universality of the 'I' in Romans 7) is not enough in this regard, we may go to the end of Romans 11 itself, with its equally universal claim that 'God has consigned all people to disobedience, that he may have mercy on all' (11:32). Indeed, embedded in our very passage, in the contrast between grace (χάρις) and works (ἔργα), are unmistakable echoes of two key passages in Romans demonstrating that Paul saw salvation as always and inevitably effected by the justification of the *ungodly*, the resurrection of the *dead*, and the gift of sheer grace to the *undeserving*. Thus in Romans 4, which emphatically contrasts ἔργα with χάρις (4:4–5), Paul claims the justification of (even) Abraham and David to be a justification of the *ungodly*. Abraham's faith was precisely that God could give life to the dead; he and his circumcised successors have to recognise that their circumcision is only a seal of a justification already received, and neither a necessary nor a sufficient basis for it (4:9–12; cf. 2:25–29). In the same way, Paul stresses through Rom. 9:6–18 that in every new present God's calling is by grace and not by human effort or will (9:11–12, 16), and he insists that God's offspring are not 'of the flesh' but of the promise (9:8). Crucially, he then supplements this by reference to God's calling of gentiles (9:24–26) so that it is clear that God's grace is not a matter of selection *within* Israel but of a levelling of all (on the stone of offence, 9:32–33), so that 'there is no distinction between Jew and Greek': God is rich in grace to all who call on Christ for salvation (10:12–13).

Thus, Paul and his fellow members of the remnant cannot be those who are exempt from stumbling (thus showing that God has not *completely* given up his people to disobedience) but, on the contrary, those who, despite their stumbling, have been put back on their feet by grace: they indicate that God's purposes for a disobedient world *include* a purpose of grace for disobedient Israel. The remnant is a sign of God's mercy on Israel, not in preserving the godly from among the ungodly (that would hardly be grace, at least for Paul) but in salvaging *even these disobedient Jews*. Thus the continuity that the remnant represents is not a continuity of ethnic descent but of the faithfulness of God: it is God's grace and God's word that is constant, even in the midst of total unfaithfulness (cf. 3:3–7). As N. Walter has argued, the root that sustains the olive tree (11:16–24) is not Israel, ethnically defined: the richness from which the olive tree draws (11:17) is, rather, the gracious kindness of God.[38] Or, even if this root be judged to relate to the patriarchs (cf. 11:29), it represents *God's promise* to the patriarchs, God's design of election, not some ethnic guarantee of continuity. The new and mysterious thing that Paul reveals in 11:25ff. is that God's faithfulness will embrace 'all Israel', but it is emphatically clear that this is not due to some inherent virtue in Israel itself—past, present, or future—but because she is the recipient of a gift and a calling that cannot be revoked by the faithful God (11:29). The final word is no special clause of exemption for an Israel that does not need grace but rather the message that she, *too*, has received mercy and will receive it in full.

Thus there never has been a time when Israel has not been called by grace, and there never will be a time when this calling will fail. But this call has become an event, specifically in Christ, and if this has caused (all) Israel to stumble, it will also be the opportunity for grace to call her into faith. Standing in the grace of God is thus, in one sense, Israel's destiny, her natural 'olive tree' (ἰδία ἐλαία, 11:24). But she learns through Christ that this is not a matter of her own righteousness (ἰδία δικαιοσύνη, 10:3) but a matter of the righteousness of God, who justifies the ungodly, both Jew (first) and Greek. This pattern of life from death (11:15) is, not surprisingly, the pattern of the cocrucifixion and new creation that moulds every believer (6:1–11). But it is not, even then, a secure possession: to presume on the goodness of God is to risk exclusion (11:19–22). If he recognises that even the receipt of grace can become a matter of pride, Paul certainly knows how subtly corrupt the church can become. Unless they continue to exist and act solely out of the grace of God, believers have every reason to fear the severity of God, which is the flip side of his infinite mercy.

Thus Paul does not in Romans 9–11 present a continuity that runs from ethnic Israel, through the remnant, to the church, and he is not a representative of God's salvation plan in this sense. The only continuity is that of the gra-

---

38. N. Walter, 'Zur Interpretation von Römer 9–11', *ZTK* 81 (1984): 172–95, at 178–82.

cious action of God, which weaves in Israel's history—past, present, and future—patterns of mercy and generosity, shaped by the death and resurrection of Christ, and now also repeated in the lives of believers. Paul has no reason to think that this pattern-weaving story has finished for Israel, nor that being a member of the church is a guarantee of participation within it. If he shares in this history, it is not because he is an Israelite—although this shows that Israelites, *too*, can continue to find their place within it. Rather, his presence in this paradoxical history is a sign of the workings of grace, and his story is worth telling as, and only as, it exemplifies that mystery.

## CONCLUSION

There are considerable differences in the way Paul tells his story of himself in Galatians and Romans (though only a larger survey would show how *relatively* large these differences are). In Galatians his first-person narrative has a high profile and contains as its pivotal component his transformation by grace. That is a moment Paul does not recount in Romans, where in general his story is woven into the story of others and not given an independent profile. In both letters his story as apostle is entangled with that of his churches, but only in Romans is it made explicit how he sees himself in relation to the story of his people. Common, however, to both letters, and the foundational reason for Paul's various testimonies, is his moulding of his story in the shape of the crucified and risen Jesus, and his conviction that this pattern, of life from death, and grace to the undeserving, is the structuring pattern of *all* the stories that could be taken to be 'salvation history'. This christomorphic historiography is applied in a new way in Romans to the story of Israel as a whole, in past, present, and future tense. But the distinctive patterning remains the same: as a story of grace.

We may therefore return to the three clusters of questions raised at the beginning and sum up our conclusions:

### Story and Gospel

We can conclude without hesitation that Paul's stories[39] are not mere illustrations of truth that could be abstracted from them without detriment. Because

---

39. David Horrell has pointed out to me the difference in nuance between those who prefer to speak of Paul's story (singular) of creation/redemption—an overarching story with multiple subplots—and those who refer to stories (plural, not necessarily implying a narrative coherence between them). I find I am drawn much more to the latter, as these conclusions make clear.

these stories are all, in different ways, narratives of God's grace, they embody 'the truth of the gospel'. The grace of God is not, for Paul, an idea, or even primarily an attribute of God, but the action of God in history. God's grace is always, and inevitably, 'storied', working in history (though often also concealed within it) to bring life out of death, power out of weakness, salvation out of sin. Thus Paul's stories convey the gospel inasmuch as they carry the pattern of grace, of justification of the ungodly, and of God's critical judgement on human pretensions. Paul does not tell his stories and *then* transmit their meaning: that meaning is embodied in the shape of the stories themselves. Inevitably, then, his story of Israel, or of his own 'Jewish' life, will not be an 'essentially Jewish story', even with a 'subversive twist' (see n. 7): they will be stories told from a different standpoint, finding the gracious call of God in events and sequences that had *not* been perceived before. His personal narrative is not a subversive *variant* on the Jewish story of the devout man:[40] it is a new story, starting with the call from his mother's womb that he had not known before and completely reevaluating (as a gross sin) what he had once considered the acme of his life's achievement (his persecution of the church of God). Paul, in other words, tells very particular grace-shaped stories, which do not so much stand as the 'foundation' of 'doctrines' such as 'justification by faith' as they tell how God has justified the ungodly—whether that be Abraham, humanity, Israel, or himself. In other words, 'justification' and 'salvation history' cannot be played off against one another: the justification of the ungodly, the gift of life to the dead, or hope to the despairing (in short, grace) is what constitutes 'salvation history', which cannot be detected other than by this criterion.[41]

## The Story Interconnections

If Paul's various stories (at least those of theological significance) all concern grace, they will derive their pattern from one central point, 'the apocalypse of Jesus Christ'. As we have seen, Paul's life is meaningful because he has been 'crucified with Christ' and because it is Christ who now lives within him. For Paul and his converts, what counts is that Christ is formed within them, and because their lives have adopted, and continue to adopt, that pattern of death to the world and self-giving in love, they carry positive significance. It is from the vantage point of the cross of Christ that Paul understands the radical grace

---

40. Wright reads Phil. 3:3–11 as a 'deliberate and subversive variant on the Jewish story of the devout Pharisee' (*The New Testament and the People of God*, 404); in my judgement, this description fits neither Philippians 3 nor Galatians 1.

41. The echoes of Käsemann (see n. 6) are not accidental.

of God, and then, in this light, perceives the gracious call (to all nations) already pre-preached to Abraham and issued to both gentiles and his 'brothers according to the flesh'. In other words, what links Paul's stories is most crucially their homology, their common 'syntax' or pattern, their cruciform or grace-moulded shape.[42] He does not trace linear lines through historical processes or human continuities: indeed, the justification of the ungodly is more likely to proceed through paradox, surprise, and the breaking of human connections. Just as Paul sees no humanly visible line of continuity through his own life, but rather an interruption, when the 'I' is overwhelmed by the agency of God (or Christ), he finds no line linking Abraham to the present except that of the faithfulness of God. By the same token, there is no line guaranteeing the future of the church, which can as readily oppose the gospel as proclaim it. Paul's stories are neither plotted on a common time line, nor linked by some other 'organic' principle: they are connected only by the common thread of the grace of God, which weaves its own independent patterns in history.

## The (Limited) Significance of Paul's Own Story

In one sense, Paul's own story is of no ultimate significance. Only as it is moulded by the 'master pattern' of the crucifixion and new creation does Paul identify the presence of 'salvation history' in his own story. Although he judged it valuable to point this out and generalise from it for the Galatians, he can write to the Romans about this same gospel and at much fuller length with far less indication that this pattern is *also* represented in his own biography. But, in another sense, the fact that Paul can and does trace this pattern in his own life, and in the life of every baptised believer, is of fundamental significance for his theology. For Paul, the believer is not simply the follower after Jesus who takes inspiration from Christ and identifies with him as the 'chief protagonist' in the story. He does not simply recall the story of Jesus as an event to be remembered, a chapter now past in whose aftermath we live. Rather, the crucifixion of Jesus is a *present* reality for Paul, present not only in the single act of baptism but also in the continuing experiences and sufferings of his life. Hence the characteristic use of the perfect tense: 'I have been [and thus continue to be] crucified with Christ' (Gal. 2:19). Paul both *lives from* the story of Jesus (it happened, crucially, once in history) and *lives in* it: it happens again, time and again, inasmuch as Christ lives in him. I doubt we can do justice to

---

42. For an explication of narrative pattern, making Christian stories generalisable without losing their uniqueness, see M. Root, 'The Narrative Structure of Soteriology', in Hauerwas and Jones (eds), *Why Narrative?*, 263–78, at 270–75.

this sense of participation in Christ if we think of this in terms of an 'imaginative identification . . . with the fate of the hero in the community's foundational story'.[43] Rather, precisely because he is *not* bound by a simple linear sense of time, Paul can keep finding in his own life—but only as a paradigm— the presence and continuance of the Christ story and the Christ grace that keeps puncturing the folds of time to reenact the new creation.[44]

---

43. Hays, 'Crucified with Christ', 242, suggests this formulation as a possible reading of 'participation in Christ'. See the earlier tentative proposals in *The Faith of Jesus Christ*, 250–54.

44. As Francis Watson observed at the corporate consultation, this sense of the 'past' being present threatens to subvert the sense of 'horizontal' narrative in Paul, though it does not, I believe, destroy it altogether. Cf. D. Ford's comments ('System, Story, Performance: A Proposal about the Role of Narrative in Christian Systematic Theology', in Hauerwas and Jones [eds], *Why Narrative?*, 191–215, 208) on the problems in stressing 'linearity' in narrative theology. I am most grateful to David Horrell and to all the members of the corporate consultation for their helpful discussion of this essay, and to two other readers, Susan Eastman and J. Louis Martyn, who made many productive observations.

# 9

# Paul's Narratives or Narrative Substructure?

*The Significance of 'Paul's Story'*

DAVID G. HORRELL

'[T]he narrative structure for which we are searching is the structure of the gospel story, not of Paul's personal story.'[1]

## INTRODUCTION

John Barclay's essay is both theologically powerful and exegetically incisive, clearly and frequently reflecting the influence of Ernst Käsemann and J. Louis Martyn. Two arguments seem most forcibly to emerge. One is deployed in opposition to any notion of Paul's story as part of some broader, temporally continuous, linear narrative of salvation history: Paul's experience, his testimony, is rather of an 'apocalypse of Jesus Christ' that fractures and interrupts any line of logic or continuity; this apocalyptic event has consequences so radical that they can only be described—in terms relating to Paul himself—as implying a total demolition and reconstitution of the self. The second argument is that Paul's 'story' is of no significance in itself. It is only told, and only has significance, insofar as it embodies the gospel of Christ—the story of God's grace—and insofar as it represents in microcosm the story of Israel and of the church in relation to this event of grace.

In responding to Barclay's essay, I shall endeavour to raise questions and issues that relate to the central question this book seeks to address: What is

---

1. R.B. Hays, *The Faith of Jesus Christ: An Investigation of the Narrative Substructure of Galatians 3:1–4:11* (SBLDS 56; Chico, Calif.: Scholars Press, 1983) 29.

the value, if any, of a narrative approach to Paul? More specifically, in relation to this subsection of the inquiry: How can an investigation of 'the story of Paul' aid us in an assessment of the narrative approach to Paul? Barclay succeeds, it seems to me, in demonstrating powerfully how Paul's story is only important (for Paul) insofar as it embodies the gospel of Christ. He offers less insight, however, into precisely how this relates to an assessment of the 'narrative approach' to Pauline theology.

## WHICH WAY UP? PAUL'S STORIES AND PAUL'S TEXTS

Barclay begins his essay with the point that although narrative analysis is more obviously applicable to the Gospels than to Paul's letters, it can be applied to Paul, since Paul 'sometimes tells stories, or parts of stories' (see page 133). Moreover, he suggests, it can be claimed that 'these are not incidental to Paul's theologising, but are in some senses constitutive of it' (see pages 133). Throughout the essay there is repeated reference to the stories Paul tells, and specifically the stories he tells about himself. Thus, Galatians 1–2 is a particularly crucial text, since it constitutes 'a quintessential narrative' (page 135); examples in Romans are also evident, though less obviously so. Indeed, Barclay's 'lead questions' all highlight this category of 'Paul's stories' and the way in which he 'tells his story' (pages 135–36). The significance of this way of setting the agenda is more far-reaching than might at first appear. For we need to note that this is precisely *not* the approach proposed by Richard Hays, in the work that to a considerable extent established the recent interest in narrative contours in Pauline thought.[2] Hays is not interested in looking at the Pauline texts as narratives, nor even at the narratives within them; that is why he looks at Gal. 3:1–4:11 and not at Galatians 1–2.[3] His claim, exemplified in his study of Galatians 3–4, is that Paul's letters, as 'reflective discourse', are based on a story, a story that provides the 'narrative substructure' for Paul's theology and that is alluded to in Paul's discourse.[4]

Barclay's approach to Paul's 'story' leads, I think, to some ambivalence over the term and its usefulness in interpreting Paul. On the one hand, he assumes that the term 'story' is a useful one to employ because it is obvious that Paul tells some stories, including some about himself. Barclay also refers to 'the story of the grace of God' and 'the story of the gospel' (pages 139, 142, and

---

2. Hays, *The Faith of Jesus Christ*.

3. Cf. Hays, *The Faith of Jesus Christ*, 23, 29–30.

4. Hays, *The Faith of Jesus Christ*, 28.

146). On the other hand, Barclay argues that Paul does not see the grace of God in terms of a linear salvation history. On the contrary (and here the influence of Käsemann and especially Martyn is clear),[5] Barclay stresses the centrality of 'the apocalypse of Jesus Christ' (page 154), the decisive moment of God's saving action, which constitutes a radical break, a caesura, which punctures, fractures, and interrupts any and every story (see pages 154–55). To the extent that he sides with those who oppose a salvation-historical reading of Paul,[6] Barclay positions himself in opposition to the thrust of the narrative approach, while his frequent use of story terminology seems implicitly to embrace it.[7] Indeed, the content of Barclay's essay seems to me, at least implicitly, to promote a perspective almost directly the reverse of that presented by Hays and others. *Where Hays sees Paul writing reflective discourse based on an underlying story, glimpsed but not narrated in the text, Barclay sees Paul writing stories based on an underlying 'paradigm pattern'.* Thus I think there is rather more difference between the two approaches than is suggested in Barclay's comment that his notion of 'pattern' may help to resolve an ambiguity in Hays' proposal (see page 134, note 6). For Barclay, what underpins Paul's theologising, *and* his telling of stories, is not so much a story but a paradigm, the paradigm of Christ crucified. This paradigm shapes, indeed determines, how all stories, Paul's own included, are rightly to be told; '[I]t punctures other times and other stories not just as a past event recalled but as a present event' (see page 146). What does not quite become clear is whether this underlying paradigm is, or is not, valuably understood as having a narrative character; it would appear that for Barclay it does not (cf. also note 10 below). Barclay answers his own question concerning the relationship between 'story' and 'the truth of the gospel' with the affirmation that God's grace is inevitably 'storied' (page 154), but what this seems to mean is *not* that the gospel itself has a temporal, story-like character

---

5. Käsemann is somewhat ambivalent on the issue of salvation history, vigorously opposing any emphasis on the idea of 'an imminent evolutionary process' of salvation (and Cullmann's work in particular) on the one hand, and Bultmann on the other, with his tendency to focus the Pauline gospel merely onto the self-understanding of the believer. Thus Käsemann states that he 'apparently stand[s] between two fronts' ('Justification and Salvation History in the Epistle to the Romans', in his *Perspectives on Paul* [London: SCM Press, 1971] 63, 76 n. 27). See further Hays, *The Faith of Jesus Christ*, 62–63 and below nn. 10–11.

6. See further below, with nn. 12–14.

7. Contrast, e.g., Martyn's emphasis on the 'punctiliar' and un-story-like character of Paul's references to Christ and Abraham (see nn. 12–14 below) with Hays' argument against a punctiliar treatment of the Christ event (see n. 14 below). Note also Hays' conclusion that Cullmann's views on *Heilsgeschichte*, vigorously opposed by Käsemann, 'are congenial with the thesis that Paul's theology has a narrative substructure' (*The Faith of Jesus Christ*, 59).

(it is not a 'Story') but rather that grace is, and must be, active in history and thus instantiated in *stories* such as Paul's own. 'Paul's stories' (plural) are all 'narratives of God's grace' (page 154); they 'convey the gospel inasmuch as they carry the *pattern* of grace' (page 155, my emphasis).

## CRITICAL QUESTIONS

### The Rhetoric of 'Newness' and the Influence of the 'Old'

While Barclay's presentation of the epistemological revolution that Paul experienced in his encounter with Christ is powerful and in many ways compelling, there are questions to be raised. First, the rhetoric of 'interruption', of radical newness, somewhat obscures the extent to which Paul's understanding and articulation of the meaning of the Christ event are inevitably formed on the basis of already existing language and tradition. Paul may see his call experience as 'an event that owes absolutely nothing to upbringing, human development, or cultural tradition' (page 139)—though the polemical context in which he narrates it surely has some impact on this presentation—but he nonetheless describes it in language that embeds him firmly in his cultural tradition. To claim, therefore, that Paul has somehow moved beyond culturally conditioned perspectives and human traditions because 'he now sees with utterly different eyes, from a perspective that radically relativises, if it does not wholly obliterate, all social and historical categories' (page 140), or that Paul experiences 'the real and total demolition of the self' (page 143), or that he 'sees no humanly visible line of continuity through his own life' (page 155) is to reiterate Paul's radical claims while ignoring, or at least downplaying, the other side of the equation. Paul may consider himself to have had an experience that renders him dead to everything in his past and that causes him to see all things from an entirely new perspective, but the fact that he narrates the experience in terms drawn precisely from that past, and describes the new things precisely in the language and categories of Judaism and its scriptures, means that there is a much more complex interrelationship between 'old' and 'new' than Barclay's essay (and Paul's rhetoric) seems to imply. Paul's new epistemology, in other words, represents, as it must in all such human experience,

---

8. The term 'reconfigure' seems to me a helpful one. I have taken it from T.L. Donaldson, *Paul and the Gentiles* (Minneapolis: Fortress Press, 1997), who speaks of Paul's Judaism being reconfigured around Christ and not Torah.

a reconfiguring[8] of his language and tradition rather than a creation ex nihilo—which would be meaningless to Paul and his contemporaries.

Barclay does rather minimally concede, for example, that Paul's 'reference to being "set apart from my mother's womb"' . . . echoes, of course, prophetic call narratives' (page 139) and that Paul's former life in Judaism (Gal. 1:13) 'at least provided him with the language in which to express the meaning of the revelation he received' (page 140). But this point needs to be stressed rather more: Paul uses, indeed depends on, the very tradition-specific language of Judaism and its scriptures to apprehend and describe a divine act that at the same time radically reorders Paul's sense of the meaning of that tradition. For instance, it is in some sense true to say, with Barclay, that Paul 'radically relativises' the distinction between Jew and gentile (page 140; cf. Gal. 3:28; 6:15; Rom. 10:12; also 1 Cor. 7:19; 12:13), but again, our description of the complex interrelationship between new and old needs to be carefully nuanced. On the one hand, while to some extent remaining aware of an identity distinction between Jew and gentile (Gal. 2:15; Rom. 9:3; 11:1), Paul sees the new community of those in Christ as one in which the distinction symbolised by circumcision is now 'nothing' (1 Cor. 7:19; cf. Gal. 6:15). On the other hand, he describes the identity of these community members in thoroughly Jewish terms: they are descendants of Abraham (Gal. 3:6–29; 4:21–31; cf. Rom. 9:8; 2 Cor. 11:22), children of the Jerusalem above (Gal. 4:26), 'sons of God' (Rom. 8:14; Gal. 3:26, etc.), and the 'people of God' (cf. Rom. 9:24–25; 2 Cor. 6:16); the scriptures were written for their instruction (Rom. 15:4; 1 Cor. 10:11); the patriarchs are their fathers (1 Cor. 10:1; cf. Rom. 4:1); they are even 'the circumcision' (Phil. 3:3; cf. Rom. 2:28–29) and 'the Israel of God' (Gal. 6:16).[9] The category distinction between Jew and gentile has not entirely been dissolved or left behind; to some extent, however, it has been relocated or transferred such that it now distinguishes those who are in Christ from those who 'remain in unbelief' (cf. Rom. 11:23). Hence it is somewhat one-sided to say that Paul's 'theological categories have been changed at the most fundamental level' (see page 149) without at the same time pointing out how thoroughly Paul's scriptural and cultural tradition continues to provide him with the categories in which he thinks.

---

9. Cf. further D.G. Horrell, '"No Longer Jew or Greek": Paul's Corporate Christology and the Construction of Christian Community', in D.G. Horrell and C.M. Tuckett (eds), *Christology, Controversy and Community: New Testament Essays in Honour of David R. Catchpole* (NovTSup 99; Leiden: Brill, 2000) 333–42. For this interpretation of the famously ambiguous phrase in Gal. 6:16, see, e.g., the still persuasive arguments of N.A. Dahl, 'Der Name Israel: Zur Auslegung von Gal. 6,16', *Judaica* 6 (1950): 161–70; and more recently J.M.G. Barclay, *Obeying the Truth: A Study of Paul's Ethics in Galatians* (Edinburgh: T&T Clark, 1988) 98.

Paul may present us with a personal story of radical disjuncture and with the rhetoric of a demolished and reconstituted self, but his frequent references to the scriptures and the language in which he describes his experiences and convictions, the identity of the members of the churches, and so on, suggest that this new self-identity has more continuity with the past than the rhetoric of interruption might suggest.

## A Story of Salvation? Linear and Punctiliar Emphases

Second, it seems to me that Barclay, like Martyn, downplays the extent to which Paul places the Christ event within—although as the climax and culmination of—the story of God's saving purposes and their enactment in history.[10] Sensitivity to the problems of a certain conception of *Heilsgeschichte*, with its notions of linear progress and evolution[11] and its potential to detract from the centrality of the death and resurrection of Christ, should not lead us to ignore the

---

10. Barclay echoes Käsemann in his assertion that 'the justification of the ungodly . . . is what constitutes "salvation history"' (28); cf. Käsemann, 'Justification and Salvation History', 75–76. On Käsemann's ambivalence regarding *Heilsgeschichte*, and specifically his rejection of the idea of a process of salvation in history, see above, n.5. Barclay's comment that justification by faith provides the only 'criterion' by which salvation history can be detected would seem to imply not that there is a connected 'Story' of salvation but that various stories (testimonies) such as Paul's are glimpses of salvation history insofar as they exemplify the recurring pattern of the justification of the ungodly.

11. Cf. Käsemann's concern to oppose 'a conception of salvation history which broke in on us in secularized and political form with the Third Reich and its ideology'. 'Our experience', he writes, 'has made a theology of history suspect for us from the very outset' ('Justification and Salvation History', 64). For an argument that 'salvation history' can be disassociated from a notion of evolutionary development, see D.J. Lull, 'Salvation History: Theology in 1 Thessalonians, Philemon, Philippians, and Galatians: A Response to N.T. Wright, R.B. Hays, and R. Scroggs', in J.M. Bassler (ed.) *Pauline Theology, Volume 1: Thessalonians, Philippians, Galatians, Philemon* (Minneapolis: Fortress Press, 1991) 247–65, 251.

12. There are parallels between the modern debate over the shape of Pauline theology and the older debate (involving especially Bultmann, Cullmann, and Käsemann) concerning *Heilsgeschichte* in Paul (see Hays, *The Faith of Jesus Christ*, 51–63, for an overview). For example, in Bassler (ed.), *Pauline Theology, Volume 1*, J.L. Martyn voices his opposition to the notion of a linear *Heilsgeschichte* in Galatians (see n. 14 below), whereas N.T. Wright, R. Scroggs, R.B. Hays, and D.J. Lull, in different ways, argue for a 'salvation-historical' approach to Paul. Scroggs ('Salvation History: The Theological Structure of Paul's Thought [1 Thessalonians, Philippians, and Galatians]', in Bassler [ed.], *Pauline Theology, Volume 1*, 212–26) makes explicit links between 'salvation history' and the 'now-popular "story theology"' and advances the bold claim that '[t]o rethink Paul's theology within the structure of salvation history does the least violence, I believe, to his own conscious thought processes' (215–16).

extent to which Paul tells a story of God's saving purposes.[12] In addition to his language of demolition and renewal and his conviction that the scriptures remain a divinely given source of instruction (Rom. 15:4), Paul also speaks of the Christ event as the culmination of a story rooted in time. One need not rehearse all that story's elements, from Adam's creation and 'fall', through the promise to Abraham and the coming of the law through Moses, and so on. It is sufficient, I think, to note how hard those who deny this must work (exegetically) to downplay this sense of a story in Paul. Martyn, for example, describes Paul's interpretation of God's promise to Abraham's seed (Gal. 3:16) as being 'as polemically *punctiliar* as it is polemically *singular*. . . . The distinction between linear and punctiliar is . . . a distinction drawn by Paul himself. In Gal. 3:16 he denies the Teachers' linear, redemptive-historical picture of a covenantal people, affirming instead the punctiliar portrait of the covenantal person, Christ'.[13] Even Gal. 4:4, Martyn insists, despite its clear setting of the coming of Christ in the context of time (ὅτε δὲ ἦλθεν τὸ πλήρωμα τοῦ χρόνου), does not refer 'to a point that lies at the end of a line'. On the contrary, 'Paul does not think of a gradual maturation, but rather of a punctiliar liberation, enacted by God in his own sovereign time'.[14] As so often tends to happen, however, the alternative Martyn wishes to refute is painted in terms that make it easier to deny. Paul does not have to think of this story as a simple 'line', nor as one that reflects a process of 'gradual maturation', in order to see the coming of Christ as something that is to be comprehended within the context of a history of God's dealings with Israel and the world, a history in which (viewed from the perspective of the Christ event) there are some moments, some points, of especial significance, as in the announcement of the promise of blessing to Abraham's seed (cf. Gen. 12:3; 13:15; 17:8–9). This story is not simply linear or steadily progressive: it is punctuated by key moments of which the coming of Christ is *the* definitive, climactic moment. This shows that the story is in its final chapter, but it is a story nonetheless.

---

13. J.L. Martyn, *Galatians* (AB 33A; New York: Doubleday, 1997) 347–48. Cf. also Martyn, 'Events in Galatia: Modified Covenantal Nomism versus God's Cosmic Invasion of the Cosmos in the Singular Gospel', in Bassler (ed.), *Pauline Theology, Volume 1*, 172–73, for his opposition to 'a *heilsgeschichtlich* reading of Paul'. Galatians lacks the sense of 'pre-Christ linearity necessary to a meaningful use of that term [*Heilsgeschichte*]. In Galatians, Abraham is a distinctly punctiliar figure rather than a linear one. . . . Thus neither history nor story is a word well linked with Paul's portrait of Abraham in Galatians'.

14. Martyn, *Galatians*, 389; cf. also 283. Contrast Hays, who writes in criticism of Bultmann: 'Bultmann also stressed the event-character of God's action in Christ, but he tended to treat the event as punctiliar. My reading of Paul emphasizes that the salvation event has temporal extension and shape; the event of the cross has meaning not as an isolated event but as an event within a story' (*The Faith of Jesus Christ*, 267 n. 1).

In Barclay's case, it is in interpreting Romans 9–11 that the hard exegetical work is done, in order to show that the passage does *not* support the idea of a 'line of continuity', in a remnant chosen by grace, 'maintained through Jewish believers like Paul' (see page 151). In Romans 9–11 'Paul does not', Barclay argues, 'present a continuity that runs from ethnic Israel, through the remnant, to the church, and he is not a representative of God's salvation plan in this sense. The only continuity is that of the gracious action of God' (pages 151–52).[15] Paul's presence in this story is 'not because he is an Israelite. . . . Rather, his presence in this paradoxical history is a sign of the workings of grace, and his story is worth telling as, *and only as*, it exemplifies that mystery' (page 153, my emphasis).

While I find much in Barclay's exegesis here that is compelling, it seems to me that the notion of continuity in the history of the people of Israel is rather too firmly excluded and the significance of Israel downplayed. Barclay rejects the idea that a 'remnant' represents a line of continuity in Israel's story to the present in which Paul stands; this interpretation has a 'fatal flaw' in its 'requirement that the remnant have remained, as it were, steady on their feet, whereas everything in Romans in general, and in Romans 9–11 in particular, shows that all, without exception, have stumbled' (page 151). There are two reasons that I find this less than a 'fatal flaw'. First, Paul's conviction that all are under the power of sin, and correspondingly that salvation is 'always and inevitably effected by the justification of the *ungodly*' (page 151) does not rule out the idea that there has always been a faithful remnant in Israel. This remnant, Paul insists, is precisely chosen by grace (Rom. 11:5) and thus, in Pauline terms, consists of those who recognise that their righteousness comes 'through faith' as undeserved gift from a gracious God and that it is not 'their own righteousness' (Rom. 10:3). Paul does not consider, let alone answer, the question as to whether this implies that they had at some point 'stumbled' in order *then* to be made righteous by God's grace, through faith, any more than he considers whether or not Abraham was at any point ἀσεβής ('ungodly') in order to be justified by 'the one who justifies the ungodly' (Rom. 4:4–5; *pace* Barclay, Paul's statement here is not quite a claim that 'the justification of (even) Abraham and David [is] . . . a justification of the *ungodly*' [page 151]).

This leads to my second point, namely that Paul's various arguments in Romans are not necessarily strictly or fully consistent or coherent with one another but are deployed to prove particular points, crucial at certain stages in

---

15. Contrast B.W. Longenecker ('Different Answers to Different Issues: Israel, the Gentiles and Salvation History in Romans 9–11', *JSNT* 36 [1989]: 95–123), who sees Paul as perceiving 'every stage of salvation history as operating through the agency of the ethnic race of the Jews' (106), though he overstresses the idea of an evolving 'process' of salvation (105).

the overall argument of the letter. The famous passage in 2:13–16, for example, where Paul insists that it is the doers and not the hearers of the law who
will be made righteous, does not sit neatly with Paul's later argument that a
righteous status can only possibly come through faith and not by works. But,
in context, 2:13–16 serves to demonstrate that Jewish possession of the law carries no automatic privilege in terms of righteous status: the argument plays its
part in establishing the equal standing (which then turns out to be an equally
guilty standing) before God of Jew and gentile (3:9–20). Similarly, in Romans
9–11 Paul is concerned to deal with specific questions about Israel and God's
promises to her. He deploys various arguments in his attempts to do this,[16] but
they all serve in different ways to demonstrate the falseness of the suggestion
that God has rejected his people. One argument to refute the suggestion is that
'not all of those from Israel are Israel' (Rom. 9:6), so only some should be reckoned as truly God's children; there is a distinction to be drawn within what
might appear to be Israel (κατὰ σάρκα; cf. 9:3, 5, 8 and 1 Cor. 10:18) since it
is only the children of the promise who are truly Abraham's seed (9:8). The
same story can be told of the generation after Isaac, again on the basis of divine
election rather than merit or deeds, for 'I loved Jacob and hated Esau' (Rom.
9:13, quoting Mal. 1:2–3). To be sure, as Barclay stresses, this is a story of
divine election and grace, but it is one in which Paul never loses sight of the
fact that this is also a story of Israel and of the continued existence within Israel
of a true Israel, or a remnant, chosen by grace, who serve as the demonstration of the truth that God has not rejected his people, has not forgotten his
irrevocable gifts and calling. At no point, despite what might seem appearances
to the contrary, would it be true to say that God had abandoned his people.

So Paul's own membership of this chosen people is not relevant *only* as an
instance of the working of divine grace. It is profoundly important that he is
an Israelite because it is precisely on this basis that he can count as a witness
to the fact that God has not rejected his people (Rom. 11:1). The story of Elijah's plea and God's response is relevant because it too demonstrates that at a
time when it seemed that Israel was entirely lost there was a faithful remnant.
This remnant was, of course, chosen by grace (11:5), since, according to Paul,
that is always the way God works, but there is no implication here that this
remnant was comprised of people who had stumbled but then been restored
by God's grace, any more than Rom. 4:4–5 implies that Abraham was ἀσεβής
before he was reckoned as righteous. Indeed, the citation from 1 Kings 19:18
refers to those who have not turned to worship Baal but have remained faithful. The point of the argument here is to establish that at other times too, just

---

16. Cf. Longenecker, 'Different Answers', 95, 112–13 with n. 73.

as now when Paul writes, when it might have seemed otherwise, God has always kept a remnant of his people, a point that is crucial to demonstrating that God has indeed never rejected them and broken his promises.

In the olive tree analogy too, whatever Paul takes to be the 'root' (cf. Barclay, page 152), it is clear that this is more than an illustration of the faithfulness of God and the constancy of God's grace and word. It is also an analogy that reflects the centrality of Israel in the story of God's saving purposes. The Israelites are *by nature* (κατὰ φύσιν) part of the tree—it is *their own tree* (τῇ ἰδίᾳ ἐλαίᾳ, 11:24)—whereas gentiles are not; they are grafted in 'contrary to nature' (παρὰ φύσιν, 11:24). Though the mysterious workings of God's grace have led to the inclusion of gentiles as well as Jews, and though salvation is available through faith to all without distinction (cf. 11:20, 23; also 3:22; 10:12), God's gifts and calling belong to Israel in a way that cannot be said of the gentiles (11:25-29).

## PAUL'S STORY AND THE STORY OF CHRIST

None of the above should be taken to imply that I disagree with Barclay on one of his central arguments: that Paul's sense of identity, his worldview, and so on, are radically reconstructed following his encounter with Christ, and that Paul's story is only of real significance 'insofar as it is moulded by the story of the crucified Christ' (see page 146; cf. pages 155–56). It is the paradigm of self-giving seen in Christ's death, and the hope embodied in Christ's resurrection, that gives Paul the new and defining pattern with which to (re)shape his personal story (2 Corinthians could, of course, provide further examples of this: e.g., 6:4–10; 12:6–10). This paradigm of self-giving also provides a fundamental motivation and pattern for Pauline ethics (Rom. 15:2–3; Gal. 6:2; also 2 Cor. 8:9; Phil. 2:4–13).[17] Paul's conviction that his own experiences and practices embody the christological pattern explains his readiness to offer himself as a pattern for imitation, indirectly an imitation of Christ (1 Cor. 4:16; 11:1; 1 Thess. 1:6). Thus Paul's own 'story' and his ethics are linked through their dependence on this central 'paradigm pattern'.

But does this conclusion mean that the partial 'stories' narrated in the Pauline letters, not least the story of Paul himself, have at their foundation not an underlying '*narrative* substructure' (so Hays) but a 'paradigm pattern', a

---

17. See further D.G. Horrell, 'Restructuring Human Relationships: Paul's Corinthian Letters and Habermas's Discourse Ethics', *ExpTim* 110 (1999): 323–25; S.E. Fowl, *The Story of Christ in the Ethics of Paul* (JSNTSup 36; Sheffield: JSOT Press, 1990).

punctiliar christological moment in which God's action shatters all previous stories and paradigms (so Martyn and Barclay)? It seems to me, siding more with Hays, that one can place due weight on the centrality and newness of the Christ event in Paul's thought, not least in determining the shape that Paul gives to his own personal story, without denying that this event is rooted in, and gains its meaning from, a temporal narrative.[18] Barclay, I think, is somewhat ambivalent on this point, for reasons outlined earlier, and does not really offer reflections on whether the *category* of story is valuable or not. This is perhaps in part a consequence of the focus on the story of Paul himself: Paul occasionally and for various reasons narrates certain aspects of his personal story, but these in themselves are not *the* story that engenders and structures Paul's discourse.[19] Barclay rightly insists that Paul's own story is significant only insofar as it serves as an example of a life stamped by the pattern of Christ's cross and resurrection. I differ from Barclay here only in wanting to stress that this paradigm pattern has its own narrative structure and context. I would also suggest that investigating 'the story of Paul', or any other 'smaller' story thought to be part of the wider theological story, is in fact rather unhelpful *as a way of investigating this broader narrative structure*.[20] For while Paul tells us bits of his

---

18. Barclay is clearly concerned to oppose the idea that Paul presumes an 'essentially Jewish story' to which Christ adds a final, if surprising, chapter, a notion that the formulation above could be taken to support. Discussion at the corporate consultation seemed to me to demonstrate the importance of distinguishing two different senses in which the gospel story has a beginning. Arranged chronologically, its beginning is the creation, Adam, and so on; in this sense the coming of Christ is a subsequent event within this temporal narrative. But we need also to make clear, as I failed to do above, that the Christ event is the 'determinative centre' (to use Andrew Lincoln's phrase), the generative beginning, of the story as Paul now perceives it. As John Barclay rightly pointed out to me, the Christ event *gives* meaning to the temporal narrative in which Paul places it, as much, or more, than it gains meaning from it. We can perhaps say that the Christ event (as generative beginning) gives meaning to a temporal narrative of God's creative and saving purposes, and then, seen within it, gains meaning from that narrative.

19. *Pace* Wright (*The New Testament and the People of God*, 404), who suggests that we could 'construct from the Pauline corpus a narrative world of Paul's own life and experience'. This 'personal narrative world', 'we may safely say, was the narrative world upon which Paul drew to make sense of his day-to-day experience'. We might rather say that it is the story of Christ, as interpreted by Paul, on which Paul draws to make sense of his experience.

20. It seemed to me to emerge from a number of essays in this book, and during discussion at the corporate consultation, that the stories of God, creation, Israel, etc., are not meaningfully separable, since they can only be understood, in Paul, as part of the story of God's saving purposes in Christ. It is a moot point, perhaps, whether Paul's story (and that of other 'inheritors'—see Lincoln's essay) is to be seen as part of that ongoing gospel narrative, or as a testimony, an exemplar of the gospel's transforming power.

personal story, for specific reasons, this personal story is *not* itself a part of the underlying narrative.[21] Rather, the fundamental story of God's gracious dealings with humanity reach their zenith in the Christ event, itself the generative centre of this story, which *then* provides the paradigmatic story with which Paul shapes his telling of any other stories, including those about himself.

## WHY NARRATIVE?

If there is a narrative substructure to Pauline thought, what is the value in identifying it? What is gained by a narrative approach? Let me begin with a caveat. It seems that the approach is attractive, at least for some, because it appears to offer a route to discerning theological coherence in Paul, despite the obvious diversity of his letters. But since we do not have a Pauline narration of the underlying story, we cannot presume that this story is an entirely stable entity for Paul. The way he construes it may vary over time and circumstance; so just as the letters vary, so, to some degree, may the underlying story Paul reflects in his discourse (cf. the essays by Adams and Longenecker in this volume). A narrative approach to Paul, then, is no easy route to recovering coherence in Pauline thought.

To some extent, the rise of narrative approaches brings scholarship full circle. In the wake of the Enlightenment, some have viewed story, or myth, as a precritical, unscientific mode of thought that can be superceded by an approach that draws out principles or ideas in their own right. The narrative framework is a mythological husk that can (and must) be discarded. Bultmann's programme for the demythologisation of the New Testament's message is a clear example of such an approach.[22] But the critique of foundationalism, and specifically of the idea that there can be tradition-independent statements of rational or universal principles, has been part of the wider intellectual scene within which narrative has been rediscovered. Now, in the context of postmodernity, it is frequently asserted that every mode of thought is essentially a narrative, a particular story about the way the world is.[23] John Milbank, for

---

21. It may be more legitimate to refer to 'subplots' that 'derive their sense and significance from their participation in the larger narrative in which Jesus Christ is the protagonist' (R.B. Hays, 'Crucified with Christ: A Synthesis of the Theology of 1 and 2 Thessalonians, Philemon, Philippians, and Galatians', in Bassler [ed.], *Pauline Theology, Volume 1*, 227–46, 234).

22. See R. Bultmann, *New Testament and Mythology and Other Basic Writings*, ed. and trans. S.M. Ogden (London: SCM Press, 1985) 1–43; Hays, *The Faith of Jesus Christ*, 51–55.

23. For a clear introduction to this postmodern context and the place of story within it, see G. Loughlin, *Telling God's Story: Bible, Church and Narrative Theology* (Cambridge: Cambridge University Press, 1996) 3–26.

example, sees capitalism, Marxism, and so on, as competing narratives seeking to outnarrate one another. Christianity, likewise, is a competing narrative that can be convincing insofar as it can '*persuade* people—for reasons of "literary taste"—that [it] offers a much better story'.[24] Stanley Hauerwas similarly stresses the importance of story in forming identity, community, character, and conduct.[25] Hauerwas sees the Christian tradition as essentially story based and in conflict with the 'liberalism' of the West that promotes its own particular story about the world: 'The story that liberalism teaches us is that we have no story, and as a result we fail to notice how deeply that story determines our lives'.[26]

It is in this wider intellectual context that I think the narrative approach to Paul should be located. Hays argues against this, though in a somewhat self-contradictory passage. He writes,

> I am making no sweeping claims about the narrative structure of human consciousness in general, nor am I arguing that we all live 'within stories.' Indeed, the point of my thesis is precisely that Paul's thinking is shaped by a story in a way that not all thinking is. If all discourse were rooted in story, it would be rather pointless to single Paul out as an instance of this universal truth.[27]

The inner contradiction here is, of course, that while the first sentence denies any attempt to make sweeping claims, the second constitutes precisely a sweeping claim, albeit one phrased in a negative way, that some modes of thought are not story shaped. Hays is of course right that not all discourse is of a kind susceptible to the literary analysis that can reveal its narrative substructure.[28] But the particular kind of analysis appropriate to discern the narrative substructure of Pauline texts can nonetheless valuably be located within the context of a broader conviction about the ubiquity of 'story'. This conviction may make it less significant to identify Paul as a writer whose thought has a narrative basis, but it does not render investigation of that narrative basis 'pointless'; in fact, it is quite the opposite.

If it is true, as some recent writers imply, that all convictions about the world

---

24. J. Milbank, *Theology and Social Theory* (Oxford: Blackwell, 1990) 330.

25. See S. Hauerwas, *A Community of Character: Toward a Constructive Christian Social Ethic* (Notre Dame, Ind.: University of Notre Dame Press, 1981) 9–35, where Hauerwas uses the novel *Watership Down* to illustrate the importance of narrative in forming and sustaining community.

26. Hauerwas, *Community of Character*, 84.

27. Hays, *The Faith of Jesus Christ*, 19.

28. Cf. the outline of Hays' Greimasian method in *The Faith of Jesus Christ*, 94–103; also Wright, *The New Testament and the People of God*, 69–77.

derive from some kind of story or tradition, recounted in a community and reflected in that community's practices, then exploring the narrative substructure of Pauline thought is important in various ways. First, in opposition to a certain kind of cerebral Christianity, it shows that Pauline thought cannot be conveyed as a series of propositions to be believed but only as a story that is 'lived', retold, and embodied in the practices of the community that celebrates that story.[29] Second, it shows that Pauline ethics, and Christian ethics more generally, is not a set of principles or judgements on issues, such as could easily be abstracted from the story and its community and recommended or implemented in wider public policy. Rather, Pauline ethics is firmly grounded in a character-forming narrative that has its essential basis in the Christian community and its corporate life.[30] Third, if other modes of thought are also deemed to have an essentially narrative, tradition-dependent basis, this implies that they too will be linked with specific communities and modes of practice, though this may be obscured or denied when those communities see themselves only as engaged in a search for rational truths, such as in the case of science perhaps. It also implies that such narratives may shape identity, values, and practice, even if they claim only to relate to a specific 'area' of life. Moreover, if all modes of thought are regarded as story based, then Paul's story is competing on a somewhat more level playing field than might have once been thought. Instead of a mythological, ancient story being contrasted with the rational truths of science or economics, we see instead—if we follow Milbank and others—competing narratives about the world. We may then ask about how Paul's story and these other stories construct a sense of human identity and shape human interaction. Capitalism's increasingly globalised story, for example, describes human beings as customers and producers and increasingly narrates their interactions in market terms (whether in hospitals, universities, or wherever); it has a very particular understanding of 'freedom'. Exploring and narrating the Pauline story can be a means to articulate a counternarrative, a challenge to this (and other) dominant narratives, a means to envisage human communities in which a different story constructs a different sense of identity and undergirds different patterns of community practice. Far from stories' ubiquity rendering such articulation pointless, I would argue that, in a world conscious of the power of stories to form identity, values, and practice, the rediscovery of Paul's gospel story *as story* is of critical value.

To return finally to Barclay's essay, it seems to me that by too closely following Martyn's emphasis on the punctiliar nature of the Christ event and the

---

29. Cf. Loughlin, *Telling God's Story.*

30. Here there are of course echoes of Hauerwas' approach to Christian ethics. See, e.g., Hauerwas, *Community of Character.*

new epistemology that results, Barclay underplays the sense of a story of salvation underpinning Pauline theology and underemphasises the extent to which Paul's 'new' Christian theology is constructed with the materials of the 'old'. Nevertheless, by convincingly showing how Paul's sense of self is moulded, reshaped, by the story of Christ, Barclay illustrates precisely this power of stories to form identity. And, for Paul, the gospel story—a story that reaches back to Adam—so completely defines his life that he is now dead to any other sphere of influence (Gal. 6:14). The story that matters is not that of Paul but the identity-defining story of Christ, the story of the gospel.[31]

31. I am very grateful to Mark Wynn for discussing this essay with me, and to John Barclay for illuminating correspondence and discussion.

# 10

# The Stories of Predecessors and Inheritors in Galatians and Romans

> Letters, Roland discovered, are a form of narrative that envisages
> no outcome, no closure. His time was a time of the dominance of
> narrative theories. Letters tell no story, because they do not know,
> from line to line, where they are going.[1]

These first impressions of A.S. Byatt's protagonist, a literary researcher, on discovering a previously unknown cache of letters from the subject of his research, Victorian poet Randolph Henry Ash, to another poet, Christabel LaMotte, turn out to be highly ironic. The letters in fact have an implied story line that helps to drive the complex and fascinating narrative of Byatt's prize-winning novel, *Possession*, and embraces not only Ash and LaMotte in the nineteenth century but also the letter's would-be possessors, particularly Roland and Maud, literary critics in the late twentieth century.[2] What, then, of Paul's letters read in a time of the popularity of narrative theories? Do these particular letters envisage any outcome or closure? Do they, too, despite first impressions produced by their epistolary form, turn out to be part of a larger story? And if so, whose story? That of Paul and the intended recipients? Or does their story also embrace that of later readers? Do Paul's letters suggest that they may be part of an even larger story

---

1. A.S. Byatt, *Possession* (London: Chatto & Windus, 1990) 130–31.
2. Byatt's work also provides an apt reminder that to talk of narrative is by no means necessarily to talk of a simple, single story line. Narratives can have large overall plots combined with complex subplots, reversals, and overlapping time perspectives in which past events become present events, all of which draw readers into their stories in a variety of ways.

that has far-reaching claims and that is the possession neither of their original author and addressees nor of later communities of readers?

The task of this essay in relation to such larger questions is to explore a reading of Galatians and Romans in terms of the stories of Paul's predecessors and his inheritors in the Christian faith. Its focus will not first of all be on Paul's *theology* and its narrative logic but on the implied narrative world of the two *letters*. Paul's letters reflect a symbolic universe that has narrative qualities. In theory, one should begin by reconstructing that universe and then locate the predecessors and inheritors within it, relating them in narrative terms to one another and to other more significant figures. Although this view provides the underlying premise of the essay, considerations of length mean that such preliminary groundwork, which would still produce debate about the number of different story lines involved, has had to give way to a more pragmatic approach. For the sake of the assignment we have chosen simply to accept initially the category of 'story' as a heuristic device for interpreting the material about the figures and groups to be highlighted. This will allow readers to make their own judgement whether the predecessors or inheritors have their own story lines and whether any illumination is provided by such a treatment. The writer will then offer his own evaluation of this exercise.[3]

Who are meant by predecessors in and inheritors of the Pauline gospel in the narrative world implied by the letters? There are a number of possible candidates for predecessors in the faith. Peter, Barnabas, the Jerusalem and Antioch churches, all mentioned in Galatians 2, could well be singled out. To make this particular aspect of the project manageable, however, predecessors will be limited to those treated in both letters and will therefore consist of the Jerusalem church and Abraham. The inclusion of Abraham as a predecessor, though at first sight an odd companion for the Jerusalem church, should on further reflection need no justification. As will be seen, he is not simply a figure in a past story of Israel. Instead, one of the striking features of both letters is Paul's treatment of Abraham as part of a continuing story in which he possesses the essential elements of Christian faith ahead of time and therefore is 'the ancestor of all who believe' (Rom. 4:11 NRSV).[4]

The inheritors of Paul's gospel in the two letters will be seen as those Paul addresses with its claims.[5] These addressees are expected to inherit, in the

---

3. Readers should be warned that the decision to proceed in this fashion means that some of the writer's early formulations, particularly those about Abraham, will need to be revised or discarded in the light of the later reflections!

4. Citations of scripture texts not designated 'NRSV' are the writer's own translation.

5. J.D.G. Dunn (*The Theology of Paul the Apostle* [Grand Rapids: Eerdmans, 1998] 18) speaks of 'the complex interactions of Paul's own story with the stories of those who had believed before him and of those who came to form the churches founded by them'. The churches founded by those who believed before Paul would presumably include the Christian groups in Rome. In this essay, however, the Roman believers addressed by Paul will not be linked with his predecessors but viewed as among his inheritors. Dunn's description at this point appears to derive from a more historical than literary approach.

sense of receive and appropriate, not only the stories of Abraham and the Jerusalem church but also the larger overarching story encompassing these stories and those of God, Israel, Christ, and Paul himself. For the purposes of reconstructing their stories, the inheritors will be treated as the implied readers of Galatians and Romans. Their stories will be discussed first, not only because they are the first of the three to surface in the letters but also because the stories of predecessors are told for the sake of the inheritors.[6] Rather than discussing Galatians and Romans entirely separately, the inheritors and the predecessors in each case will be treated together in order to facilitate a comparison between the different versions of their 'stories'.[7]

## THE STORIES OF THE READERS

### Galatians

The story of those to whom Paul writes in 'the churches of Galatia' (1:2) is one that had begun promisingly enough ('You were running well', 5:7 NRSV). They had had a pagan past in which they did not know God and instead were enslaved to beings that by nature are not gods (4:8). But all that had been turned around as they had come to know God or rather to be known by God (4:9). In fact, they had been called by God in the grace of Christ (1:6). This decisive event had occurred when Paul had graphically proclaimed the gospel to them (1:8; 3:1). They had received the gospel (1:9), that is, they had believed what they heard (3:2, 5). As a result they had also had the experience of receiving the Spirit and of God's working miracles among them (3:4–5; cf. also 4:6). What is more, when they had received Paul's gospel, they had also received Paul himself. This had happened under far from favorable circumstances. Paul had not been at his best or most attractive in their initial encounter with him. He had in fact ended up in Galatia as a result of a debilitating physical affliction, caused either by illness or by persecution. Although the readers might

---

6. Because of our attention to the world implied by the letters, we shall use the term 'readers' in speaking of this group. From a historical perspective, of course, for most of them 'hearers' would be a more accurate term to describe the nature of their exposure to the letters.

7. Galatians does not treat the rival missionaries who are mentioned either as predecessors, since they are purveyors of a different gospel (cf. 1:6–8), or as inheritors, since it does not address them directly. Their distinct story will only be registered here as it impinges on the other stories. It should also be noted that there is a group of opponents mentioned in Romans with a much more minor role at the margins of the letter (cf. 16:17–18).

well have had good reason to scorn or despise him, their welcome and hospitality had been generous in the extreme. From Paul's perspective the blessing they pronounced on him then was simply evidence of the fact that they would have done anything for him—they would, proverbially, have torn their eyes out and given them to him (4:12b–15). In short, in their response to Paul they had shown all the signs of a life transformed by the gospel.

But the present aspect of the readers' story is in stark contrast to this brightest of starts in the Christian faith and had come about astonishingly quickly (1:6). Some people, to whom Paul imputes the motive of perverting the gospel, are upsetting and disturbing the Galatian believers by their teaching (1:7; cf. 5:10, 12). They want the gentile Galatians to be circumcized as part of the requirement to observe Torah (6:12–13). Indeed, in line with this teaching, some of the readers are already observing the Jewish liturgical calendar (4:10). They have been persuaded that, in addition to believing in Christ, they need to keep the Jewish law, whether or not they would have accepted Paul's interpretation of their new view as desiring to be 'under the law' (4:21) or 'justified by the law' (5:4 NRSV). Not surprisingly, this new persuasion has also entailed a different attitude toward Paul. Under the courtship of the new missionaries, a certain alienation toward their founder has set in (4:16–20). They are now inclined to perceive the absent apostle as having imparted to them a deficient message, one that he had trimmed of more difficult requirements in order to please people and gain converts (cf. 1:10), one that was out of line with the teaching of the Jerusalem church and its leading apostles (cf. 1:13–2:21), and one that elsewhere he was perfectly willing to change by actually advocating circumcision (cf. 5:11).

Where the story of the Galatian readers will lead from here is on one level entirely dependent on their response to this letter and on whether they will be persuaded to accept Paul's analysis of their present situation as one of dire danger. Put another way, the issue is whether they will be prepared to reconfigure their story in the light of the overarching story of the gospel on which Paul's attempt to persuade them draws. Seen in that light, their attraction to the teaching of the other missionaries has set them on the path of deserting the one who initiated the whole story, the God who has called them in the grace of Christ, and of turning to a different gospel with a significantly different implied overall story line (1:6). They were committing the folly of thinking that their own story, which had made a decisive new start with the Spirit, needed the flesh (and an emphasis on the removal of the foreskin) to complete it (3:3). They had started on the right track but had allowed the other teachers (with their message about cutting off the foreskin) to cut in on them and divert them from the goal of obedience to the truth (5:7). To continue on this diversion would be to take themselves away from Christ and to plunge out of the sphere of grace (5:4). What is more, the reversal of their story will be complete as they end up back again in the same situation as their pagan past—under the elemental spirits and their enslaving hold (4:9). So the decisions they make about this letter are fraught with ultimate consequences. On another level, however, what is finally decisive for their story will be neither Paul's persuasion (cf. 1:10) nor their own ability to judge its validity and to reshape their own story but rather the continuing activity, through the grace and power of the gospel, of the God who called them into a new creation.

The letter's rhetoric nevertheless attempts to urge them on in the right direction. While 'you foolish Galatians' (3:1) underlines the incongruity of what they are considering, the repetition of 'brothers and sisters' (1:11; 3:15; 4:12, 28; 5:11, 13; 6:1, 18 NRSV) and the designation, 'my little children' (4:19 NRSV), reinforce the confidence expressed that they will come to their senses and not think otherwise than Paul does on these crucial matters (5:10). More specifically, the future he envisages for their story will mean that the Galatians embrace the freedom Christ has secured for them in such a way that male gentile believers do not allow themselves to be circumcised (5:1–3), that they appropriate the life of the Spirit in such a way that the notion that the law is needed to deal with the evil desires of the flesh becomes entirely superfluous (5:16–26), and that they dismiss from their assemblies the rival teachers: 'Drive out the slave and her child' (4:30 NRSV). If the letter becomes the catalyst for this sort of future story, then the readers, in repeating its final 'amen' authentically (6:18), will not find themselves entangled in the law's curse (3:10) but will be among those who experience this letter's blessing of peace and mercy on the Israel of God (6:16). Their story will then play its part in the larger story suggested by this letter, as they cooperate in the drama of deliverance from this present evil age and its onward movement to the completion of a new creation and to its hope of righteousness (cf. 1:4; 6:15; 5:5–6; cf. also 3:28).

## Romans

The implied readers of Romans did not owe their coming to faith to Paul's gentile mission (cf. 1:10–13). They would, however, have been reminded by his list of greetings in 16:3–15 that, although he had not been to Rome, he knew a considerable number of their leaders from elsewhere and that these kept in communication with the controversial figure whom they recognized as the apostle to the gentiles. They would no doubt also have been gratified to learn that, despite his lengthy rehearsal of key features of his own gospel message, Paul cast no aspersions on their past Christian experience but rather respected the foundations that had been laid by those who introduced the gospel to Rome (15:20), was thankful to God for their faith (1:8) and their obedience to the teaching they had received (6:17), expressed confidence in their virtue and understanding (15:14), and treated them as in solidarity with his mission and message (1:12; 15:24, 30–32).

At the time of the receipt of Paul's letter, the Roman Christians were meeting in a variety of house churches (cf. 16:5, 14, 15, and possibly 16:10–11). Gentile Christians constituted the substantial majority of their number (cf. 1:5–6, 13; 15:15–16), but there were also some Jewish Christians among them, including some of the leaders known to Paul, who were likely to have been in agreement with the Jewish Christian apostle's views on the implications of his law-free gospel for gentiles (cf. 16:3, 7). Some among the Jewish Christian minority, however, insisted on maintaining, as part of their obedience to God, the observance of food laws, sabbaths, and festivals (cf. 14:2, 5–6). The differences were producing strong tensions. These were not helped by the practice of those who saw no continuing necessity for observance of cultic aspects of Torah and were predominantly gentile Christians styling themselves 'the strong in faith' and labelling the predominantly Jewish Christian others 'the weak in faith' (cf. 14:1–2; 15:1 NRSV).[8] It was not simply that there were theological differences about the role of the law. The attitudes that accompanied these differences were proving the real threat to harmony. There were continuing disputes, in which the gentile Christians stressed their faith and the freedom it engendered, despised those who did not share their stance about the abrogation of the law, and, in the case of some, were arrogant enough to think that God's purposes for ethnic Israel as a whole were also at an end (cf. esp. 11:20, 25). The Jewish Christian minority condemned the 'strong' for what they viewed as the latter's moral laxity, and the disputes may well have heightened the suspicions some of them already entertained about Paul and his law-free gospel.

The letter that circulated among them indicates that the future aspect of the story of these Roman believers is to a large extent dependent on whether they agree to become part of Paul's story. A number of questions confront them: Having heard the rehearsal of the gospel he proclaims, are they convinced that they are among those for whom Paul claims to have received apostolic responsibility (1:5–6, 14–15)? Will they welcome him, have fellowship in the gospel with him, and support him on his projected mission to Spain when he arrives on the visit he has promised (1:10–13; 15:22–24, 32)? In the meantime, will they pray for his more immediate visit to the Jerusalem church (15:30–31) and respond positively to his exhortations designed to ensure that

---

8. The gentile/Jew categories in 15:7–13, which constitutes the climax of the exhortations to the two groups, provide strong support for this interpretation of their ethnic makeup.

they are not only known for their emphasis on faith but also for the obedience that accompanies faith (1:5, 8; 6:16–18; 15:18)? In particular, on the basis of the gospel that is for 'everyone who has faith, to the Jew first and also to the Greek' (1:16b NRSV) but in which Jew and gentile are also one and equal, will they cease their quarrelling, welcome one another, and live in harmony (14:1–15:13), so that when Paul comes to Rome he will find Christians united in their glorifying of God and united in their support for his mission to Spain? Again, as we saw in the case of the Galatians, the answers to these questions about their future do not lie simply in the hands of the Roman readers. In Paul's view, they are also ultimately tied up with the power of God at work in his gospel (1:4, 16), a power that is able to bring life out of death (4:17–25) and harmony, joy, and peace out of dissension and quarrelling (15:5–6, 13).

## Comparison

The future of both groups of readers will depend on how far their values and actions are shaped by the gospel mediated to them through Paul's story. An important difference in the past aspect of their stories is that the Galatians were introduced to the gospel by Paul himself while the Romans' reception of the gospel had been independent of the Pauline mission. The clearest difference between their stories, however, lies in the present stage reflected in the letters, where that of the Galatians is more fraught with peril. In their case there is the real danger that some of them will actually abandon the Pauline gospel. In the case of the Roman readers what is at stake is the implications of their adherence to the gospel for issues of unity—primarily between gentile Christians and Jewish Christians. This points to another significant variant. The role of Jewish Christians, though they were in a minority, is explicitly in view in the latter story. But in Galatians, if there were any Jewish Christians among the readers, they do not figure in Paul's construal of his audience, whose story is that of gentile believers who could well be persuaded that they need circumcision. While Rom. 16:17–20 could be read as an attempt to put the Roman Christians on their guard in the event of the arrival among them of a group similar to the missionaries in Galatia, no explicit connections are made between the stories of the two sets of readers.[9]

---

9. From a historical perspective, however, Romans' treatment of topics common to the two letters in a way that appears to be designed to avoid possible misinterpretation raises the possibility of a link. It may reflect an awareness not only that choice excerpts from the Galatian letter had been communicated to the Jerusalem church by the missionaries, for which its writer would imminently be held to account, but also that conflicting reports about its content had reached Rome and added fuel to the tensions among its readers.

# THE STORIES OF ABRAHAM

## Galatians

Abraham's story enters Paul's argument in Galatians following the rhetorical questions he has posed for his readers in 3:2–5. Did they receive the Spirit, and does God supply the Spirit and work miracles among them by means of 'works of the law' or by means of 'the hearing of faith', that is, the hearing accompanied by faith? Since the answer to this question should be obvious (i.e., the Galatians' experience of the Spirit took place before and independently of any considerations of the need to observe Torah), the reason for enlisting Abraham at this point in order to expand on the notion of believing is not immediately apparent. This observation makes highly plausible the view that this is not the first time the story of Abraham has intruded into the readers' story. In all probability, as part of their teaching, the rival missionaries had made the case that circumcision and other requirements of Torah were necessary if gentile believers were to become full members of God's covenant with Israel, bona fide children of Abraham. After all, they would have claimed, Abraham is the father of proselytes. The covenant initiated with him in Genesis 17 makes clear that he and his male descendants had to undergo circumcision as the sign of this covenant. So, if they wish to become true descendants of Abraham, male Galatian converts should follow suit.

Paul's version of the story of Abraham highlights the themes of believing, blessing, promise, descendants, and inheritance. It immediately intertwines Abraham's story with that of the Galatian believers with its introductory 'just as'. The obvious answer to the rhetorical questions of 3:2–5 is developed not in direct reference to the Galatians' story but in reference to Abraham's story. 'Things were the same with Abraham'.[10] In the words of Gen. 15:6, he 'believed God, and it was reckoned to him as righteousness'. It was not by means of works of the law but simply through trust in the preceding promise about his descendants (cf. Gen. 15:5) that he was credited with a right relationship with God. This speaks to the issues with which the readers have been confronted by the rival missionaries: (1) How does one become a descendant of Abraham? and (2) Who, therefore, are the true descendants of Abraham? The answers are given: (1) by believing what has been heard (3:5–6), and (2) those, therefore, who like Abraham are identified by their trust (3:7).

Such descendants are no longer limited to physical descendants within Israel. Here the narrative point of view is explicitly spelled out. It sees the time

---

10. J.L. Martyn's translation of 3:6a; cf. *Galatians* (New York: Doubleday, 1997) 294, 296.

of Abraham both anticipating and overlapping with the time of the Galatians. Abraham and the Galatians occupy the same positions in a unified narrative because the same gospel that had been preached to the Galatians (cf. 1:8, 11, 16; 4:13) had been declared to Abraham ahead of time. In this retelling of Abraham's story Paul sees his law-free gospel for the gentiles already antici- pated in the earlier promise to Abraham in Gen. 12:3 (conflated with the word- ing of Gen. 18:18) that he now cites: 'All the gentiles shall be blessed in you' (3:8 NRSV). Abraham's story was never meant, then, to be solely a story about and for Israel and those proselytes prepared to take on Israel's distinctive eth- nic identity marker of circumcision. The extent to which the two time per- spectives—that of Abraham and that of the Galatians—is compressed in this retelling is remarkable. Abraham heard God's word but not, of course, its inscripturated form, yet the promise that he received about all nations being blessed in him can now be said to have been preached to him by scripture, which, as a personification, foresaw that God would justify the gentiles by faith (3:8). So the scriptures, in which the original story of Abraham is found and which allow for Paul's creative construal, can be retrojected as a character in the story of Abraham Paul is now telling the Galatians. Scripture, from this narrative point of view, is correlated with Paul's law-free gospel for gentiles, and the latter decisively shapes his rehearsal of Abraham's story. In his version, to be blessed by being in Abraham, incorporated into the patriarch, is to share in the experience of the benefits of the covenant relationship, and since Abra- ham has already been depicted in terms of his trust in the promise, it is those who are identified by their trust who are blessed with 'faithful Abraham'. The latter is not Abraham as faithful in his observance of the commandments or in his obedience to the injunction to circumcize but the believing Abraham of Gen. 15:6.

Throughout Galatians 3–4 Paul's telling of Abraham's story is bound up with his telling of the story of the Mosaic law, and the latter is interpreted by and subordinated to the former. While not ignoring this other story, our atten- tion must remain focussed as clearly as possible on Abraham, and Paul's next explicit move in rehearsing the story of Abraham for his readers is to relate the blessing of Abraham to their experience of the Spirit, which had been the start- ing point of the discussion (3:14). But in order to highlight this blessing, elab- orate on how the readers share in it, and connect it with Christ, he first contrasts it with the law's curse. According to Paul, those who identify them- selves not by trust but by works of the law are subject to the curse of Deut. 27:26, expanded to include anyone who fails to do all that is written in the law (3:10). So justification does not come by the law. Instead, as Hab. 2:4, when read in the light of the gospel, asserts, 'the one who is righteous through faith will live', and this is quite different from the law's tenet in Lev. 18:5 that obtaining life is through doing its commandments (3:11–12). The transfer from an identity based on doing the law and a status of being under the curse to a shared identity and status with Abraham in terms of faith and righteousness has been brought about by Christ. By being crucified and becoming a curse for those under the law, Christ redeemed them from the enslaving power of the law's curse. This redemption opened the way for the blessing promised to Abraham to flow to the gentiles and enabled both Jews and gentiles to experience that promised blessing in the form of the Spirit and through faith (3:13–14). The Galatians' new story, marked so decisively by their experience of the Spirit, is one of having been blessed in Abraham (cf. 'All the gentiles shall be blessed in you', 3:8 NRSV) and has been made possible by what has taken place 'in Christ Jesus' (3:14 NRSV).

This vital link through Christ is underlined in 3:15–29, where the Abrahamic covenant of promise is played off against the later provision of the law. Here Paul claims that the latter cannot annul the former and was a temporary measure designed for very different purposes than the covenant of promise. For Paul a major indication that the promise to Abraham was not annulled can be seen in the fact that it was made to both Abraham and his offspring, and his offspring par excellence is Christ. Through the highlighting of the singular form of the noun 'seed' (3:16), Paul's christological point of view in telling the story becomes explicit. His later usage of the same singular term with a plural sense (cf. 3:29) means that he is well aware of its usual connotations. Nevertheless, in keeping with the Jewish exegesis of his day that could find meaning in minor details of a formulation, he seizes on the significance of the singular at this point. Viewing Abraham's heir as Christ underscores that it is the relation to Christ and not submission to circumcision that determines qualification as Abraham's offspring. This is driven home at the end of the section, after Paul has put the law in its place: 'And if you belong to Christ, then you are Abraham's offspring' (3:29 NRSV). So Christ is seen as the singular fulfilment of the promise of descendants to Abraham while preserving that promise's corporate overtones, because he is also a representative figure in whom all who believe are incorporated (3:26–28). The way has already been prepared for a return to the notion of Abraham's offspring in 3:29 through the assertion that in Christ believers are 'sons of God' (3:26), a more comprehensive designation for God's people and one previously seen as Israel's exclusive prerogative (cf. Exod. 4:22–23; Deut. 14:1–2; Hos. 11:1). Whether the readers are viewed as children of God or children of Abraham, this identity has been achieved in Christ and cannot possibly require completion.

Another important strand of the Abraham story is introduced explicitly in 3:15–29 and continues into 4:1–7 (cf. also 4:30; 5:21), even though the name of Abraham does not appear in the latter pericope. Abraham had been promised not only descendants or heirs but also an inheritance of which they would be the beneficiaries, namely, the land of Canaan. In Paul's retelling, Abraham's heirs are Christ and those who are incorporated into him through faith, and Abraham's inheritance is the Spirit. What was promised is referred to first as the blessing or benefit (3:14) but then, in the assertion that God's gracious disposal comes through the Abrahamic promise and not from the law, it becomes designated as the inheritance (3:18). It is natural, then, that, when Paul concludes in 3:29 that the Galatian believers are already Abraham's offspring, he should add that they are also 'heirs according to the promise'. Just as earlier he had elaborated on their blessing as Abraham's offspring in terms of the work of Christ and their experience of the Spirit, so now in 4:1–7 he explains their status as heirs in a similar fashion. In contrast to full heirs, minors (Jews) are no better off than slaves (gentiles, cf. 4:7–8) in regard to actual possession of the inheritance. What was needed to bring the situation of minority and enslavement to an end was the sending of God's Son to be born under the law in order to redeem those under the law (cf. also 3:13) and in order that both Jews and gentiles could receive adoption as sons (4:4–5). The confirmation that the Galatian readers are the sort of sons (and daughters) who are full heirs already experiencing the inheritance is that God has sent the Spirit of *the* Son into their hearts (4:6–7). Through the mention of the readers' experience of the Spirit, the story of Abraham and his descendants is reconnected to its starting point in 3:2–5. Here that experience is specified in terms of the indwelling and empowering Spirit crying out to the Father through the Galatian believers in the distinctive form of address used by the Son. Those who were previously in slavery are already Abraham's heirs by having been adopted into God's family and, because of Christ and the Spirit who were sent to bring about that status, they can be said to be heirs through God.

Since the story of Abraham in Galatians pivots on the relation between the patriarch and his offspring, Paul's turning to an allegory about Abraham's sons in 4:21–5:1 is an integral part of that story. We shall pass over the allegorical details about Hagar and Sarah in order to concentrate on Abraham's sons.[11] The earlier motifs of promise, slavery, the Spirit, and inheritance all play a role in this final twist to the story, which begins with Paul's reminder that scripture speaks of Abraham having two sons and therefore two quite different lines of descent. One, who is not named but is clearly Ishmael, was born of a slave woman and 'according to the flesh', while the other, Isaac (cf. 4:28), was born of a free woman and 'through the promise' (4:22–23). The evaluative point of view is already clear in these descriptions. Abraham's son through Hagar is

---

11. For an earlier fuller treatment of this passage, see A.T. Lincoln, *Paradise Now and Not Yet* (Cambridge: Cambridge University Press, 1981) 9–26.

associated with slavery, the situation of Jews and gentiles before faith in Christ (4:1, 3, 8–9; cf. also 2:4), and with the flesh, the negative sphere contrasted with the Spirit in Paul's earlier question designed to expose his readers' folly (3:3). By contrast, Abraham's son through Sarah is associated with freedom, the liberation from slavery brought about through Christ (1:4; 2:4), the situation of those who are no longer slaves but sons and heirs (4:7). This son is associated with the promise, God's original promise to Abraham about offspring that has been fulfilled in Christ and those who are in Christ by faith (3:16–18, 29). The characterization is clearly intended to enable the Galatian readers to find themselves in this story as the children or products of a gospel in which promise and Spirit are at work rather than as products of another gospel in which the flesh is to the fore in a way that leads to enslavement.

The notion that gentile converts were to align themselves with Abrahamic descent through Isaac and to associate the Jewish Christian missionaries who insisted on observance of the Mosaic law with Abrahamic descent through Ishmael was likely to have been outrageously counterintuitive. Paul thus has to spell out that this is precisely how he wishes his storytelling to be interpreted. In 4:24–27 he insists that scripture is indeed speaking with another meaning, or allegorically.[12] On the one side, Hagar is to be aligned with the Sinai covenant and with the present Jerusalem, both of which are characterized by slavery; on the other side, Sarah is aligned with another covenant (presumably the Abrahamic covenant of promise now fulfilled in Christ) and with the Jerusalem above, the symbol of the salvation of the age to come, with its freedom and life that can be experienced now by faith.

Having set the framework for its meaning, Paul can now return to his main thread and make explicit the parallels between the story of Abraham's sons and the story of the Galatians. The Galatians are to identify themselves as children of the promise in line with Isaac (4:28). But there is another identification to be made. In dependence on a Jewish exegetical tradition of Gen. 21:9 that sees Ishmael as harassing and mocking Isaac,[13] Paul talks of the child born according to the flesh persecuting the child born according to the Spirit and claims that the same holds in the present situation. In the Galatians' story, what matches this persecution is, from Paul's perspective, the impact of the missionaries who are teaching the necessity of Torah observance. Their activity is described as confusing and unsettling to the Galatians (5:10, 12), who are being compelled to be circumcised (6:12). Yet this story is inviting the readers

---

12. As S.E. Fowl points out (*Engaging Scripture* [Oxford: Blackwell, 1998] 133), the use of this term 'does not signify a radical departure from Paul's previous pattern of interpretation'. Throughout Galatians 3–4 the pattern is 'counter-conventional'.

13. Cf. e.g., *Tg. Ps.-J.* Gen. 21.10; *Gen. Rab.* 53.11.

not simply to make identifications but also to act out the consequences of such identifications. After the reference to Ishmael's harassment of Isaac, the next words, from Gen. 21:10, are Sarah's instructions to Abraham. These now become scripture's command to the readers: 'Drive out the slave and her child; for the child of the slave will not share the inheritance with the child of the free woman' (4:30 NRSV). The rehearsal of the story of Abraham's sons has been heading to this point from its start: 'Tell me, you who desire to be subject to the law, will you not listen to the law?' (4:21 NRSV). This section draws its readers into its distinctive adaptation of the Genesis narrative in order that they might then be directly addressed by that narrative's discourse. They are to take measures designed to ensure that the missionaries and their enslaving influence no longer jeopardize their experience as heirs of the Abrahamic promise. This is confirmed by the summarizing exhortation in 5:1 NRSV: 'Stand firm, therefore, and do not submit again to a yoke of slavery.'

The impact of the readers' story on this retelling of the Abraham story can be seen to extend to its sequence. First, in line with the Galatians' initial experience, Abraham's faith is highlighted. The next issue faced by the readers is how adherence to the law should be related to such faith. This in turn leads to the discussion of living as heirs or as slaves—the decision the readers now face, and finally the allegory confronts them with the further implication of such a decision—the driving out of the missionaries who do not share their inheritance. The Abraham story is also related to the story of Paul. The plausibility of this new version is dependent on the credibility and character of its narrator, reflected in the story he tells about himself and his relation to God and Christ in the rest of the letter.[14]

## Romans

The story of Abraham fits rather more smoothly into the argument of Romans than it had done in Galatians. Paul has just asserted that his gospel of the righteousness of God in Christ is available to all who believe, so that just as all, Jew and gentile, were in sin and under the condemnation of God's wrath, so now all, Jew and gentile, are justified not by works of the law but by faith (3:21–28). He has also employed the further argument that, since God is the one God of all, both Jews and gentiles, there is a oneness in this God's saving action of justifying both groups by means of faith (3:29, 30). The direct link into the story of Abraham is provided by 3:31. To the objection that he knows will be raised

---

14. See especially Fowl, *Engaging Scripture*, 145–50; also B.W. Longenecker, *The Triumph of Abraham's God* (Edinburgh: T&T Clark; Nashville: Abingdon Press, 1998) 168–71.

by some Jewish Christians, namely, that his formulation about justification means the abrogation of the law, Paul replies that, far from this being the case, he upholds the law. The Abraham story substantiates this claim because it brings forward a witness from the law (cf. 3:21). Despite what many would have thought about the exclusive relation of Abraham to Israel, it offers another argument for the universal scope of the gospel of justification by faith. Aspects of the law's story of Abraham are retold in such a way that he is characterized both in terms of the story of Paul's gospel and in relation to the story of the readers.[15]

Because Gen. 15:6 is chosen as the key text (cf. 4:3), Abraham is portrayed first and foremost as a man who was justified by faith. Indeed the question with which he is introduced and which is formulated with Jewish Christians in mind ('What then shall we say that Abraham our forefather according to the flesh has found?' [Rom. 4:1]) is probably meant to recall LXX Gen. 18:3 where Abraham says, 'If I have found favor/grace before you. . . .'[16] and therefore already implies that Abraham's status before God is a matter of grace (cf. also 4:4, 16). This means that, contrary to other versions of the Abraham story (cf. 1 Macc. 2:51–52; Sir. 44:19–21; CD 3.2; *Pr. Man.* 8), Abraham was not justified by works, which would have given him a cause for boasting. The Abraham presented here is, instead, in full conformity with the gospel in which justification is through faith by God's grace as a gift and in which boasting, as a possible stance before God, is ruled out (3:24, 27). Gen. 15:6 confirms this portrait, because, in speaking of Abraham's being reckoned righteous, it does not talk of works but simply mentions faith. Abraham was not, then, owed justification on the basis of his successful performance (4:4). In fact, the statement that it is faith in 'him who justifies the ungodly' that is reckoned as righteousness (4:5) implies that Abraham was at one time among the ungodly who deserve only God's wrath (cf. 1:18) and therefore have to receive justification as a gift. Such a depiction of Abraham not only shows him to be a representative of the principles of Paul's gospel but also suggests his links with the readers' story. For Jewish Christians, both 'their forefather according to the flesh' and, by extension, they themselves can be said to be in exactly the same position as gentiles in regard to receiving justification.

After the appeal to David and LXX Psa. 31:1–2 for further evidence that God pronounces blessing on the one to whom righteousness is reckoned apart from

---

15. I have reflected previously on Paul's imaginative correlation between scripture, his gospel, and the situation in Rome in 'Abraham Goes to Rome: Paul's Treatment of Abraham in Romans 4', in M.J. Wilkins and T. Paige (eds), *Worship, Theology and Ministry in the Early Church* (Sheffield: JSOT Press, 1992) 163–79, esp. 176–79.

16. Cf. also e.g., U. Wilckens, *Der Brief an die Römer*, vol. 1 (Zurich: Benzinger, 1978) 261.

works (4:6–8), a return to the Abraham story enables the point to be made that such a pronouncement does not just apply to Jews. After all, when Abraham was reckoned righteous by faith, he was uncircumcised (4:9–11a), as should be clear from the sequence in the Genesis narrative, in which the statement of Gen. 15:6 comes before the account of Abraham's circumcision in Genesis 17. So when he became circumcised, that sign was simply the seal of the righteousness he already had by faith. This sequence in the Abraham story allows all the Roman readers to connect their story with his because it makes him the father of both uncircumcised and circumcised believers (4:11b–12). Gentile Christians can claim him appropriately as their father because when he was justified he was in precisely the same position as they (i.e., uncircumcised) and circumcision played no role in his being reckoned righteous. And Jewish Christians can now see him not only as 'their forefather according to the flesh' (cf. 4:1) but also as their father in the faith because they too are not only circumcised but have exercised the same justifying faith that was the means of his being reckoned righteous before his circumcision.

What Abraham believed when he was reckoned righteous was God's promise that he would have innumerable descendants (cf. Gen. 15:5). To this was added the further promise that these descendants would inherit the land of Canaan (Gen. 15:18–21). In Paul's retelling, this promise to Abraham and his descendants is extended to inheriting the world and, from the point of view of the apostle's own contrast between promise and faith, on the one hand, and law, on the other, such a promise did not come through the law, and adherents of the law cannot be its heirs. Because Abraham believed this promise before the law (seen here as anticipated in the requirement of circumcision) was given, he is characterized not only as being justified without circumcision but also as being justified without law (4:13–14). If there is to be any guarantee about inheriting the promise, the whole process has to depend on faith, for only in that way is the principle of grace rather than of law and performance brought fully into play (4:15–16a). On this view of Abraham's story, his offspring, for whom the promise of inheritance is guaranteed, can be said to be all believers and again be identified in the same terms as the two groups among the readers in Rome (4:16b–17a). The promise is 'guaranteed to all his descendants— not only to those of the law [i.e., Jewish Christians who observe the law] but also to those [simply] of the faith of Abraham [i.e., gentile Christians], for he is the father of us all'.[17] Whether the formulation about Jewish Christians is in terms of circumcision (4:11–12) or, as here, in terms of law, Abraham's

---

17. On any view, Paul's wording is difficult and requires filling out. For the view taken here, cf. e.g., Wilckens, *Der Brief an die Römer* vol. 1, 271–72; D. Moo, *The Epistle to the Romans* (Grand Rapids: Eerdmans, 1996) 278–79.

fatherhood extends to all believers, and the inclusion of gentiles in his family is simply the fulfilment of the divine assurance to him in Gen. 17:5: 'I have made you the father of many nations.'

This version of the Abraham story not only reflects the issues among Jewish and gentile Christians, including those in Rome, but also has the potential for reshaping the story of the Roman readers. To perceive Abraham as 'the father of us all' and therefore as a symbol of unity would require altered attitudes on the part of both groups. Previously they might well have seen Abraham primarily as the great dividing point in the history of humanity, the symbol of God's particularism in choosing out one nation. But this new portrayal makes Abraham 'the great rallying point for all who believe, whether circumcised or uncircumcised'.[18] In a setting in which faith and its implications had become a divisive issue, the insight that they both share Abraham's justifying faith ought to help Jewish Christians and gentile Christians see each other as equal members of one family. This entails Jewish Christian readers' reconsidering any view of Abraham as simply 'our forefather according to the flesh' and accepting gentile believers as equally children of Abraham solely on the basis of their faith. It also entails gentile Christian readers, who may have been inclined to write off Israel's past as no longer of any significance, recognizing that they are part of a larger family that can trace its ancestry back to Abraham and seeing that the blessings of salvation they experience are an inheritance that was promised to Abraham and his descendants (cf. also 9:5a; 11:28b).

In this rehearsal of his story, the significance of Abraham's faith has not yet been exhausted. When he believed the promise that God would make him the father of many nations, Abraham had to believe in a God who gives life to the dead and calls into existence things that are not. It was this kind of faith that was reckoned to him as righteousness (4:17b–25). Abraham's God is the creative, life-giving God, and the language that depicts this God is also the language employed of the God of Paul's gospel. Giving life and choosing the things that are not are formulations for the power of God at work in the gospel (cf. Rom. 8:11; 1 Cor. 15:22; 1 Cor. 1:28). From this vantage point, Abraham's justifying faith was already belief in the God of the gospel, the God 'who raised Jesus our Lord from the dead'.

The aspects of Abraham's story of faith that are related to the two attributes of God singled out in 4:17b are set out in reverse order. In believing in the promise that many nations would be his offspring (4:18), Abraham trusted in a God who was able to summon into existence those things that did not yet exist. Such faith can also be portrayed in terms of hope: 'against hope, in hope

---

18. A. Nygren, *Commentary on Romans* (Philadelphia: Fortress Press, 1949) 175.

he believed.' The theme of hope or confident assurance will not only prove to be of significance for Paul's later exposition of his gospel (cf. 5:1–11; 8:18–39) but will also play a role in the final part of his paraenesis about mutual acceptance. There his prayer wish, which constitutes the climax of his exhortation, is 'May the God of hope fill you with all joy and peace in believing, so that you may abound in hope by the power of the Holy Spirit' (15:13 NRSV; cf. also 15:4). As in the case of Abraham, hope is connected with believing. Just as Abraham's hopeful belief that he would be the father of many nations impelled him to positive action in the present despite the seeming impossibility of his situation, so, in terms of the future of the readers' story, the faith that abounds in the hope of the salvation in which Jew and gentile are one and equal (cf. 11:30–32) is to provide the motivation for them to accept one another and worship together in unity and equality in Rome despite the present seemingly unsurmountable obstacles.

Abraham's belief in the God who gives life to the dead was displayed in the attitude that looked at the negative factors in his own situation and yet still trusted completely that God was able to do what God had promised and would bring life (Isaac) out of Abraham's 'body which was already as good as dead' and the deadness of Sarah's womb (4:19, 21). The depiction of this trust in God's promise is remarkably influenced by what the letter indicates about its readers' story and the language employed in their disputes. Abraham 'did not weaken in faith . . . but he grew strong in faith' (4:19–20). He does not merely exemplify the Pauline gospel as one who is righteous by faith but is portrayed in such a way as to be aligned with the strong in faith, possessing the qualities that Paul will later stress are essential in the situation in Rome. He did not doubt (4:20). Later in 14:23 doubt while eating meat is a characteristic of the weak, who will be condemned because they are not acting out of their own faith. Again, Abraham is said to have been 'fully convinced' (4:21), and in 14:5 the Roman Christians will be told that whether they hold that one day is more important than another or treat all days alike, what matters is that they have the kind of faith that enables them to be 'fully convinced' in their own minds. For those Jewish Christians with ears to hear, this characterization of Abraham as having strong faith, not doubting, and being fully convinced may be suggesting that the basic stance of the strong, which Paul endorses (cf. 14:14a; 15:1), need not be thought of as forsaking one's heritage but as emulating the strength of faith of father Abraham. For gentile Christians, recognition that strong faith is found already in Abraham would provide a further reminder that the gospel in which they believe is 'to the Jew first, and also the Greek'.

Since it was his hopeful and strong faith in the promise of the God who is creative and life-giving that was reckoned to Abraham as righteousness (4:22), it can be said, in a formulation that makes explicit the point of view that has been so clearly driving the depiction, that the words about Abraham in Gen. 15:6 'were written not for his sake alone, but for ours also' (4:23b–24a NRSV). Via the story of Paul's gospel, in which Christ 'was handed over to death for our trespasses' and then vindicated in the reversal of the condemnation of death through resurrection, Abraham's story of being reckoned righteous through faith becomes that of the readers who believe in the God who raised Jesus from the dead for their justification (4:24b–25). In this typological pattern of thinking, which brings together the stories of Abraham and of Christian believers, a person being placed in a right relationship with God is like Isaac being born despite the death in the bodies of Abraham and Sarah. The readers' justification involves nothing less than a radical intervention on God's part, through the death and resurrection of Christ, in which humanity is rescued from its situation of death and brought into the realm of life.[19]

## Comparison

At almost every turn, both versions of the Abraham story are shaped decisively in the light of the gospel story of God's actions in Christ and formulated with the stories of the readers in view, so that, as we have seen, there is an intricate interplay of all three stories. The same scriptural text (Gen. 15:6) is the interpretative key for both versions, which have in common the themes of Abraham's faith, Abraham's offspring, inheritance, and the contrasts between promise and law and faith and works.

There are, however, significant differences, most of which are dictated by the different stories of the readers that are being addressed and by the different places the Abraham stories occupy in the overall exposition of the gospel in each letter.[20] Romans emphasizes the notion of 'reckoning', whereas this is absent from Galatians after the citation of Gen. 15:6. Romans has a far more elaborate characterization of Abraham in terms of a faith that is hopeful and strong. Galatians makes the link to believers through the redemptive death of Christ and the work of the Spirit while in Romans, where the inheritance is seen as the world to come, the Spirit drops out of the account, and the resurrection comes into play alongside the death of Christ as a major aspect of the antitype of the gospel that draws believers and Abraham into the same typologically patterned narrative. Romans

---

19. Cf. also H. Moxnes (*Theology in Conflict* [Leiden: Brill, 1986] 275–76) and D. Patte (*Paul's Faith and the Power of the Gospel* [Philadelphia: Fortress Press, 1983] 214–22), who clearly set out the typological relationships within Romans 4.

20. For a discussion of the relation between the contingent formulations and the basic coherence of the Abraham story in Galatians 3 and Romans 4, see J.C. Beker, *Paul the Apostle* (Philadelphia: Fortress Press, 1980) esp. 94–104.

drops any reference to Gen. 12:3 and blessing, and it contains no contrast between such blessing and the curse of the law. Instead, since the condemnation of all under the law has already been dealt with earlier in the letter (esp. 3:9–20), there is simply the assertion that the law brings wrath (4:15a). Galatians makes use of the argument from temporal priority in pointing out that the promise to Abraham came before the giving of the law, but it ignores Abraham's circumcision in Genesis 17, presumably because Paul did not think it would help his case. Romans makes amends for what opponents would no doubt have pointed out as a flaw in the Galatians' portrayal by bringing that text into play. Making a different use of the argument from temporal priority, it spells out that faith was reckoned to Abraham as righteousness before he was circumcised.

There are two interrelated points at which, having given due allowance to contextual factors, it might be questioned whether the two versions contain what is identifiably the same story. First, the treatment of Christ as the singular offspring of Abraham in Galatians 3 highlights the way in which the Galatians' story line about the Abrahamic promise appears to leap straight from Abraham to the fulfilment in Christ with no positive evaluation of Abraham's relation to ethnic Israel or recognition of any progressive history of salvation between Abraham and Christ. The version in Romans 4 omits the notion of fulfilment in a singular seed, Christ, and thus appears to make believers' relation to Abraham as their father dependent simply on sharing his faith. Second, because not only gentile Christians but also Jewish Christians are in view in the relation to Abraham in the Romans story, there is a more positive perspective on a continuing ethnic aspect of that relationship. While the decisive factor in determining who are Abraham's offspring remains faith, the reference to 'our forefather according to the flesh' (4:1) and the inclusion among Abraham's genuine offspring those who are circumcised (4:12) and 'those of the law' (4:16) allow for a continuing subordinate relationship to Abraham through circumcision and observance of the law on the part of Jewish Christians. We have concentrated on Romans 4, but the difference is reinforced by the explicit return to the Abraham story in 9:6–9, where the two types of his descendants are described as children of the promise and children of the flesh, language similar to that of Gal. 4:23, 28–29. But this text in Romans is part of a discussion designed to show that God has not proved unfaithful to the divine promises. God never intended that all Abraham's physical descendants would be his true offspring but that, instead, from Abraham's time onward God's sovereign election would be operative *within* ethnic Israel. Such was the case in the period of the patriarchs (9:10–13), and in the time of Elijah the true descendants were a remnant (11:2–4), as they would also be at the time of Isaiah (9:27–29). In Paul's time the continuation of that remnant within ethnic Israel is constituted by Jewish Christians, among whom Paul himself as 'a descendant of Abraham' is a prime example (11:1, 5). Again, then, the line of physical descent from Abraham is not to be dismissed but is a significant factor in the midst of which God's overriding salvific purposes have been at work. Such observations justify the broad conclusion that in Galatians Abraham is part of a narrative that emphasizes discontinuity in the history of Israel between Abraham and Christ, while in Romans he is part of a narrative that takes account of continuity.[21]

This depiction of the differences between the two stories requires two important qualifications. To claim that 'nowhere in Romans' depiction of Abraham as believer does Paul specify that Christ is involved' and that 'all who believe as Abraham did become Abraham's children directly, not through Christ'[22] is to distort the Romans story by downplaying both its context and the extent to which its whole telling is determined by the starting point of the gospel about Christ. Paul has already made clear that believers' faith is faith in Jesus Christ (3:22, 26), and it is this faith, further described in 3:27–31, that is attested in the law in the case of Abraham. In addition, the premise on which the entire portrayal of Abraham is based is revealed at the end, namely, that his faith is equivalent to believing in the God who raised Jesus from the dead (4:24).[23] It would also not be accurate to say that there is no recognition of some continuing role of ethnic Israel within God's salvific purposes or of the existence of Jewish Christians in the midst of Galatians' presentation of the Abraham story. The later allegorical expansion already qualifies such an assertion with its treatment of Isaac as a child of the promise in contrast to Ishmael (4:23, 28), and the blessing of Abraham only comes to gentiles after Christ has entered the line of physical descent as one 'born under the law' in order to remove the law's curse. This also means that Jewish Christians do appear in the exposition of the narrative in the 'us' of 3:13 and the redemption of 'those under the law' of 4:5.[24] These qualifications suggest that, however different

---

21. Cf. also Beker (*Paul*, 99): 'Romans 4 allows for the continuity of salvation-history, whereas Galatians 3 focuses on its discontinuity.'

22. As does J.P. Sampley, 'Romans and Galatians: Comparison and Contrast', in J.T. Butler, E.W. Conrad, and B.C. Ollenburger (eds), *Understanding the Word* (Sheffield: JSOT Press, 1985) 325, 327.

23. H. Boers, *The Justification of the Gentiles* (Peabody, Mass.: Hendrickson, 1994) 110 makes similar points in claiming that 'notwithstanding the remarkably non-christological discussion of the faith of Abraham in Romans compared with Galatians, Romans 4 is no less christological than Galatians'.

24. On the significance of these passages, see Longenecker, *Triumph of Abraham's God*, 90–95, 177; cf. also R.B. Hays, *The Faith of Jesus Christ* (Chico, Calif.: Scholars Press, 1983) esp. 116–21. On the relation between continuity and discontinuity in Galatians, see also J. Barclay, *Obeying the Truth* (Edinburgh: T&T Clark, 1988) 96–105.

their point of view, sequence, and formulations, the two stories are by no means incompatible.[25]

## THE STORIES OF THE JERUSALEM CHURCH

### Galatians

The Jerusalem church's story emerges in this letter as an integral but subordinate part of both the stories of Paul and of the Galatian readers. The Christians in Jerusalem, along with other churches in Judea, had at one time been the object of Paul's violent persecution. More than three years after Paul had received his revelation of Christ and commission to preach to the gentiles, however, they had still not set eyes on him and had only heard of his transformation that had become a cause for giving glory to God. The formulation of the report of his new activity ('is now proclaiming the faith he once tried to destroy', 1:23 NRSV) allows no suggestion that they thought Paul to be proclaiming something other than what they themselves believed. Only two of their number had had any contact with Paul, and then it had not been until three years after the revelation to him. At that time Paul had sought out Peter and stayed with him for fifteen days, during which period he had also briefly seen James, the brother of Jesus. That Paul is prepared to go on oath about these details suggests that he is responding to another story about the Jerusalem church put out by the rival teachers in Galatia in which it was claimed that the Jerusalem church taught Paul and authorized his mission and that therefore he ought to conform to its views.

In contrast, Galatians emphasizes that only after a considerable time, either eleven or fourteen years after the initial revelation to him (cf. 2:1), did the Jerusalem church have any major contact with Paul. In the account of this occasion the Jerusalem church is represented by three groups, each characterised differently: its leaders (described as 'those of repute', 2:2, 6, 9), a group labelled 'false brothers' (2:4), and a broader stratum of its members designated 'the poor' (2:10). In addition to Barnabas, Paul had taken Titus, an uncircumcised gentile believer, with him, and his presence had served as a test case for the legitimacy of Paul's law-free gospel. Despite the efforts of some Jewish Christian members of the Jerusalem church who advocated circumcision for gentile believers, Titus remained uncircumcised. There is, significantly, no indication that the Jerusalem church leaders took any action against this group, but Paul regarded them as false brothers because their view constituted a blatant con-

---

25. Indeed Boers (*Justification*, 159–60) claims that their overall point is the same.

tradiction of the truth of the gospel (2:5). The narration of what happened explicitly has the readers in view and draws clear parallels to their story. Titus was not *compelled* to be circumcised (2:3) while, of course, the missionaries in Galatia were trying to *compel* the Galatians to be circumcized (6:12). The false brothers were wanting to enslave those who had freedom in Christ, and Paul asserts that he, Barnabas, and Titus did not submit to them even momentarily 'so that the truth of the gospel might remain with you', in other words, that it might be preserved for his gentile converts, of whom the Galatians are now a part. When the readers' story is later directly addressed, the impact of the rival missionary teaching is also depicted as leading to slavery rather than freedom and as preventing the Galatians from obeying the truth.

But the main players in Jerusalem are the leaders, later specified as James, Peter, and John, with whom Paul met in private. His way of speaking about them combines an acknowledgment of the role and status they were given in the church with an ironic distance that makes clear he does not see their standing in relation to the gospel as in any way superior to his own. Most important, they are not swayed by the strict Jewish Christian line on circumcision for gentiles. In fact, Paul can report that they added nothing to his formulation of the gospel but rather recognized the grace of God at work in his ministry, just as it was at work in Peter's among the circumcised. The essential harmony between the Jerusalem church and Paul was demonstrated by the right hand of fellowship extended to Paul and Barnabas by the three so-called 'pillars' of the church, in an agreement that there were two parallel missions (one to the gentiles and one to the circumcised) in furtherance of the one gospel. For Paul this concord was sealed by the agreement on the part of Barnabas and himself to do what he had already been eager to do at that time, namely, 'remember the poor', that is, raise financial support for needy members of the Jerusalem church from believers in Antioch and possibly other converts from his work in Syria and Cilicia (cf. 1:21). So at this stage in Paul's narration, the Jerusalem church in the persons of its leaders and of its poor members are seen as in solidarity with Paul and his mission, but the pressure group demanding that gentile converts be circumcised is not characterized as part of the true church, despite the role its adherents were playing among Jerusalem believers.

The Jerusalem church plays a much less favorable role in the next incident Paul narrates, where its story continues through the presence of Peter in Antioch and the mention of James and 'those of the circumcision' (2:11–14). Peter by this time had evidently left his leadership position in Jerusalem and was pursuing his mission to the circumcised in Antioch. During this time, he had been happy in a mixed church to have table fellowship with gentile believers without imposing on them any dietary regulations. But then certain people came from James with a message to Peter that caused him to withdraw from the Antioch church's practice. Presumably James warned him that such a practice would jeopardize Peter's mission to Jews, and Peter complied with the warning. Paul's interpretation of this action was that it was taken out of 'fear of the circumcision faction'.[26] This group within the Jerusalem church was determined that Jewish Christians should strictly maintain their ethnic distinctiveness and that as a consequence any eating with gentiles could only be under conditions of the latter's accepting Jewish dietary practices and becoming, to some extent, law observant. Those earlier-dubbed 'false brothers' would no doubt have been part of this group but would have represented an even more rigorous approach to the law's requirements. Peter's compliance with James' message, which was in turn followed by the other Jewish Christians in Antioch, including even Barnabas, is interpreted by Paul as a going back on the earlier agreement, since it added law observance to faith in Christ as a condition for full fellowship in the one people of God. The controversy had moved from circumcision to table fellowship and food laws, but for Paul the basic issue was the same. Peter is now in the same position as the 'false brothers' on the previous occasion and, by extension, as the rival teachers in Galatia, jeopardizing the truth of the gospel and *compelling* gentile believers to live like Jews (2:14). Although Peter is the butt of Paul's charges, the clear implication is that Paul believes that the Jerusalem church has also shifted its position. With Peter's absence from Jerusalem, James' position as leader (and James was already listed as the first of the three pillars in 2:9) had consolidated, and James was evidently under the influence of the conservative 'circumcision faction'. The implied characterization of the Jerusalem church as a whole is now a rather different one from that of 2:1–10.

It should not be too surprising, therefore, if the final, decidedly negative mention of Jerusalem in the letter has the Jerusalem church in view. As we noted earlier in passing, in the midst of the allegory in 4:21–5:1 Hagar represents the Sinai covenant and can be said to correspond 'to the present Jerusalem, for she is in slavery with her children' (4:25 NRSV). This formulation has frequently been taken as a general reference to Jerusalem as the symbol of an Israel that adheres to the Mosaic law. But, given the context, it is likely to be a more pointed reference to the Jerusalem church that, with its present stance on some form of law-observant gentile mission, is in bondage (in Paul's view) and, like Hagar, is 'bearing children for slavery'. In each of the previous references in the letter (1:17–18; 2:1) 'Jerusalem' signifies the geographical location of the Jerusalem church. Whether or not the rival mission-

---

26. On the identity of this faction, see Martyn, *Galatians*, 236–40.

aries had any direct connection with or authorization from Jerusalem, the shape of Paul's earlier narration in 1:11–2:10 suggests that he has had to respond to a Jersulem-oriented viewpoint that is influencing his readers and claiming the approval of that church. Immediately after indicating that the present Jerusalem is in slavery, Paul stresses that the Jerusalem above is the true mother of believers and thereby subverts any notion that the Jerusalem church is the mother church on whose authority he and the churches of the gentile mission should be dependent. If this reading is correct,[27] the story of the Jerusalem church in Galatians is a tragic one—seen as moving from fellowship in the gospel to slavery under the law, from being a helper and supporter of Paul's mission to aligning itself with the opponents.

## Romans

That the story of the Jerusalem church features at all in a letter to Roman Christians makes clear that, however polemical he had felt it necessary to be in Galatians about leaders and activities associated with the church, Paul had certainly not written it off. Indeed, in Paul's account of his own story, the place it takes is remarkably positive. As he thinks of the geographical extent of his mission to this point, he can speak of having proclaimed the gospel 'from Jerusalem and as far around as Illyricum' (15:19 NRSV). This reference is not to the beginnings of the Christian movement but to Paul's own ministry, and it is not a chronological reference to that ministry. To place its beginnings in Jerusalem would be far too problematic in the light of Galatians 1. The event most likely to have led to such a positive association of Jerusalem with Paul's proclamation of the gospel was his laying out of that gospel in the meeting with the leaders of the Jerusalem church (cf. Gal. 2:1–10). The Jerusalem church has an equally positive potential part to play in the apostle's immediate plans. In view here are not so much its leaders as its members as a whole (i.e., 'the saints') and in particular 'the poor' among them (15:25–26). What Paul had originally agreed to undertake when he was based in Antioch is now back at the top of his agenda, as this time he is about to take a collection from his gentile churches in Macedonia and Achaia in order to serve the needy believers in Jerusalem. The reason he gives for gentile churches having such an obligation reflects his conviction that the gospel is 'to the Jew first and also to the Greek'

---

27. For a recent justification of this interpretation, see Martyn, *Galatians*, esp. 457–66 and *Theological Issues in the Letters of Paul* (Nashville: Abingdon, 1997) 25–36. As Martyn allows (*Theological Issues*, 205), Judaism may well stand somewhere in the background because Paul does hold the conviction that the law leads to enslavement, but it is the teaching of the rival missionaries rather than Judaism as a whole that is the focus of his polemic in this passage.

(1:16; cf. also 11:17–24). He recognizes a temporal priority of the Jerusalem church in the experience of the gospel's blessings, and he feels gentile churches who have come to share in these spiritual benefits owe the poor among the Jerusalem believers a material debt (15:25–27). From Paul's point of view, this collection would constitute a practical symbol of the solidarity between the Jewish Christian Jerusalem church and the churches of the gentile mission, a sign of the successful completion of his mission in the eastern part of the empire before he turned westward to Rome and beyond Rome to Spain (15:23–24, 28–29). But his ambivalence about the Jerusalem church surfaces when he asks his readers to pray earnestly not only that he would be delivered from unbelieving Jews in Jerusalem but also that the believers there would find his ministry through the collection acceptable (15:30–32). That he conceives of the possibility that financial resources would be spurned by those in great need suggests the seriousness of the hostility towards his mission that he knows to exist in Jerusalem among the strict law-observant Jewish believers whose viewpoint is so dominant. Whatever Paul might wish to see as the denouement of the Jerusalem church's story in relation to his own, influential parties in Jerusalem have a different script in mind. Their rebuff of what he views as an attempt at unifying service would mean a negative outcome of the story.

Because, through this letter, the story of Paul now impinges on the lives of the Roman Christians, the Jerusalem church's story also becomes a factor in their story. It is not simply that the issues Paul faces in regard to the impending Jerusalem visit are likely to have been one of the catalysts in his rehearsal of the gospel in terms of the unity of Jewish and gentile believers that he wants to see realized among the readers. Whether, when, and in what frame of mind Paul shows up among them in Rome depends on what happens in Jerusalem, and the exhortation they have received to pray about the outcome of this visit means that they can play their part in God's purposes for the development of this story. What is more, making Paul's concerns their own in prayer would strengthen their commitment to work at the local level for the unity for which they recognize Paul is prepared to risk his life at the translocal level.

## Comparison

Both stories contain positive and negative features. Which of these predominates depends on which grouping within the Jerusalem church is in view and which stage of the relationship between Paul and the Jerusalem church is being reflected. The two stories are therefore connected through Paul's story. Indeed, the collection in Romans can be seen as Paul's taking up again the request of the original Jerusalem leadership at the meeting recounted in Gal. 2:1–10, and the confrontation with the Jerusalem leadership that Paul fears may result from this collection would be a replay of the issues in the Antioch confrontation related in Gal. 2:11–14. A negative outcome would have even more disastrous consequences at this later stage for the vision he still maintains of the relationship between Jewish and gentile believers.

The Galatians version of this story moves from a predominantly positive to a predominantly negative portrayal, while the more positive present state of the story in Romans has the strong possibility of a negative future hanging over it. Romans makes clear that in principle the Jerusalem church continues to have a vital role to play in the story of Paul's mission. It is striking that in this account, in contrast to Gal. 2:4 and 4:25, there is no explicit association of the Jerusalem church with slavery. This should not be taken to mean, however, that in Romans Paul considers the Jerusalem church to be the authoritative mother church. When Paul envisages the place of ethnic Israel in the climax of salvation in Rom. 11:25–27 and talks of all Israel being saved, he cites the scriptures to indicate that this will occur through the coming of Christ: 'as it is written, "Out of Zion will come the Deliverer; he will banish ungodliness from Jacob".' His wording of Isa. 59:20 follows neither the MT where the Deliverer comes *to* Zion nor the LXX where he comes *on behalf of* Zion. Since elsewhere Paul talks consistently of Christ coming from heaven at the end of history (cf. e.g., 1 Thess. 1:10; 4:16; Phil. 3:20), it is plausible that he has made the change to conform to this perspective so that Christ is conceived of as coming from the heavenly Zion to include all Israel in the salvation of the end time.[28] As in Galatians, then, the Jerusalem above still appears to be Paul's focus in considering God's eschatological purposes.

## DID SOMEBODY SAY 'STORY'?

By employing the category of story loosely, it has been possible to construct accounts of predecessors and inheritors in Galatians and Romans and to engage in brief comparisons of the two versions of each story. In doing so, we have restricted ourselves to the data of the letters and therefore to Paul's own point of view on the readers, on Abraham, and on the Jerusalem church. No attempt has been made to establish a more critical or 'real' story of the Jerusalem church or the letters' addressees by, for example, including data sifted from Acts, from other letters, or from external evidence about conditions in Rome or north or south Galatia.[29] The object has not been to speculate on how Paul's mind worked nor, because of space restrictions and because the implicit gospel story line was not the specific topic of this assignment, to penetrate to the worldview or symbolic universe presupposed by the stories—although the readers' stories in particular

---

28. Cf. e.g., J.D.G. Dunn, *Romans 9–16* (Dallas: Word, 1988) 692–93; Moo, *Romans*, 728.

29. This is to take as axiomatic the distinction of N.R. Petersen (*Rediscovering Paul* [Philadelphia: Fortress Press, 1985] 6–14) between the referential-contextual narrative world of the letter and history as story.

give expression to answers to such worldview questions as, Who are we? Where are we? What's wrong with the world? What is the solution? How should we then live? The aim, instead, has been to discover how far a treatment in terms of 'story' might enhance our reading of the two letters.[30]

The most obvious result of a treatment employing this category has been to see that none of the stories treated has been independent or discrete. Instead, we see a pervasive overlap and interplay between them. In particular, the different stories of the readers have influenced the shaping and discourse of the Abraham and the Jerusalem church stories—in the latter case, especially through the readers' relation to Paul's story. But it is the overarching story evoked by the gospel and mediated through Paul's story that has been most determinative for the telling and interrelation of the stories of predecessors and inheritors. The past, present, and future of the readers' stories are dependent on their relation to the gospel story. The Abraham stories are told as witnesses to the gospel story, and Abraham takes his place in the larger story of God's purposes for the world, of which the gospel of the crucified and risen Christ is the determinative centre. In the stories of the Jerusalem church, this gospel story provides the evaluative point of view that produces the resulting characterizations of that church.

But has anything been achieved by using categories drawn from discussion of narrative that could not have been gained by using other interpretative categories? Here the answer will depend on the goal being pursued. Is that goal simply an accurate as possible exposition of the letters? Is it to reconstruct the historical Paul behind the texts in dialogue with his churches? Is it to find an alternative way of depicting Paul's theology? If so, what is meant by Paul's theology: his theologizing, or a synthesis of the results of that theologizing in the extant letters? Is it to do justice to the narrative world implied by these texts? Or is it to help present day readers, with a renewed awareness of the significance of narrative in a late modern setting, appropriate Paul's letters?

If one's goal is an accurate exposition of the letters in their historical setting, the honest answer, in the case of predecessors and inheritors, has to be that very little has been gained. The readings above, pruned of the continual mentioning of the term 'story' and the more occasional use of other narrative categories, would remain substantially unaltered.[31] Abraham and the Jerusalem church

---

30. Even in the case of the larger gospel narrative, our ability to construct it and our finding it illuminating are not the same as establishing that it would have been known to Paul in this form or that he consciously formulated his arguments with it in mind.

31. The same might also be said of more extensive projects (e.g., B. Witherington III, *Paul's Narrative Thought World* [Louisville, Ky.: Westminster/John Knox Press, 1994]), where narrative categories often function as not much more than an alternative framework within which to discuss topics in Paul's thought.

would be seen as topics in the argument of each letter, whose treatments could be compared, and the readers would be viewed in terms of either the rhetorical audience or the situation of the addressees.[32] Correlations among the topics, the readers' settings, and Paul's gospel would still be drawn. Only in the case of the readers, as we shall argue below, might anything be lost by having employed other categories for analysis.

If one is working with traditional interpretative goals in view, one will also inevitably want to ask whether and in what sense story is an appropriate category for the way in which the three subjects are treated in the letters. When I began this assignment, I had expected, somewhat naively, that the material about Abraham would most readily lend itself to analysis in terms of narrative, but that treating the material on the Jerusalem church and discussing readers in such a fashion might involve more of an imposition of an alien framework. Is not Abraham already a character in the Genesis narrative, and is not Paul, in both Galatians and Romans, retelling the story of this character? As we shall suggest, however, the material about Abraham is the most resistant to being treated in terms of stories of Abraham in their own right. Instead, it is with the discussion of the Jerusalem church that one comes closest to a match between analysis in terms of story and the form of most of the relevant material in the letters. Nevertheless, as we have seen, this is not because the Jerusalem church has a story in its own right but because it features as an integral part of Paul's own story, related in Galatians in the *narratio* section of his argument and in Romans in the section that outlines his travel plans.

In the case of Abraham, if our goal is to follow the discussion of Abraham in the text or to discover how Abraham functions in Paul's theologizing, then we shall not be helped by any insistence that Paul is straightforwardly telling a story about Abraham. Instead, he assumes the Genesis narrative about Abraham and is concerned to point out in a selective manner the significance of various aspects of *that* story. Describing Paul's discussions of Abraham as stories or even as retellings of the Abraham story obscures what is really going on in these sections of the letters. They are applied commentaries on the scriptural story of Abraham. The form that most of the material about Abraham takes—creative exegesis of the Jewish scriptures—should have given pause before subsuming it within story. The discussion of Abraham's significance in Gal. 3:6–16 proceeds through the juxtaposition and interpretation of specific texts, and the allegory of Gal. 4:21–5:1 actualises an already existent narrative, giving its details another referent. Both letters also employ typological exegesis

---

32. As Petersen (*Rediscovering Paul*, 2) points out, however, in depicting the occasion of a letter, which includes the readers' setting, commentators in fact end up telling a story.

in their treatment of Abraham. In addition, Romans 4 takes the form of a midrash, where the key text from the law (Gen. 15:6) is cited in 4:3, and the significance of its major terms is then unfolded. The verb 'reckoned' is taken up in 4:4–8, with a text from the writings (Psa. 32:1) included in the process. 'Righteousness' had already been discussed in 3:21–26, and so the other major term 'believed' is treated in 4:9–21, as material from Genesis 17–18 is woven in and Gen. 15:5, the verse immediately preceding the main text, is also cited. Finally there is a return to the original text in 4:22–25.

What is said about Abraham in the biblical narrative is crucial for shaping the understanding of the identity of the people of God, but in the setting of Paul's gentile mission its meaning is disputed. The narrative itself is not enough; it needs interpretation. In Galatians and Romans that interpretation is supplied not so much by a new telling of the Abraham story but by a focus on those elements in the Genesis version (1) that support the apostle's perspective on the one new people of God formed out of Jews and gentiles by God's actions in the death and resurrection of Christ and (2) that supply connections with the stories of the readers. Although Paul's commentary on scripture is done in the light of the grand story,[33] there is an implication to be drawn here about the danger of indiscriminately applying the notion of narrative. The scriptural narrative about Abraham, the implied gospel narrative, and even the stories of Paul and the readers are all contested and need interpretation; it is the epistolary form with its theological argument and paraenesis (though these may still be dependent on the underlying gospel narrative) that provides the highly effective vehicle for doing so.

If, however, one is convinced that texts reflect symbolic universes that have narrative elements (Petersen) or worldviews that come to expression primarily in stories (Wright), then one will wish to evaluate the readings we have offered rather differently. The criterion will be how far justice has been done to the implied narratives of Galatians and Romans about the readers, the Jerusalem church, and Abraham. We have already noted that the Jerusalem church is best viewed as part of an implied narrative about Paul. As regards Abraham, a sequence of basic events underlying a narrative can be inferred from Galatians 3–4 and Romans 4. In Galatians the key episodes are as follows: God made a promise to Abraham about descendants and inheritance; Abraham believed the promise; God reckoned his faith as righteousness; God sent Christ to be born and to die redemptively (thus fulfilling the promise about offspring in Christ);

---

33. R.B. Hays (*Echoes of Scripture in the Letters of Paul* [New Haven, Conn.: Yale University Press, 1989] 157) talks of Paul 'reading the Bible through the lens of a narrative hermeneutic', while N.T. Wright (*The New Testament and the People of God* [London: SPCK, 1992] 79) claims Paul's 'repeated use of the Old Testament is designed not as mere proof-texting, but, in part at least, to suggest new ways of reading well-known stories, and to suggest that they find a more natural climax in the Jesus-story than elsewhere'.

gentiles believe in Christ and are baptized into him (thus also becoming Abraham's offspring); God gives the Spirit to them (thus fulfilling the promise about blessing or inheritance). There is then a further story line, not sufficiently related to the previous one to be seen as its subplot, in which the two sons of Abraham appear. In Romans God made a promise to Abraham about descendants; despite appearances to the contrary, Abraham believed the promise of this God who gives life to the dead; God reckoned his faith as righteousness; Abraham was later circumcised (thus sealing his righteous status); God raised Jesus from the dead; Jews and gentiles believe in the God who raised Jesus from the dead (thus sharing the faith of their father Abraham); God also reckons their faith as righteousness.[34] What is readily apparent from such an analysis is that in neither Galatians nor Romans is there really a story about Abraham himself. Abraham is rather a character in an implied story line in which God is the main actor and which will include God's actions in Christ and the actions of Christian believers.[35] The bracketed explanations above, which give the story line coherence, are primarily dependent on grasping the christological theme of the whole narrative. So, if we are interested in an implied narrative, Abraham has to be included with God, Israel, Christ (the subjects of other essays in this volume), and believers. Although, for the sake of the assignment, the expositions above have talked of the Abraham story, they have at least underlined repeatedly that in both letters this story can only be appreciated if it is seen as part of such a larger narrative. Our earlier language of 'retelling' the Abraham story has a little more justification if it is clarified that it is the Genesis story that is being retold and that the retelling consists of placing particular parts of that story within an implicit overall narrative whose shape is now determined by Paul's gospel.

When it comes to the inheritors, although their relationship with Paul is sometimes the topic in narrative sections, the stories we have told have in any case been implied ones, constructed from clues in a variety of places in the letters. These stories have the essential features usually attributed to a narrative, with past, present, and future events related to one another in a basic plot and with elements of tension or conflict. Of course, viewed historically, at the time of the letter writing, the resolution still awaits, but it is clear from the letters' narrative worlds what the options are. It was suggested above that, in the case

---

34. Since this larger narrative is not the specific remit of this essay, no attempt is made to discuss the significance of the reordering of these events in the texts.

35. It is, of course, the story of Christ that is uncovered as the narrative substructure of Gal. 3:1–4:11 in the groundbreaking work of Hays, who states that 'the Abraham story is for Paul taken up into the Christ story, and the Christ-story is understood, with the hindsight of narrative logic, as the fit sequel of the Abraham story' (*The Faith of Jesus Christ*, 226); cf. also Witherington, *Paul's Narrative Thought World*, 38, 50. It will be evident from my earlier exposition, however, that I disagree with major elements of what Hays holds to be the narrative logic (see *The Faith of Jesus Christ*, esp. 193–235).

of the readers, there might well be a dimension that an analysis in terms of story rather than other categories helps to highlight, even if one has more traditional interpretative interests. Whereas talk of the rhetorical audience or the setting of the readers tends to encourage a static conception of the inheritors, the story approach enables a more dynamic construal. A common hermeneutical approach to Paul's letters is to ask, 'If this is what the gospel meant when addressed to the Galatians or to the Romans in their settings, what might that same gospel mean when addressed to today's readers in their particular settings?' Given that stories play a vital role in the way that people make sense of who they are and of the unfolding events in their lives, the construction of the inheritors' stories can help present-day readers, conscious of their own stories, to draw analogies with the implied readers in a way that enhances the sense that they too are being addressed by Paul's gospel. The way in which the formulation of Paul's gospel takes in the contingencies of his readers' stories also demonstrates the need for adjustment and reformulations of the gospel story as circumstances change. At the same time, the open-endedness of their stories leaves the challenge, for both the intended readers and today's readers, of whether they are prepared to realign their lives with the goals of the overarching story of God's dealings with the world in Christ. What has been said here is also part of a frank acknowledgment that it is legitimate to evaluate the narrative approach to Paul, where it is carried out responsibly, in terms of its perceived value for contemporary Christians in their appropriation of scripture and their mission in the world. If its construction of implied stories for the readers and for other major figures in the letters is found to be helpful in such a context, then a narrative approach is certainly none the worse for that.

On the basis of this particular probe of predecessors and inheritors, I would urge greater clarity about the goals that the category of story is being made to serve. Story or narrative is first of all a *literary* category, and before we relate it, as we should, to theological or historical analysis, we need to ensure we do justice to its distinctive focus on the world of the text. On the basis of this particular assignment, I would also provisionally conclude that, if the category of story is to prove a useful tool for analysis of Paul's letters, it should not be made to do too much work but be limited to analysis on three levels that most directly affect the letters.[36]

---

36. This might be seen to correspond more closely to the three levels of theologising than to the five stories isolated by Dunn, *Theology*, 18; cf. also 713–15. It differs, however, in making the story operative at the first foundational level not primarily one about God and Israel but a larger story, in which Christ is the determinative centre. Christ functions in this way not simply at the level of Paul's story, as Dunn argues. He is not so much 'the plumb line by which Paul measured the alignment of what could and should be built on the stable foundation inherited from his past' (723) as the new foundation on which the formulation of the overriding story presupposed in Paul's letters is built, and in that story even previously foundational elements are now decisively reconfigured.

The first level is that of the message of Paul's gospel with its underlying story of God's activity in Christ. This implied story should be seen as taking into itself and reconfiguring the story of God's dealings with the created world and with Israel, for which the Jewish scriptures are essential and in which Abraham is a significant participant. But since Paul's gospel announces the paradoxical introduction of the life-giving power of the end time into history through the crucified and risen Christ, it has the effect of disrupting and transforming human categories, including that of story. Any formulation of this implied narrative, therefore, will need to beware of domesticating such a gospel and to allow for radical disjunctures (Galatians) as well as definite continuities (Romans). And if the problem of grand stories is that they induce oppression and violence, this one ought to subvert any such use, because at its centre is the divine love displayed in the weakness of the crucified Christ.

The second level is the story of Paul and his apostolic mission, and it is to this story that the story of the Jerusalem church properly belongs as a major component. Paul's story is a major factor in his shaping and formulating of the gospel's larger story as it comes to expression in the letters, and because his story includes letter writing, it mediates between the gospel's overarching narrative and the stories of the letters' readers. This third level—the stories of the inheritors of Paul's letters—also decisively shapes the form in which the gospel comes to expression within the letters.[37] As we have noted, it is a level that, by extension and analogy, can also include the stories of present-day readers. Both types of readers are inheritors of Paul's gospel but not its possessors. It is not a question of subsuming the gospel within their story but of allowing the gospel's story to shape the stories they live out in Galatia, Rome, or elsewhere.

Talk of possession returns us to where we started and also to the notion that 'letters . . . are a form of narrative that envisages no outcome, no closure'. Paul's letters to the Galatians and to the Romans are not a form of narrative, although they refer to narrative worlds. In doing so, they reflect an implicit gospel story line that is still on the way to an envisaged closure that will also be a new beginning—the completion of a new creation. They also reflect readers' stories that, in their open-endedness, envisage not so much closure as a desired outcome precipitated by the letters themselves—the conforming of readers' stories to the continuing story of the God who has acted in Christ and the Spirit.

---

37. An analysis on these three levels also corresponds to the cosmic, apostolic, and local story lines isolated by W.T. Wilson in his fine analysis of the worldview and narrative substructure of Colossians in *The Hope of Glory* (Leiden: Brill, 1997) 183–218.

# 11

## Response to A.T. Lincoln

### The Stories of Predecessors and Inheritors in Galatians and Romans

I. Howard Marshall

There are at least two possible stages in a response to Andrew Lincoln's paper on the stories of 'Paul's predecessors and his inheritors'. The first is a discussion of the actual exposition of these stories, assessing the validity of the exegesis offered in Lincoln's paper. The second is an assessment of methodological issues that arise, asking whether the use of the category of 'story' is appropriate and helpful in the study of Paul's letters and, specifically, whether it leads to new insights that might not have been uncovered without the development of this approach. These two aspects of the discussion are obviously interrelated.

## STORIES OF INHERITORS AND PREDECESSORS

In the present assignment, the two groups of predecessors and inheritors form an odd combination with fuzzy and even overlapping boundaries. 'Inheritors' implies an ongoing story, one that must be related to the letters in a rather different way from past stories. The inheritors are taken to be the people addressed in the two letters, two separate groups of people in Galatia and Rome. Their stories will be ongoing stories in that they already had a past story before the letters were written and there is a future for them. The story of the Galatian Christians began with Paul's intervention in their lives, but the story of the Roman Christians began independently of him. Both groups will have an ongoing story, in the sense that their lives will go on after the receipt of the letters, and the question will be what difference the letters will make to that story. Yet this 'future story' can hardly be said to underlie the letters.

For the purposes of the essay, the predecessors are limited to those held in common by the two letters, but they are very different in character: Abraham, in the distant past with a finished, written story; and the Jerusalem church with its unwritten, ongoing story in the immediate past and present. Do these two predecessors form a real category or rather two quite different species that have ended up in one cage in the zoo—dinosaurs with ostriches, if that were possible? Despite Lincoln's disclaimer, it still seems to me to be distinctly odd to couple together two such disparate entities.

Moreover, if Paul had intended Romans to go to other destinations as well as Rome,[1] then it is conceivable that Jerusalem could have been one of those destinations, in which case the predecessors would also have been the inheritors. And in any case, if you had asked Paul, 'Would you think it appropriate to forward copies of your letters to Rome and Galatia to Jerusalem?' he might well have said, 'Yes', even if he might have wanted to say some things a bit differently. The distinction between immediate predecessors and inheritors is somewhat accidental and therefore not to be pressed.

## The Inheritors of Galatians

Lincoln's account of the inheritors of Galatians raises no real problems. There is an ongoing history of a people who follow in the footsteps of Abraham (as understood by Paul) as the exemplar of faith and who can be counted as his children. The issue is whether the readers, who are under pressure to withdraw from this succession (and some of them may even have done so), will respond to Paul's appeal and stay 'in'. You can express this in Lincoln's words in terms of 'play [their] part in the larger story suggested by this letter' (see page 176), but I am not sure that we gain anything by using such language.

## The Inheritors of Romans

The question at issue is whether the Christians in Rome accept Paul's understanding of the gospel by faith, and so agree to regard questions of foods and festivals as no longer causes for division and debate. This can be put as 'agree to become part of Paul's story' (page 177). Lincoln also puts this in something more like a traditional form by saying, 'The future of both groups of readers will depend on how far their values and actions are shaped by the gospel mediated

---

1. My own view is that Romans was meant purely for Rome, and other destinations, such as Ephesus for a variant form of the letter, are unlikely. Yet the possibility that Paul would have regarded the contents of Romans as relevant for other destinations is a very real one.

to them through Paul's story' (page 178). But was Paul telling them a 'story'? It seems to me much more that he was arguing a case that he backed up by scriptural quotations, and the question is simply whether they will let themselves be shaped by Paul's account of the gospel.

However, an important point arises here. As Lincoln puts it, the question is whether '*they* will be prepared to reconfigure their story in the light of the overarching story of the gospel' (page 175; my italics). As thus put, the implication is that we are considering a *human* response to a message. What will the readers do? Call a church meeting and discuss 'How do we go forward from here?' But for Paul the gospel is more than a story! It is the power of God leading to salvation for all who believe (Rom. 1:16). So instead the question may be whether the power of God at work in the gospel will cause a change in the configuration of their story. Lincoln rightly recognises this point when he writes of 'the continuing activity, through the grace and power of the gospel, of the God who called them into a new creation' (page 176).

Of course, it could be argued that God acts simply through the power of the story as a story to change lives, and the two explanations, the one on a more human level in terms of what stories can do, and the other on a divine level of what God can accomplish through stories, may be complementary. But the impression given by Paul is that the power of the gospel is something more than the power of a story: 'Our message of the gospel came to you not in word only, but also in power and the Holy Spirit and with full conviction' (1 Thess. 1:5 NRSV).

## Is 'Stories of Inheritors' a Helpful Concept?

To put it bluntly, the past and present 'stories' of the inheritors are nothing other than what would be gained by a traditional mirror reading of the letters, supplemented by any relevant external information, in order to ascertain information about 'the readers and their situation.' The use of the category of 'story' has not made any significant difference to the approach and the results obtained at this point, except perhaps in one respect.

What is new is the raising of the deliberate query; What difference did the letter make to their ongoing story? What did Paul hope would happen? And what in fact was the actual effect of the reception of the letter? This is a question that has not often been asked in past scholarship with regard to these two letters. It has certainly been asked about the letter to Philemon: What did Philemon do about Onesimus? It has also been asked to some extent about Corinth, and also about Rome,[2] but the question has arisen less because of a desire to

---

2. R.E. Brown and J.P. Meier, *Antioch and Rome: New Testament Cradles of Catholic Christianity* (New York: Paulist Press, 1983) 122–27.

know how the Pauline letters were received than because of later evidence to be taken into account that scholars want to know how to get—for example, from the Corinth of Paul to the Corinth addressed by 1 Clement.[3] J.L. Martyn does raise the issue with regard to Galatians by suggesting that Paul failed to win the day and that a small number of his followers departed to Ephesus.[4]

In fact we do not know what happened in these two cases as a direct result of the reception of the letters. In the case of Philemon, it has been suggested that the fact that Philemon kept Paul's letter is an indication that he responded favourably to its request. If so, it would be helpful to know whether we have the two letters to Galatia and Rome preserved because the recipients valued them or simply because Paul himself kept copies of them. If the former is the case, we may presume that their response was positive,[5] although we should still have to ask whether the response was in fact what Paul was hoping for.

If we have no external evidence to guide us on this point, we have to fall back on the alternative question: In what ways did Paul expect that the lives of the readers would be reconfigured in the light of his letter? And again this is an old question in a slightly different wording: What is the purpose of the letter?

But to ask these questions about how the stories of the readers would be influenced by the reading of the letter is to raise a different issue from that of how the stories of the inheritors affected the writing of the letters. There is no existing 'underlying story' here.

## STORIES OF PREDECESSORS: ABRAHAM

From the inheritors we turn to the story of the common predecessor, Abraham. By way of introduction, I fall back on my favourite comparison of New Testament study with the reading of a detective story of the 'Who dunnit?' variety. In the classical form of this literature, a murder is committed, and then the investigator gathers such material evidence as may be available and also interviews and cross-questions the various people who might be suspected of

---

3. Cf. the classic but questionable approach of W. Bauer, *Orthodoxy and Heresy in Earliest Christianity* (London: SCM Press, 1972).

4. J.L. Martyn, *Theological Issues in the Letters of Paul* (Edinburgh: T&T Clark, 1997) 38–39. He finds support in the observation that, if Galatians was composed between 1 Corinthians and Romans, then Paul was able to count on Galatian support for the 'collection' in the earlier letter (1 Cor. 16:1) but not in Romans (Rom. 15:26), where Galatia is conspicuous by its absence (against this kind of view, see J.D.G. Dunn, *Romans 9–16* [Dallas: Word, 1988] 875).

5. But Martyn thinks that it was a dedicated minority that retained and preserved the letter to the Galatians.

having done the dastardly deed. Somewhere by page 150 the investigator can say to his sidekick, 'Well, it's pretty obvious who did it, and how', but the reader is perplexed. And the reader's perplexity lasts through some forty more pages to the final chapter where the characters are gathered together and the investigator proceeds to tell a series of stories in which it is shown how each character in turn could have had the motive and the means to carry out the murder. In every case, however, something does not quite fit into a coherent story, until eventually we come to the 'perfect' story in which all the clues fall into place and the real murderer is unmasked. Here we have a combination of (a) stories told by the individual characters, which may include some deceit and untruth, some twisting of the facts in their own favour; (b) the various penultimate stories told by the investigator at the end, each of which is an unsuccessful but at first sight plausible attempt to make sense of the ambiguous evidence; and (c) the final story that accounts for all of the evidence.

This analogy will perhaps hold for the story of Abraham, for which (a) the evidence consists in the narrative about him in the OT. This evidence (b) was interpreted in particular ways in Judaism and very probably by some Christians with views different from Paul's. Paul then (c) retells the story, or rather picks up certain elements in it and tells them in such a way that he expects his readers to be persuaded that this is the right way to understand it—with the hope that they will say, 'Gosh, why didn't I see it like this before?'

To be sure, one complication is the considerable uncertainty about what the 'facts' in the story of Abraham actually were, or indeed whether there were any facts at all.[6] We have no choice but to take the 'story' in Genesis (whether basically fact or basically fiction) as the 'original story' and ask what subsequent readers made of it.

## Abraham in Galatians

Clearly, as Lincoln says, Abraham may well be introduced by Paul because appeal was already being made to him by the rival missionaries. There is a prima facie reading of the story in Genesis that Abraham's example is one of observing circumcision and of establishing his position with God by what he did.

According to Lincoln, what Paul offers is a new version of the story of Abraham developed under the impact of the story of the readers. What is going on? Is it simply a rereading that may or may not be true? Certainly, from Paul's point of view, it is the new 'authorised version' that he hopes his readers will

---

6. For an unfashionably positive assessment of the evidence on this question, see A.R. Millard, 'Abraham', in D.N. Freedman (ed.), *Anchor Bible Dictionary*, vol. 1 (New York: Doubleday, 1992) 35–41.

accept because it is self-evidently convincing. In his eyes there is no place for a plurality of competing stories of Abraham. And this rejection of other versions of the Abraham story stands despite the fact that his own version offers an incredible inversion of normal understanding of the story.

I have no problems with the idea of Paul using Abraham's story or of asking what happens when Paul tells the story in a manner that was different from the way in which the 'opponents' would have read it, or that James read it. Thus this section raises the question of the relationship between the various versions of the story of Abraham: Are we to say that what lies behind the letters is the raw material in Genesis and also Paul's interpretation of that story in his own particular way? How would Paul have justified his telling of the story if somebody had said, 'No, it wasn't like that at all' and had offered a rival version?

Paul achieves his point by pointing first to Abraham's faith (Gal. 3:6). He can assume that what he means by faith, the faith displayed by Christian believers, is essentially the same as that which Abraham displayed. To put this point by saying with Lincoln that the times of Abraham and the Galatians 'overlap' (see page 180) is perhaps not quite right; rather the good news was announced to Abraham ahead of time in a prophetic manner through the statement that the nations would be blessed in him. The new interpretation comes in when Paul says that scripture foresaw that God would justify the gentiles by faith.[7]

We can pass over most of Lincoln's exposition of the Abraham story in Galatians without comment, although I would perhaps frame some details differently. However, we should take note of the allegory of the two sons of Abraham in Galatians 4. On the usual understanding of the story, Abraham's son Ishmael is the ancestor of the non-Jewish peoples, and he receives a limited divine promise that he will be made into a great nation (Gen. 21:13, 17). And Isaac is the ancestor of the Jews to whom the covenants are further made. But Paul reverses this imagery. The 'descendants' of Abraham who believe are the children born of the Spirit (assumed to be the power by which Isaac was born). Those who keep the law and do not believe are the children of Hagar, who corresponds to Sinai.

What is going on here? Evidently Paul is drawing a contrast between those who believe (whether Jew or gentile) and those who depend upon the law (again whether Jews or gentiles). The former are children of God by the Spirit, like Isaac, while the latter are trying to be God's children by ordinary human efforts, and so in a sense correspond to the child of Hagar, born in the ordinary human

---

7. To make the scriptures 'a character in the story', as Lincoln suggests (see page 180), seems to me to be a piece of unnecessary daring! Which 'story' is in mind now? Paul's expression is admittedly odd because in fact God is the speaker of the promise. The expression is not so problematic in 3:22 where it simply refers to the trend of scriptural statements.

way. Jerusalem corresponds to the latter in that it is the site of the temple and the centre of the law. But Paul takes a daring leap and identifies a new Jerusalem as the free mother of God's children.

Galatians 4 seems to me to be drawing a typology or allegory out of the story rather than being a part of telling the story, as Lincoln suggests. It is seeing principles at work in the Abraham story that still apply in terms of God's action and how humans behave, or ought to behave.

## Abraham in Romans

In Romans Paul views Abraham as being 'justified' like contemporary believers through believing in a God who can raise the dead (i.e., through bringing life out of a barren womb, not the metaphorical raising of Isaac from the dead, as in Heb. 11:19). Thus Paul finds things in Abraham's life and experience that are sufficiently like what happens in the case of Christian believers for him to claim real parallels between them. Paul also sees that God has established in the case of Abraham how God will deal with people, and he sees in Abraham a paradigm of how people should respond to God.

Lincoln can refer to two 'versions of the Abraham story' (see page 189) or to 'two stories' (page 191), and the question arises as to which of these phrases is more apt. There is no problem about Paul having two 'different' stories of Abraham, one in Galatians and one in Romans. He is drawing different points out of different aspects of the one story, although it might be necessary to ask whether he does so consistently and convincingly. Lincoln rightly recognises that the different uses made of the Abraham story fit in with the different needs that Paul is addressing in the two letters. Romans 9:6–9 is an example of a further use of the story of Abraham's children: not the children of the flesh but the children of the promise are counted as descendants. Here 'flesh' refers to the normal process of conception and birth, as in the case of Hagar's son, whereas 'of the promise' refers to God's intervention to give a child to the barren Sarah. The further refinements found in Galatians 4 do not occur here. In any case, however, Rom. 4:11–12 and 4:16 confirm that the children of Sarah include both believing Jews and believing gentiles.

## STORIES OF PREDECESSORS: THE JERUSALEM CHURCH

The church in Jerusalem, by which Paul is thinking principally of its leadership, is a predecessor of a different kind. There is no written story here to be reinterpreted; no canonical form to which respect must be paid. And this story is interwoven with the stories of Paul himself and his readers, although it is distinguishable from them.

In Galatians, Paul is responding to a different 'story' (i.e., perspective), on the church at Jerusalem put about by his rivals; Galatians 1–2 is clearly written as a response to a different understanding of the events. Lincoln's suggestion that Paul is describing a shift in the position of the Jerusalem church is cogent. Paul implies this but does not state it directly. He says nothing to clarify how the James of 2:1–10 could lie behind the position of 'the men from James' in 2:11–14 or how Cephas could have felt compelled to shift his own practice.

Especially interesting is Lincoln's suggestion that the Hagar typology refers particularly to Paul's rivals who were geographically located in and inspired by Jerusalem. Thus the story of Jerusalem in Galatians is that of a tragic decline in Paul's eyes from acknowledging and commending his mission to becoming its opponents.

But was that the end of the story? Is this story of tragedy Lincoln's story or Paul's story about the Jerusalem church?

Some reason for caution is provided by the favourable mention of Peter in 1 Corinthians, where there is nothing to suggest any major differences between him and Paul, nor indeed between Paul and James (1 Cor. 15:9). The various Pauline chronologies currently on offer all place 1 Corinthians with its references to Peter after the incident in Gal. 2:11–14. Can the story then refer to a temporary aberration on the part of Peter? On the whole, it seems more probable that Peter himself was not permanently opposed to Paul. This does not, however, exclude the possibility of a continuing hard-line group in Jerusalem (or in Galatia) whose influence may have gone up and down. Certainly Lincoln has no difficulty with the hypothesis that there were various groups in Jerusalem and that Paul's ambivalence is related to this, depending on which group has the upper hand.

Lincoln's identification of the Judaisers with Hagar in the allegory is intriguing.[8] Is the driving out of the slave woman and her child to be taken as an instruction to push the troublemakers out of the churches?[9] This would tie in with the strong language in Galatians 1, where a curse is pronounced on the purveyors of a different gospel. However, it seems more probable that Hagar stands for the Judaism with which the Judaisers identified themselves, and Hagar's children, for the Judaisers.

---

8. A.T. Lincoln, *Paradise Now and Not Yet* (Cambridge: Cambridge University Press, 1981) 9–26; cf. Martyn, *Theological Issues*, 25–36.

9. Martyn, *Theological Issues*, 36.

# THE USEFULNESS OF THE CATEGORY OF 'STORY'

## History and Story

What I may call 'the Petersen principle' excludes history from the kind of exercise in which we are engaged. N.R. Petersen recognises that the historical world exists and that reconstruction of it is a legitimate task, but he confines himself to the 'fiction' of Paul's narrative world.[10] While I can appreciate the necessity to work out exactly what Paul is doing before proceeding to use it to find out what history lies behind it, it is equally clear to me that one cannot exclude history in attempting to work out the narrative world; history determines the parameters of what Paul may have thought or constructed. In brief, a dialectical process that moves to and fro between the events and the story corresponds better to what we actually do than an isolation of either historical or literary study.

## Story and Salvation History

Lincoln himself asks 'how far a treatment in terms of "story" might enhance our reading of the two letters' (see page 198). He makes the candid admission that the 'story' category has not really made much difference so far as 'an accurate exposition of the letters in their historical setting' is concerned (page 198). My general impression with regard to these 'stories' is that he is right.

He comments that the Abraham material is the most resistant to this 'story' treatment. Abraham is simply a character in an implied story line. Instead, Paul places particular parts of the story of Abraham within 'an implicit overall narrative' (page 201), which would suggest that for Paul there is a 'salvation history' (that also is a 'judgement history').

This point may be of greater importance than may appear at first sight. It would mean that for Paul there is a linear *Heilsgeschichte*, despite J.L. Martyn's denial of this.[11] This conclusion is not surprising, for two reasons. First, people have a strong tendency toward unification and synthesis, particularly evident in the composition of the Bible, so that, however the various narratives in the Bible arose, there would be a tendency to ask how they fitted together and to mould them into an all-encompassing story. The other reason, of

---

10. N.R. Petersen, *Rediscovering Paul: Philemon and the Sociology of Paul's Narrative World* (Philadelphia: Fortress Press, 1985) 6–10.

11. 'Events in Galatia: Modified Covenantal Nomism versus God's Invasion of the Cosmos in the Singular Gospel: A Response to J.D.G. Dunn and B.R. Gaventa', in J.M. Bassler (ed.), *Pauline Theology, Volume 1: Thessalonians, Philippians, Galatians, Philemon* (Minneapolis: Fortress Press, 1994) 160–79, e.g., 173.

course, is that the Bible is essentially a book about God, with a firm belief in one God who is sovereign in history and who has been active since creation; there is thus a built-in unifying factor that would lead to the various subplots being seen as parts of one overriding plot. Out of this, one can pick various self-contained units, and in particular the careers of individual men and occasionally women, and of specific groups, families, tribes, and nations. The question that then arises is whether God is consistent and engages in an ongoing action. Many parts of the Bible operate within their own confined horizons, but it is plausible that there is an attempt to weld together the material into one story through various devices that need not be specified here. The story of Abraham is such a story, one taken up by Jews and Christians alike, that contains forward-looking elements that could be picked up and used to create continuity. Paul does this by taking up the biblical story and using those parts of it that are appropriate for his purposes.

It would be fair to say, then, that Paul does have a sense of an ongoing, underlying story. What he does is to give 'applied commentaries' (page 199). It is correct that Paul does not retell the story as a story but focuses on the elements that he can use and makes use of them.[12]

## Is Your Story Really Necessary?

According to Lincoln a better example of a 'story' is the story of the Jerusalem church, which is told to some extent as a 'story' only because it is part of Paul's own story. But does saying that it is 'story' really take us anywhere new? The identification of Galatians 1–2 as autobiography or narrative says all that is necessary and is perhaps more appropriate in that it reminds us that here Paul is relating what happened. He may be interpreting it, selecting those items that are most significant and telling them from a particular angle, but this is what historians do.

But to agree that the Jerusalem church is the subject of a story or narrative is not the same thing as saying that Paul's theology is narrative theology or that this particular story is a foundational story of some kind. It is, rather, a report of an episode in the impact made by the gospel, a story of how people responded in different ways to the gospel and its demands on them, and it manifestly does not function like the story of Abraham in providing a 'canonical account' that can be interpreted to show how the readers ought to behave.

---

12. Here I tend to side with those scholars who think that what we have is more of an underlying story that has shaped Paul's theology and the way in which he expresses it, rather than the retelling of a story; see R.B. Hays, *The Faith of Jesus Christ* (Chico, Calif.: Scholars Press, 1983) 17–20.

## Stories, Propositions, and Relationships

Finally, Lincoln suggests that we should limit the use of the category of story to three levels of analysis: (1) the message of Paul's gospel; (2) the story of Paul and his apostolic mission (which includes the story of the Jerusalem church); and (3) the stories of the inheritors of letters. All of these stories form, as it were, the furniture in Paul's mind, but his actual letters are not in story form, apart from small elements of narrative.

The various stories are, of course, one story in that they are inextricably linked to one another. The inheritors are described by Paul as his children, and their story is his, although he cannot control it, just as the story of my children is part of my story and yet is independent of me. The gospel is a combination of stories about events that happened and continue to happen as the mission advances, with stories explaining the significance of those events. The gospel story, then, is 'fixed' in terms of events (Christ died and rose again) and their significance ('God was in Christ reconciling the world to himself; be reconciled to God') as well as continuing to be written as people write themselves into the story or refuse to do so.

David Lull raises the question of whether Paul's theology is more propositional or more narrative in its structure.[13] This antithesis is no doubt a false one, and the question should be whether one term is more generally applicable and useful than the other. Nevertheless, my clear impression is that Paul usually offers something much more akin to propositions than to narrative. However, an underlying 'story' or explanation of things shapes his thinking and hence his writings, but that story is also plastic and reshaped by Paul's theological work on it. From one point of view, the gospel is an account of things that God has done and is doing, but to a large extent Paul's message is an explanation of the significance of these events in terms of *Gabe* and *Aufgabe*. From yet another point of view, the Christian life, both of individuals and communities, is to be understood as the spiritual equivalent of a personal relationship expressed by such terms as love and faith and even personal knowledge. Out of such a relationship you can make a 'love story' if you will, but more fundamental than the story is the actual relationship between God and his people that underlies and gives birth to the story.

---

13. D.J. Lull, 'Salvation History: Theology in 1 Thessalonians, Philippians and Galatians: A Response to N.T. Wright, R.B. Hays and R. Scroggs', in Bassler (ed.), *Pauline Theology, Volume 1*, 247–65, 247.

# PART 3

# In Retrospect

# 12

# The Narrative Approach to Paul

*Whose Story?*

James D.G. Dunn

What has been the attraction of introducing the concept of narrative to Pauline studies? The chief attractions, I suggest, are twofold. First, to see history as narrative is to make sense of it. History then can be seen not merely as a random series of events or as an incredibly complex sequence of intricately related events, but as a story, with a beginning, middle, and end, a story with a recognisable plot, a story whose participants can be identified and their respective roles characterised. Whether the story is inherent to history or a grid imposed upon the endless flux of history is a question whose pertinence is usually recognised, but the value of the approach does not hang on a decision being reached on the issue.

So the first value of reading Paul in narrative terms is that we are thereby enabled to assume that behind the particularities of his letters is one or more stories, coherent stories about creation, about Israel, about Jesus, about Paul, and about recipients (and targets?) of his letters. Even if the allusions are obscure, even if the particularities give only the most fragmentary glimpses of Paul's understanding of creation, of Israel, of Jesus, we can assume that there is a coherent story behind each, a narrative or narratives with beginning, middle, and end, a well-defined plot and clearly identifiable characters.

The second benefit is that by assuming the underlying narrative or metanarrative, we can refer to it in order to fill out the allusions, to complete what Paul did not deem it necessary to spell out to his readers (who, we have also to assume, knew the story for themselves). By setting the individual letter within the context or framework of the foundation story, we, like the first auditors, are enabled to fill in the 'gaps of indeterminacy' and thus to recognise a coherence that will remain invisible to those who remain only on the surface of the text.

The classic example of this is the 'faith of Christ' reading of the phrase πίστις Χριστοῦ. As a phrase it is seen to sum up a complete story line, a substantial sub-plot in the narrative of Jesus. Never mind that the subplot is never spelled out in those terms in Paul, or indeed elsewhere in earliest Christian writing. The phrase encapsulates the whole story in itself and enables us to 'plug into' a whole dimension of Paul's story of Jesus to which we would otherwise be blind.

Richard Hays is quite properly credited with (re)introducing both emphases to Pauline studies,[1] though in his subsequent writing on Paul he has not pressed much further along that line, and his work on Pauline allusions[2] makes less use of the logic of assumed narrative structure than we might have expected. His good friend Tom Wright has pressed the logic most thoroughly, though principally in relation to Jesus' own mission. Behind the Jesus tradition there is what he calls a 'controlling story', the story of Israel's exile and restoration. By constant reference to this story, he claims, we are enabled to recognise allusions and hear reverberations that would otherwise be lost to us.[3] The argument is Wright's, but the logic is that of the underlying or overarching story.

The appeal of this narrative approach to Paul is obvious. To those who want to find a coherent theology in Paul's letters, theology as narrative, theologising as telling a story, with its implicit promise of discernible plot, beginning, middle, and end, is bound to be attractive. Given that there are/were bound to be *aporias*, 'gaps of signification', in what are/were occasional letters, the possibility of setting these letters into one or more larger stories to provide an exegetical and hermeneutical context within which particular textual cruces can be resolved (and resolved not in a series of ad hoc ways, but in ways that are compatible with and integrate into the larger story) could hardly be other than welcome.

However, there are innumerable problems bound up with the approach, which such an initial somewhat naively optimistic evaluation as I have just indicated inevitably invites. Several of the problems were indicated in the papers themselves, and the discussion that followed each of the papers elaborated them and exposed still others. In this final overview chapter, therefore, I have been charged to supplement my own initial critique by incorporating the main points and issues that emerged in what proved to be very stimulating and fruitful discussions.

---

1. R.B. Hays, *The Faith of Jesus Christ: An Investigation of the Narrative Substructure of Galatians 3:1–4:11* (Chico, Calif.: Scholars Press, 1983).

2. R.B. Hays, *Echoes of Scripture in the Letters of Paul* (New Haven, Conn.: Yale University Press, 1989).

3. N.T. Wright, *Jesus and the Victory of God* (London: SPCK, 1996).

# WHERE IS THE NARRATIVE?

Is the narrative to be found (1) *within* the text—to be read off the page, perhaps with some slight assemblage here and there, but nonetheless integral to the text? Or is it (2) *behind* the text, informing, enriching, and constraining the logic within the text's discourse? Or is it (3) *in front of* the text, constructed by the reader from discursive elements in the text, without any claim that Paul himself imagined the narrative in this way?

Those in the consultation who had also participated in the seminar discussion on Pauline Theology at the annual meeting of the Society of Biblical Literature (SBL) in North America recognised at once an issue that had plagued the seminar's decade-long discussions.[4] What do we mean by 'the theology of Paul'? (1) Is it the theology *of the letters themselves*, that is, of each individual letter—Paul's theologising as he reacted to a sequence of particular churches and specific situations? If so, can we do more than describe the theology of each letter individually? (2) Or is it the theology *of Paul himself*, conceived as a sort of large reservoir on which Paul was able to draw and from which the particular letters were drawn off? The challenge is then to reach through the partialness of the separate letters to a whole, envisaged as lying behind them, in which the idiosyncrasies of the different letters are somehow merged by taking into account the particularities of each situation that have skewed each presentation and by 'unskewing' somehow the separate theologies. (3) Or is it the theology *of the reader of Paul*, or of the tradition to which the Pauline letters have given rise? Is what we call 'the theology of Paul' nothing more than the order that we impose on the peculiar and recalcitrant elements in the Pauline letters? In my own *Theology of Paul the Apostle*[5] I have attempted an exposition chiefly along the lines of the second option. At the same time, in taking Romans as the template, I also emphasise that Paul's theology was not something static but that it developed and changed in emphasis over the years and adapted to different situations. I also emphasise the dialogical nature of any attempt to write a 'Theology of Paul', for a contemporary 'Theology of Paul' cannot be other than an encounter between Paul theologising and a reader reading. The most challenging reviews of my *Theology of Paul* have been those that argued that it is neither possible nor desirable to move beyond the first option.

---

4. J.M. Bassler, (ed.), *Pauline Theology, Volume 1: Thessalonians, Philippians, Galatians, Philemon* (Minneapolis: Fortress Press, 1991); D.M. Hay, (ed.), *Pauline Theology, Volume 2: 1 and 2 Corinthians* (Minneapolis: Fortress Press, 1993); D.M. Hay and E.E. Johnson, (eds), *Pauline Theology, Volume 3: Romans* (Minneapolis: Fortress Press, 1995); D.M. Hay and E.E. Johnson, (eds), *Pauline Theology, Volume 4: Looking Back, Pressing On* (Atlanta: Scholars Press, 1997).

5. *The Theology of Paul the Apostle* (Grand Rapids: Eerdmans; Edinburgh: T&T Clark, 1998) particularly 13–19.

Equally, those familiar with the history of biblical interpretation will recognise that the issue being raised here is simply another form or example of the
well-known and inescapable 'hermeneutical circle'. The circle takes several
forms. In its classic form it is the circularity of part and whole: the parts can
only be understood in terms of the whole; but understanding of the whole is
built up from the parts. More recently it has been reexpressed as the circularity of subject matter and the speech used to convey it—between Word and
words, *Sache und Sprache*; between *langue* and *parole*, signified and signifier—
or again in terms of the circle of reader and text and all that is implied in Bultmann's much-quoted observation that 'there cannot be any such thing as
presuppositionless exegesis'.[6]

The question is, then, whether the promotion of narrative theology as a way
of doing 'the theology of Paul' actually succeeds in escaping the hermeneutical circle? Or whether the problem of locating 'the narrative' simply drives us
in yet another series of dances round what is actually the same old hermeneutical circle under another name?

The fact that this project had to restrict itself to only two of Paul's letters
(Galatians and Romans) simply compounds the problem. Of course, these two
letters lend themselves to some kind of narrative analysis, dominated as they
are by questions of continuity and discontinuity of Paul's gospel with Israel's
past. But to the degree that Paul's other letters do not invite such an analysis,
to that degree the question is raised whether a narrative analysis is capable of
engaging the fuller sweep of his theology as indicated by the full range of his
letters. By confining ourselves to Galatians and Romans, it may be fairly asked,
have we not limited too much the 'whole' of which they are 'part'? A dance
round a too narrowly constricted hermeneutical circle is likely to induce feel-
ings of dizziness or nausea.

## DISCERNING THE FORM

I have to confess to a fair degree of unease about the way 'story' is usually
defined and applied. If we think simply in terms of plot and characterisation I
have no difficulty. It is when we go on to specify a fuller form for the story, a
universal story form or type, and then attempt to fit Paul's stories into that
form that my unease begins to quicken. I confess that when I see a Greimasian
diagram laid out in preparation for the analysis of a text I groan inwardly. I
have a not very shrewd suspicion that soon I am going to see features of the

---

6. R. Bultmann, 'Is Exegesis without Presuppositions Possible?', in his *Existence and
Faith* (London: Collins, Fontana, 1964) 342–51.

textual treatment pressed into the role of 'agent', 'helper', and so on, in order to fit the Greimasian structure—as, for example, when Eddie Adams identifies 'Christ's obedience' or again 'grace and the gift of righteousness' as 'the helper' (pages 31–32). My reservations on structural analysis are much the same: the more elaborate and extensive the chiastic structure discerned, the less persuaded I find myself; and the deeper the structures discerned, the more banal they usually seem to me. I confess that I do not find such analyses informative or helpful, though I recognise that others do and readily acknowledge that there may well be a value here that I am simply missing.

Right or wrong, my concern is lest the text (both *Sache* and *Sprache*) is being forced into some Procrustean bed, or lest some grid is filtering out what does not 'fit'. I am reminded of the mistake made by the early form critics who assumed that in the beginning there was the 'pure form', so that anything less than 'pure' was bound to be later. They had to settle uncomfortably to the recognition that many of the Gospel pericopes were after all 'mixed forms'. Or again I think of the debate about rhetorical form as it applies to the Pauline letter. Are we talking about an 'epeidectic' or a 'deliberative' or a 'protreptic' letter? they ask. When the letter in question does not seem to fit straightforwardly into any one of these categories, what does it matter? I ask.

The danger in all these cases is of postulating an established form and deducing *from the postulated form* the function and significance of various particulars within the letter, sometimes even despite the internal logic of the letter itself. The application of a too-idealised form of 'story' to Paul's theology raises the same unease.

In the consultation discussion, we were reminded of the danger of imposing a particular concept of story form on the Pauline material. Are the Pauline stories necessarily *linear* in character? More like an arrow, or more like a web? asked Barry Matlock. To make coherence depend on linear, chronological progression raises Bruce Malina's question of whether we are right in assuming that Mediterranean time is/was the same as Swiss time.[7] Does Abraham belong to 'the story of Israel', or is he a figure whose significance for Paul depends on Paul's being able to excerpt him from the story of Israel and to reinsert him into Paul's own story, as the convolutions in the arguments of Galatians 4 and even Romans 4 indicate?[8] Alternatively expressed, are we thinking of stories that proceed from beginning to end by the unfolding of a coherent plot, or do we rather have to think in terms of *fractured* or broken stories, particularly on

---

7. B.J. Malina, 'Christ and Time: Swiss or Mediterranean?', *The Social World of Jesus and the Gospels* (London: Routledge, 1996) 179–214.

8. The discussion was largely stimulated by Andrew Lincoln's inclusion of Abraham among Paul's 'predecessors'.

the role of the law in relation to Paul's gospel? Or again, does the story form, with its expression of historical continuity, horizontal linearity, give enough weight to the apocalyptic discontinuities, the vertical disruptions, marked not least in Paul's theologising by the sending of the Son and his own conversion?[9]

## STORY OR STORYTELLING?

Story implies storytelling. Storytelling implies performance. The work I have been doing on oral tradition has underlined for me the inescapable character of performance as a blend of stability and variability, of fixity and flexibility. In most cases the performance (*die Sprache*) is of a recognised story (*die Sache*): the story is the stable element. But given the variability of performance, the question will unavoidably arise on at least some occasions as to how varied a performance may be before it has to be designated the performance of a different story. Two questions arise from this observation.

First, where the stability of the story is maintained, it is the audience's familiarity with the story that both allows the storyteller to make allusive comments, confident that the audience will pick them up, and enables the audience to fill out the ellipses and shorthand references that the performer uses, wittingly or unwittingly. To take up the language of recent literary discussion, the performer operating within the audience's 'horizon of expectation' (H.R. Jauss) can expect it to fill in the 'gaps of signification' (W. Iser) in his/her performance. J.M. Foley in particular has offered a fruitful blend of insights from oral tradition and reception theory (reader response) in his concept of metonymic referencing—the part evoking the whole.[10] A good performance will use various phrases and formulae that trigger off associations in the hearers, allusions that work.

This applies more directly to Paul's letters than to most other New Testament writings, for they are the next best thing we have to live performances of Paul's theology. As has been widely recognised in the last two or three decades, Paul's letters are a substitute for his personal presence. He writes them as though addressing his audience through the one who was to read the letter to the recipients. I recall being deeply impressed by this insight when I witnessed a 'live performance' of Paul's letter to the Galatians at one SBL meeting.

We can assume that Paul was an accomplished performer of his theology.

---

9. These were issues raised particularly by Francis Watson.

10. J.M. Foley, *Immanent Art: From Structure to Meaning in Traditional Oral Epic* (Bloomington: Indiana University Press, 1991).

Which is also to say, we can assume that Paul was aware of his audience's 'horizon of expectation'. Just as we can assume that he did not have to spell out every point he wanted his audience to take from his letter; he could confidently expect that key members of his churches would fill in the 'gaps of signification' that he no doubt deliberately left. This line of reflection thus fills out and gives more substance to the second benefit initially postulated in regard to a narrative approach to Paul's theology. So far so good.

Second, however, the trouble arises when we take seriously the variability of storytelling as well as the stability of the story told. The problem in the Galatian churches is that there was no single story of Israel to which Paul could appeal. The story of Israel was what was contested: What was the story of Israel? Evidently there was another version of the story of Israel that was being circulated by 'the agitators', a story that had become influential among the Galatian churches. It is equally evident that Paul set out to subvert that story and to establish his own version. Now, should we actually say that he tried to subvert the story of Israel? Or that he tried to subvert his opponents' *version* of the story?

One test might be where Paul makes allusive indications of continuity. Where he could simply allude to the story of Israel without arguing the point, we could deduce that the matter was uncontested, part of the stability provided by the (uncontested) story of Israel. In contrast, where he deemed himself unable to advance his version of Israel's story simply by allusion but had to argue for it, we can deduce that the versions of Israel's story as told by the two protagonists were quite diverse. Galatians 3–4 obviously invites such an analysis in terms of what needed to be argued and what could be conveyed allusively or metonymically.

The problem then arises as to how the present-day reader can discern when Paul's silence on a subject within his retelling the story is an allusion that he intended his audience to fill out and when it is an omission that he intended his audience to recognise as such. In reworking the story he tells, no doubt hoping that his audience would recognise it as a performance of the same story, has he actually transformed it into a different story? Expressed differently, in the language of the consultation, how do we distinguish the (assumed) theological stability from the (evident) rhetorical flexibility?

My concern here, then, is that the concept of story is treated too woodenly, as though it were, one might say, a textual artefact, which, by careful excavation, could be discovered lying at the deepest stratum of Paul's theologising. This again is a problem most familiar from Jesus studies, where the Jesus tradition is conceptualised as layers down through which one might dig to discover at or under the bottom layer 'the historical Jesus'. The hunt for Paul's theology, or the story being told by Paul, is not unlike the quest for the historical Jesus. The danger in both cases is that we forget how dynamic was the transmission of the tradition, the theologising, the retelling of the story. Simply because we encounter these performances, whether of the Jesus tradition or of Paul's theology, in frozen literary form, we should not assume that there was a fixed something that could be uncovered simply by stripping away later or contingent features. Paul's theologising was his theology. In Paul's perspective, the story he told was the story. To abstract a fixed story from within the variable rhetoric of various tellings would be to misunderstand the character of Paul's theology.

## A SINGLE STORY?

As noted already, the attractiveness of talking in terms of 'story' is the implication of a dominant (single) plot line and a clear sense of progression from beginning to end. To see history as narrative is what gives history its temporal flow, his-story, God's story—God as ultimate storyteller (story maker) and the central plot line as determined by God. But this once again raises the question of whether the story perceived is only in the eye of the beholder. Are we falling into the trap of constructing a 'grand narrative' from what are discordant insights and disjointed encounters with the divine? The question has been posed by postmodernism to the grand narrative of modernity, of scientific progress as understood by the West in the sure confidence that the West is in the vanguard of that progress. That confidence owed more to a biblical concept of unfolding divine purpose than many of the proponents of that grand narrative cared to admit. So if the validity of the grand narrative of modernity has to be called in question, can we avoid posing the same question to the originating grand narrative of divine providence? To what extent is the story of divine purpose and providence a harmony imposed on the discords of history by the theologian? Can we really construe the messiness of history into the coherence of a 'story' without serious question?

We are not, however, talking about a single story. Or are we? Are the stories of creation, of Israel, of Paul, and so on, simply facets or phases in a single story? Should the tensions between the stories of Israel, as told on the one hand by the Galatian agitators and on the other by Paul, be simply resolved by asking which best fits into the overarching story? Paul evidently thought so, as he pressed for his version of the overarching story. But the problem then emerges that if the overarching story is the solution, the solution is not yet complete; the story remains unfinished; we have reached the story's middle but not yet its end. Of course, that is part of Paul's way of resolving the tensions: the story of Israel is not yet complete, and only with its completion, when all Israel will be saved (Rom. 11:26), will the conundrums wrestled with in Romans 9–11 be resolved. And

Bruce Longenecker's question remains: whether Paul's Romans resolution of the tensions in his former storytelling in Galatians can be so easily reconciled.

Or should we focus on one of the proposed five stories and either allow it to absorb all the rest or conform all the rest to it? Could Paul's theology perhaps be construed as the story of creation, of creation darkened and subjected to futility, but finally to be liberated into the glorious liberty of the children of God? Rom. 8:19–21 invites such an overview. We could envisage salvation as God's creative intention for the first Adam, distorted by sin, but fulfilled through the last Adam. Everything else could certainly be fitted into that framework. If we start with creation, does that predetermine the shape of the controlling story, even if we then concluded, with Eddie Adams, that Galatians does not have much about creation? Alternatively, one could argue that it is precisely the notes struck in Gal. 1:4 and 6:15 that signal the way Paul tries to subvert the agitators' story of Israel by reference to the larger, cosmic story.

Or surely the story of Christ has a strong claim to provide the dominant story for Paul; certainly that claim was frequently voiced and echoed around the consultation table. Important as Rom. 8:19–21 is, does it sufficiently express the centrality of Christ for Paul? After all, Paul makes a point elsewhere of reckoning with Christ at and as the beginning of creation (1 Cor. 8:6). And is it not the case that Paul did his theologising by fitting the other stories into that of Christ, that he read off the 'plight' of humankind from the 'solution' that he experienced in Christ (to use the terminology of Ed Sanders)? The problem, then, is the difficulty of integrating the story of Israel, as predominantly told in scripture, with the lead story of Christ—as signalled by the unsatisfactoriness of Paul's attempts at integration through his christological interpretation of the seed of Abraham (Gal. 3:16). In which case, does Paul simply use the story of Christ to override the most obvious alternative and traditional reading of the story of Israel?

## HOW MANY STORIES?

Our discussion envisaged and worked with five stories—of creation, of Israel, of Jesus, of Paul, and of Paul's predecessors and inheritors. But the concept of 'story', its relevance and value in relation to Paul's theology, is most effective in reference to the background stories of creation, Israel and Jesus. The extension of the concept to Paul's own story works well particularly for Galatians 1–2, for his understanding of his mission (Rom. 11:13–14), and of the process of salvation as that of being conformed to Christ (notably Gal. 2:19–20). It works also for the personal nature of Paul's pastoral interaction with his churches, though that aspect is less apparent in Romans and Galatians. But the fifth category is more problematic. The indeterminate nature of 'predecessors and inheritors' already warns that a category is being stretched too far, especially when Abraham can be counted as one of the 'predecessors'.[11] And in both cases we are uncomfortably dependent for the two stories on Paul's own letters. In the case of the first three stories we can compare and check out Paul's reading of these stories from the many other references to them elsewhere in biblical and related writings. But the only access we have to the stories of Paul's converts is through the letters themselves. Story construction by mirror reading alone is likely to produce a much less satisfactory 'story'. The dynamic of the fourth and fifth stories is in fact not primarily narratological so much as dialogical.

Of course we have the same problem of filling in the allusions and 'gaps of indeterminacy' in reference to Paul's own past and his congregations' situations and points of view. But the value of being able to appeal to a story is that its basic plot and characters can be assumed to be familiar to both letter writer and recipients. The stories of Paul's Christian congregations, however, had hardly begun and what their plot line should be was a subject of recrimination and dispute.

When the issues here were run together with those indicated previously (see 'A Single Story?'), the consultation discussion proved indeterminate. I had suggested that, if we are to get the most out of a narrative approach to Paul, we are better advised to focus on the three primary stories (creation, Israel, Jesus). The dynamic of Paul's theology is his attempt to hold these three together and to conform his own story and, by extension, that of his Christian contemporaries, to that three-fold story. Andrew Lincoln, however, preferred to collapse the first two stories into the story of Jesus as the primary story and to regard the last two stories as embodiments of the primary story, whereas Francis Watson wanted to collapse the last two together. Perhaps we should be asking whether Paul's theologising is more likely to be 'captured' by approaching it in terms of 'intertextuality', or even 'myth', than 'narrative'.

## CRITIQUING THE STORIES

What about our own critical theological engagement with these stories— assuming that the theologian's task is not simply to describe what Paul is saying but to engage with it critically?

---

11. My own reference for the fifth category (*Theology of Paul*, 18) was the other Christians who were in some measure interacting with Paul, both those who had influenced him (thinking of such passages as 1 Cor. 15:1–5 and Gal. 1:18–19; 2:1–10) and those who had been influenced by him (the churches founded by him).

For example, the story of creation. The category of story actually blurs the distinction between the creator of the story and the character within the story, not to mention the storyteller. Is God to be understood as merely a character in the story of creation? Or is God outside the story? But in the latter case, where theological analysis is proceeding narratologically, how can we bring God into the picture? And in the former case, has the narrative approach not condemned itself by its inability to reckon appropriately with God? Again, can the story of creation be narrowed down to or focussed on Adam without serious loss? The story of Adam, after all, did not resolve for all Jews the problem of evil and its origin or the function of death. Just as for historical theology it did not explain sufficiently the character of human nature. Just as for us today it does not adequately deal with human gender and sexuality. The simple linear model of cause and effect is as problematic as it is evocative—those problems being implicit in Romans 5 and 7, as Paul probably realised. Paul makes rich use of Adam. But the story of creation did not stop with Adam and Eve.

Or consider the story of Israel. Does a narrative approach mean that we simply take Israel's story as given and work from it? That story starts with Israel's election from out of all the other nations of the world, the chosen people, with the corollary that the others have been rejected. Paul was evidently content with the story of Israel's origin, and he did not shirk from its disturbing corollaries (Rom. 9:14–23). But in a time when every day's news reminds us of the confrontation between Israel and Palestine, can we be so content? The story of Israel's election is itself a reading of divine purpose that at best cuts across the story of the one God who is Creator of all nations and peoples. And the story of Israel and the nations comes to uncertain climax, uncertain as to whether the nations will be converted, enslaved, or simply destroyed—somewhat like a modern interactive drama on TV, where viewers can press different buttons to determine the outcome of the plot—one prophet presses one button (destruction); another, a second button (enslavement); another, a third button (conversion). There were, we should not forget, voices within Israel's story that raised questions regarding the standard reading (Amos 9:7; Matt. 3:9/Luke 3:8), and Paul too was not slow to identify strands within Israel's story that in his view had been too much ignored (Gal. 3:8). But still we can hardly avoid asking how African or Asian Christians, or particularly Palestinian Christians, should hear the story of Israel—as their story too?

Equally there are legitimate questions with regard to the story of Jesus—in particular, whether we today read Paul's story of Jesus too much in the light of subsequent, classic Christian confessional faith. Do we hear his story within his horizons of expectation or our own? Do we fill in the gaps of signification from the later Christian tellings of the story or from the story as it was being remembered and told at the time of Paul? Or again, bearing in mind that Paul's story of Jesus seems to have been less controversial for many of Paul's Jewish contemporaries than his story of Israel and Israel's law, should we not attempt to hear the story of Jesus with more sympathy for those tellings that would be recognisable within the Second Temple Judaism of Paul's day?

Such questions, of course, move well beyond the normal limits of 'Paul's theology'. But in invoking the category of story, I assume we are looking for fresh ways to 'read' and 'hear' Paul and are trying to open up fresh possibilities for him to be read and heard in dialogues with traditions and other cultures than our own.

## RELATING THE STORIES TO EACH OTHER

One of the disappointing features of many of the papers in first draft was the lack of attention they gave to the question of how the different stories related to each other.

1. I refer first to the stories of Adam/creation and Israel. One of the fresh insights that came to me when I wrote my *Theology of Paul* was that in each of the key Adam passages we also meet Israel. I think of the way the Adam allusion in Rom. 1:19ff. is blended with allusions to Jer. 2:5–6 and Psa. 106:20, referring to Israel's failure in the wilderness. Similarly in Rom. 5:12–21, the coming of the law is set in parallel to the coming of death. Also striking is the degree to which the 'I' of Rom. 7:7ff. is illuminated equally by the 'I' of Adam and the 'I' of Israel.[12] In a real sense the story of Adam is repeated in the story of Israel. How does that feed into the evaluation of the latter?

2. Second, I liked what Douglas Campbell and John Barclay said about the integration of the story of Christian salvation by incorporation into Christ's story. But I was surprised that Campbell did not do more to elucidate how for Paul the story of Jesus integrates with the story of creation and the story of Israel; nor did he ask whether the story of Christ requires any radical revision of the two earlier stories. After all, a key question in elucidating Paul's theology, probably the key question arising from the papers, is whether the 'revelation', or if you like 'apocalyptic revelation' of Christ, constitutes a *new* story. Or is the story of Christ rather a renewed or climactic expression of what was *always* true of God's dealings from the first (Rom. 4:17 demands more attention here), and of what was true of God's dealings with Israel for those with faith to recognise it (like Abraham and the 7,000 faithful ones of Elijah's time)? Is there a continuity (*Heilsgeschichte*?) underlying the discontinuities—a divine

---

12. *Theology of Paul*, 93, 97, 99–100.

'plot' hidden within/behind the several stories of humankind? Paul is surely struggling to articulate such in Romans 9–11. And does the story of Jesus so completely override the story of Israel as several imply? I think again of Romans 11, where the climax of all is in terms of the story of God and Israel, without explicit reference to Christ! Reference is made to the 'gospel', certainly (11:28), but the primary category of divine 'mercy' is drawn directly from the definitive revelation of Exod. 33:19 and 34:6–7. There is no continuity in terms of 'Judaism'; that is true. But there certainly is continuity in terms of *Israel* in both Galatians and Romans.[13]

3. Here too I would need to take issue with Bruce Longenecker, in many ways the most stimulating and provocative of the contributors. I do so on three points. First, he polarises the elements of continuity and discontinuity too much. Despite purporting to deal in terms of the dynamic of the story, he seems to conceive the determinative factor of Paul's 'fundamental theological sensibilities' in rather static/fixed terms. In *Theology of Paul* I preferred the model of 'dialogue' precisely because it recognizes that Paul's theologising was an ongoing process, a dialogue, with several different emphases in interaction with each other as well as with the other dimensions of his theology.

Second, I was hoping for a fruitful discussion of the tensions in that theologising between the three foundation stories—of the Jesus story with the Adam/creation story as well as with the Israel story. Galatians poses not just stories two and three (Israel and Jesus) in an antithetical way, but also stories one and three (old creation and new creation), whereas Romans subverts the dominance of the story of the Torah by going behind it, not simply to Abraham but also to Adam. Both subvert the second story. But Galatians does this by a new creation scenario; Romans, by an old creation scenario—the God who gives life to the dead and calls into existence what does not exist (Rom. 4:17), the God who creates both vessels of wrath and vessels of mercy (9:22–24), is ultimately the same God as revealed himself to Moses, a God of mercy and grace (Exod. 33:19; Rom. 11:30–32). At this point it is important to recognise that despite frequent reference to it in contemporary discussion, Paul does not make 'covenant' a leading category or distinguishing feature of his own theological position.[14] His dialectic is more between promise and inheritance.

---

13. Here I resonate with David Horrell's response (see page 164) to John Barclay.

14. In Gal. 3:15, 17 the Greek term διαθήκη means 'testament', and in 4:24 'covenant' serves equally on both sides of the antithesis between the children of Hagar and the children of Sarah. In Romans the 'covenants' are those of Israel (Rom. 9:4), and the covenant held out in 11:27 is that promised to Israel in Isa. 59:21. In 1 Cor. 11:25 he refers to 'the new covenant' in tradition he received. And even in 2 Corinthians 3, the dominant motif is that of 'ministry' (2 Cor. 3:6–9; 4:1) more than 'new/old covenant' (3:6, 14).

Third, I struggle to recognise the contrast Longenecker draws between Galatians and Romans, primarily because the stories he draws from both letters are so selective. As Morna Hooker observes, the notion of organic continuity ('organic linearity'!) is hard to escape when the talk is of seed and heir. I waited in vain for Longenecker to comment on Gal. 4:1–7—Israel as heir, albeit in an immature slave-like state, but heir nonetheless. Even in his response to Hooker, Longenecker continued to ignore the key motif of 'inheritance'. It surely makes no sense of either Galatians or Romans to talk of gentiles as heirs in waiting; the whole point is that gentiles have been brought into an inheritance that was *not* previously theirs. Nor can the continuities that Paul in effect claims in 5:14 and 6:2 be so easily dismissed. Nor the fact of the benediction on Israel (not the seed of Abraham) in 6:16; here again the response to Hooker's challenge was hardly adequate. How different, in the end, is Paul's redrawing of the definition of Israel in Rom. 9:6ff. from that in Gal. 4:21ff? In both cases 'Israel' and 'election' are redefined in terms of promise, grace, and divine call. My concern here is that Paul's loudest rhetoric in Galatians has made Longenecker (and behind him Lou Martyn!) too deaf to the continuities between the story of Jesus and the story of Israel that Paul does not bring to the fore but still assumes. In this case the 'gaps of indeterminacy' have been filled from only one of strand of Paul's two(-or-more)-stranded dialogue.

4. I would have liked to see a greater appreciation of the stories of Paul and his congregations as incomplete, still to be fully told, and of the degree to which the other stories help fill out that 'not yet' element: a liberation that awaits the 'redemption' of the body and of creation; a salvation that awaits the conversion of Israel; a cocrucifixion with Christ that is ongoing and a resurrection with Christ that is still to come. John Barclay talks of the reconstruction of identity but, in my view, does not give enough emphasis to the degree to which this is an ongoing process. Nor does he address the question of whether the 'I' who has somehow been replaced by Christ can somehow reassert itself and lose Christ. Is it still possible for the one who now defines his/her identity in terms of the story of Christ to relapse, as it were, back into the story of the Torah or the story of the flesh? What does that say about the effectiveness of the different stories in actualising identity and in ensuring its ongoing integrity? Here again we see the danger of failing to appreciate the dynamic quality of Paul's storytelling and story living-out.

In short, as with all attempts to understand and interpret Paul and his theology, the narrative approach provides valuable insights at various points, including several crucial points, but when the narrative approach is pressed into service beyond its obvious competency, it raises more problems than it solves and becomes more of a hindrance than a help.

# 13

# Is There a Story in These Texts?

FRANCIS WATSON

Reading through my colleagues' insightful reflections on the various kinds of 'story' that Paul may be telling or retelling or presupposing, I am struck by their ambivalence towards the term 'story' (or 'narrative'). The writers of these papers and responses have undertaken to *investigate* the significance of 'narrative' within Pauline thought or theology, but unqualified, enthusiastic *endorsements* of this concept are not much in evidence here.[1] The book as a whole does *not* argue that all earlier Pauline scholarship has failed to grasp what we, the authors, have now grasped, which is that 'narrative' is the magic key that unlocks the innermost recesses of Paul's thought. This book is an exercise not in scholarly triumphalism but in scholarly circumspection; and this caution derives not from any narrow-minded suspicion of someone else's proposed paradigm shift, but from the sense that central Pauline theological emphases may be lost if the apostle is converted without remainder into a storyteller.

On the other hand, this book certainly does not amount to a *critique* of the concept of 'story' as applied to Paul. All of the contributors agree that there is a topic here that is worth investigating, and I do not think that the book as a whole confirms the occasional suggestion that the term 'story' really adds nothing to our understanding of Paul. At the very least, this concept is so central to our current intellectual culture that the Pauline texts demand to be reread in the light of it; and the results are by no means uniformly negative.

---

1. The contributions of Edward Adams and David Horrell may be partial exceptions.

In this response to the book as a whole, I should like to offer an interpretation of the ambivalence I think I detect here. I shall argue, first, that the reason for the contributors' caution is clear: it is that Paul is simply not a storyteller. Unlike the Gospels according to Matthew, Mark, Luke, and John, the gospel according to Paul just isn't a story. Is that an overstated claim? Surely, like the evangelists, Paul too knows of interconnected events in sequence: 'Christ it is who died, yes indeed, who was raised, who is at the right hand of God, who also intercedes for us' (Rom. 8:34). Yet the Pauline gospel typically conceives of sequential events in their unity and coherence as representing the *singular* saving action of God. Second, and in contrast to the first point, I shall argue that there is indeed a 'narrative substruc- ture' to Pauline theology, but that this consists in the scriptural narratives relat- ing to Israel's history with God, whose significance Paul contests with Jewish or Jewish Christian opponents in Romans and Galatians.[2] Paul offers a reinterpre- tation of these narratives in the light of the singular divine saving action. He does not himself retell the scriptural stories, but he does give a number of indications as to how they should be understood.[3]

The Pauline gospel announces a definitive, unsurpassable divine incursion into the world—'vertically, from above', in Karl Barth's celebrated phrase—that both establishes the new axis around which the entire world thereafter revolves and discloses the original meaning of the world as determined in the pretempo- ral counsel of God. So unlimited is the scope of this divine action that it com- prehends not only the end but also the beginning—although it takes the highly particular form of an individual human life that reaches its goal not only in death but also in resurrection. The question is whether, for Paul, this life can be pre- sented *both* as the singular divine saving action *and* as a narrative.

This crucial issue is most sharply raised in Douglas Campbell's excellent and thought-provoking paper. Campbell rightly acknowledges that narratives 'tend to presuppose a linear temporal framework', in some tension with the 'vertical' rather than 'horizontal' plane of the trajectories of descent and ascent at the heart of the Pauline gospel. The presence of both vertical trajectories in Phil. 2:6–11—where they bracket and inhibit the linear, horizontal unfolding of the life of Jesus—is con- firmation that Campbell's synthesis of material scattered through Romans 8 is broadly correct. If I read his paper correctly, he also assumes that this 'vertical' con-

---

2. Contributors to this book generally hold that Paul assumes a single scriptural meta- narrative, 'from Adam's creation and "fall", through the promise to Abraham and the com- ing of the law through Moses, and so on', as David Horrell puts it (see page 163). But on a number of occasions, Paul appears to focus on the individual scriptural narratives with- out much attention to their context within the 'grand narrative' of scripture as a whole. In Romans 4–5, for example, Abraham and Adam are not coordinated with one another. I have therefore usually referred to scriptural 'narratives' (plural) rather than 'narrative'.

3. I am indebted to Andrew Lincoln for this distinction between scriptural narrative and Pauline interpretation or commentary—which is not 'retelling' (see pages 199–200).

strual of the gospel is characteristic of Paul and not peculiar to Romans. This would rule out two ways in which this 'vertical' construal might be relativised, as identified by two of the respondents (Graham Stanton and David Horrell, respectively). First, one might argue that the relative absence of linear extension in Paul's 'story of Jesus' is an optical illusion created by the nonavailability to us of Paul's original missionary preaching. When he preached, Paul *must have* told the story of Jesus as unfolding on the horizontal, linear plane; when he wrote, he could therefore *allude to* this story, without ever restating it in full; and so the authentic Pauline gospel is to be located in the inaccessible and hypothetical preaching rather than in its extant but secondary textual embodiment. (Not for the first time, a 'conservative' interpretative move here has the effect of undermining the authority of scripture.) Second, one might argue that the vertical construal of the gospel is evidenced in some Pauline texts but not in others, where greater weight is given to temporal extension on the horizontal plane (compare Bruce Longenecker's concept of 'organic linearity'). Yet there seem to be no Pauline exceptions to the claim that the horizontal unfolding of the life of Jesus is everywhere constrained and inhibited by the dominant vertical construal of his significance—which, as Campbell rightly points out, also entails coordinating statements about the Father and the Spirit.

If this vertical construal of the Pauline gospel is justified, that would make it difficult to understand this gospel as a 'story'. Campbell summarises as follows the 'narrative substructure' of Romans 8 (see page 108):

> (1) God the Father (2) sends, delivers up, and does not spare (3) his own (4) Son, Jesus. (5) Jesus suffers (6) and dies, (7) in an act of identification. . . . (10) The Spirit of God and Christ, (11) also the Spirit of life, (12) resurrects Jesus, that is, creates new life in and for him, (13) and glorifies him, (14) to the right hand of the Father, (15) from which point he reigns, (16) and also intercedes.

This is an interesting synthesis of the christological material in Romans 8, but is it really a story? It is true that Jesus' incarnation, death, and resurrection are necessarily in sequence. Yet when it is said that God 'sen[t] his Son in the likeness of sinful flesh and as a sin-offering' (Rom. 8:3), the temporal, horizontal space between incarnation and death is compressed almost to a vanishing point. In the one statement in this chapter where death and resurrection are referred to together, they are simply juxtaposed: 'Christ Jesus it is who died, yes indeed, who was raised.' The Greek participles serve to identify a living individual, 'Christ Jesus', and they no more require narrative expansion than do the clauses that follow: 'who is at the right hand of God, who also intercedes for us' (Rom. 8:34). It is also less than obvious to me that the various christological statements of Romans 8 *should* be brought together in a synthesis of this kind. When Paul says that God 'did not spare his only Son but gave him up for us all', he does not refer merely to a 'narrative motif' that needs to be set within an overarching story if it is to be correctly understood. Instead, he refers to God's saving action *in its totality, but under a particular description*, that of 'giving up'. The death of Jesus is not an event within a temporal flow; it is an absolute and unsurpassable event that determines who Jesus is, who God is,[4] and indeed who we are—since the one who died and was raised is, as Campbell rightly emphasises, the 'template' for the transforming work of the Spirit. For Paul, neither the death nor the resurrection of Jesus recede into the past as they are overtaken by subsequent events within an unfolding narrative.[5] Although they do not lack their own unique spatiotemporal location, they cannot be absorbed into the temporal process, for they are themselves the foundation and the meaning of that process.

It seems, then, that the Pauline gospel is not in itself a 'story'. No doubt the concept of 'story' *could* be bent and stretched enough to accommodate its idiosyncrasies, but it would hardly be worth the effort. At some point, every concept reaches its limit. Yet, in claiming to be 'in accordance with the scriptures', this gospel does align itself with a prior 'story', encompassing both the creation of the world and the history of Israel. Scripture for Paul is not simply narrative, but he does draw freely on scriptural narrative texts—especially from Genesis and Exodus. This use of scriptural narrative is not just a response to contingent situations in his congregations, for it is essential for Paul both that his gospel is attested by scripture and that it is itself the hermeneutical key to scripture. For that reason, his gospel must be correlated with 'the story of God and creation' and 'the story of Israel'. These stories, however, are not exactly *Paul's* stories. They are scriptural stories; Paul is their interpreter but without becoming a teller or reteller of stories. More specifically, what Paul does *not* do is to incorporate his gospel into a linear story of creation and Israel as the end and goal of that story. If the 'vertical' construal of Paul's gospel is correct, then the event of Jesus' life, death, and resurrection *cannot* be located on the same horizontal plane as the events of (for example) exodus, conquest, and exile—or even the creation and the fall.[6] These

---

4. If God *is* 'the one who did not spare his own Son', then it cannot be said that 'God is by definition outside history', as Morna Hooker does (see page 86). Where does this definition come from?

5. As John Barclay rightly notes, 'Although the crucifixion of Christ was indeed an event in history, it punctures other times and other stories not just as a past event recalled but as a present event. . . . In the preaching of the gospel, time becomes, as it were, concertinaed, and the past becomes existentially present' (see page 146). The obvious Bultmannian affiliations of this claim do not necessarily mean that it is wrong.

6. Contra David Horrell, who, in response to John Barclay, argues that a 'punctiliar' or 'vertical' emphasis 'downplays the extent to which Paul places the Christ event within—although as the climax and culmination of—the story of God's saving purposes and their enactment in history' (see page 162). But Horrell is right to identify the 'linear versus punctiliar' issue as crucially important to the discussion of narrativity in Paul; this is perhaps the major unresolved tension in the present book.

events are susceptible to linear narration, whereas the event that Paul announces is not. Paul's appeal to scriptural narrative does not incorporate the gospel into that narrative; rather, it aims to show how the narratives in their different ways attest this or that aspect of the gospel.[7]

I shall develop this point in dialogue with the contribution of Edward Adams (see page 33), who seeks to reconstruct from Romans 1–8 'a basic and coherent "story of God and creation"'. This comprises

> a unified series of events with characters, setting, and trajectory, tracing the history of God's creative aims from their foundation at the beginning of creation, through their frustration due to Adam's fall and subsequent human fallenness, to their ultimate fulfilment in the eschaton. The focus of the story is Christ, who functions as a new Adam, sent to repair the damage done by the first Adam.

Adam and Christ are here located on the same horizontal plane, as 'fate-determining individuals' (page 27). They are the main characters within a single story, which tells how the disastrous consequences of one person's action were put right by the action of another. Indeed, the 'positive effects' of Christ's action 'more than outbalance the negative results of what Adam did' (page 27). Yet if Christ comes to repair the damage done by Adam, then it is Adam who determines the scope of Christ's work.

It is true that Paul can on occasion place Adam and Christ in logical and chronological sequence. In 1 Cor. 15:21–22, he writes, 'For since through a man came death, also through a man came resurrection of the dead. For as in Adam all die, so also in Christ shall all be made alive.' Adam and Christ are here related to one another in two subtly different ways. In the first statement, they are related by way of a *logical sequence* of the form: *A*, therefore *B*—where *B* follows from *A* in a chronological as well as a logical sense. Comparable statements are found later in the chapter, where 'the first man Adam' is correlated with 'the last Adam', 'the first man' with 'the second man' (1 Cor. 15:45–47). The 'logic' of these statements is that of the extended 'sowing' metaphor in 15:35–44. *A*, therefore *B* is, arguably, an embryonic narrative—in this case, one that embraces the beginning and end of God's purposes for creation. In the second statement, however, Adam and Christ are related to one another by way of *analogy*: as is *A*, so is *B* (1 Cor. 15:22). Analogy is less

---

7. This account contrasts with Bruce Longenecker's concept of 'organic linearity', that arises out of the organic metaphor of Rom. 11:17–24. This passage is said to imply 'a view of salvation history in which gentile Christians find themselves incorporated within the story of Israel's own salvation' (page 61). Since the olive tree passage tells of an excision of 'natural' branches and an 'unnatural' ingrafting of branches from a wild olive tree, 'linearity' is hardly an appropriate term. One might indeed read Romans 9–11 as a whole as the Pauline *critique* of the concept of a linear salvation history.

clearly related to narrative than is logical sequence, since it sets two entities
alongside one another without attempting to derive the second from the first.
Admittedly, the formal distinction between the two types of statement does
not make much semantic difference within 1 Corinthians 15. Whether by way
of logical sequence or analogy, Adam and Christ are apparently set on the same
horizontal plane, as 'fate-determining individuals'. There are two individuals
in this category, not just one.[8]

In Rom. 5:12–21, analogy predominates over logical sequence (n.b. the 'as/so'
statements in 5:12, 18, 19, 21)—although the references to the time 'from Adam
to Moses' (5:14) and to the coming of the law (5:20) indicate that chronology
has not been forgotten. Yet Paul's argument here serves to undermine the
assumption that Adam and Christ share a single linear history, in which Christ's
task is to undo the effects of what Adam did. However obvious it may seem that
Paul must have meant that, it is not what he actually says. The basic analogy
between Adam and Christ, as stated in 1 Cor. 15:22, is subjected to two far-
reaching qualifications. First, the specific form of the analogy is said to be that
of the 'type': Adam is 'a type of the coming one' (Rom. 5:14). The analogy still
takes this form: as is $A$, so is $B$. However, $A$ is now both oriented towards $B$ and
radically subordinated to it, so that $A$ and $B$ no longer coexist on the same level.
Second, the analogy, announced in 5:12 ('Therefore *as* through one man . . .'),
is in its full form postponed until 5:18–19, being interrupted by clarifications
relating to sin, death, and law (5:13–14) and, more important, by a series of statements to the effect that the deeds of Adam and of Christ are *incommensurable*
(5:15–17). These two points must be discussed in more detail.

1. Adam is a 'type [τύπος] of the coming one' (Rom. 5:14). Elsewhere, Paul
sees the Israelites' experiences of divine judgement in the wilderness as negative 'types' or warnings intended for our benefit: 'These things happened to
them as types [τυπικῶς], and were written for our instruction, upon whom the
ends of the ages have come' (1 Cor. 10:11; cf. 10:6). Paul here uses these 'types'
or negative models for ethical rather than christological reasons, but the two
references to scriptural 'types' appear to share the same basic structure. What
was written (about the Israelites, about Adam) was written *for us*, in order to
shed light on the realities that concern *us* (Christian conduct, Christ as the

---

8. The 'logical sequence' model has been especially influential within the Christian
theological tradition—which is why it is so easy to assume that this is the only model
available. For example, Athanasius is paraphrasing 1 Cor. 15:21 when he writes, 'For
since it was from a human source that death prevailed over humans, for this reason by
the Word of God becoming human has come about the destruction of death and the
resurrection of life' (*On the Incarnation*, 10.5).

divine gift of righteousness and life). The scriptural type exists for the sake of its Christian realisation, toward which it is oriented from the beginning. If, then, Adam is a 'type of the Coming One', then the analogy between the two figures is radically asymmetrical, or as Paul himself writes in Rom. 5:18–19 (REB; emphasis mine):

> It follows, then, that *as* the result of one misdeed was condemnation for all people, *so* the result of one righteous act is acquittal and life for all people. For *as* through the disobedience of one man many were made sinners, *so* through the obedience of one man many will be made righteous.

The element that is common to both members of this analogy is that of the individual human action that determines (for good or ill) the eschatological destiny of humankind as a whole; hence the reference to 'one' action and 'all people', or to 'one man' and 'many', on both sides of the equation. Searching for a scriptural analogy that will shed light on Christ's act of self-giving in its universal scope, Paul finds his analogy at the very dawn of human history, in the figure of Adam. Adam is a 'type' of Christ, 'the Coming One'—an expression that suggests that the coming of Christ is determined not simply by Adam's transgression but by the eternal divine decree (cf. Rom. 8:29). Like the Israelites in the wilderness, Adam is a negative type, who in certain respects represents the opposite of the reality to which he points forward. The opposition is in both cases central to Paul's argument, but without detriment to the real though asymmetrical analogy between Adam and Christ, the Israelites and the Corinthians. In neither case does the typology imply a single linear history that unites both parties.

2. Although Paul's 'as/so' statements (5:18–19) bestow a formal symmetry on the Adam/Christ analogy, the typological relation between the two has the effect of radically subordinating Adam to Christ. The *incommensurability* of the two is, however, most emphatically asserted in statements that go so far as to deny that there is any real analogy between them. Although in 5:18–19 Paul does assert an analogy between Adam's action and Christ's, 5:15 opens with a rejection of a similar analogy: 'The gift is *not* like the trespass'—or, more accurately, 'It is not the case that *as* is the trespass, *so* is the gift'. The following verse opens in similar vein: literally, 'Not *as* through one having sinned [is] the gift'—that is, the outcome of the one man's sin is quite unlike the logic of the gift (5:16a). In these statements, Paul is not simply making the banal point that 'trespass' and 'gift' are not synonyms, or that the two acts lead to opposite outcomes.

Two issues are at stake here. First, Paul intends to deny that there is any *equivalence* between the two actions—as though Christ came merely to remedy the aftereffects of Adam's action, as if to restore the balance. So he writes in Rom. 5:15–17:

> For if by the trespass of one many died, much more did the grace of
> God and the gift in grace of the one man Jesus Christ abound for
> many. . . . For if by the trespass of one man death reigned through the
> one, much more will those receiving the abundance of grace and the
> gift of righteousness reign in life through the one man Jesus Christ.

In these statements, the formula of equivalence ('as/so') is replaced by a formula of disproportion ('much more'), which is to be understood in the light of
the repeated references to 'abundance'. 'The abundance of grace' implies that the
scope of God's gift is incomparably greater than Adam's 'trespass' or offence (cf.
also 5:21, where the compound verb, 'hyperabounded', makes the point still more
emphatically). God's act in Christ is, in relation to Adam's sin, utterly dispropor-
tionate, and there is no equivalence or symmetry between the two.

Second, Paul asserts that the logic of divine grace is quite different from the
logic of Adam's action and its consequences (Rom. 5:16): 'The judgement that
followed one offence led to condemnation, but the gift following many
offences led to justification.' According to Paul, the logic of the early chapters
of Genesis is one of *retribution*. Adam's single action opens the floodgates to
sin and its nemesis in death, for himself and for his descendants (5:12). Those
who sinned and died between Adam and Moses were somehow still implicated
in Adam's sin and were judged accordingly (5:13–14). In contrast, the logic of
God's grace is one of *transformation*. The divine response to the 'many
offences' of humankind is the transcendent, transformative act of justification:
'Where sin increased, grace abounded all the more' (5:21).

From these two points (nos. 1 and 2 above) it is evident that Paul's emphasis on typology, asymmetry, and disproportion in Romans 5 makes it difficult
to envisage Adam and Christ as equivalent figures within a single linear history.[9] Paul does not incorporate Christ into the scriptural narrative; instead,
he seeks to interpret the divine gift and the scriptural narrative in the light of
each other. He interprets the scriptural narrative in the light of Christ, but it
is more important for him to interpret Christ in the light of the scriptural narrative: for it is his vocation as an apostle to interpret scripture not for its own
sake but for the sake of its testimony to God's act in Christ. Paul finds that
scriptural testimony in narrative texts as well as prophetic ones, and in the narrative texts too that testimony is *direct*. Adam is a type of the Coming One; he

---

9. As Barth rightly says, 'Paul does not simply place Adam and Christ . . . in juxtaposition as if they were figures and factors of equal dignity and equal value and as if
they were the bearers of an equally powerful destiny. Adam and his many are meant to
stand by the side of Christ and his many merely as a shadow and an example . . . [Adam]
is only apparently the first. The first is Jesus Christ' (*A Shorter Commentary on Romans*
[Eng. trans; London: SCM Press, 1959] 62).

is not simply the beginning of a long story that will eventually issue in the coming of Christ, for the Christ event is sui generis and does not exist on the same horizontal plane as the scriptural narrative(s) that nevertheless bear witness to it. The grace of the one man Jesus Christ is the gift of God, and the divine act of giving occurs within the vertical plane rather than the horizontal one.

Paul's gospel, then, is not itself a 'story', since its vertical construal of God's act as a movement of descent and ascent inhibits the linear, temporal extension that a 'story of Jesus' would require. Nor does this gospel become part of a story, its climax indeed, through insertion into a scriptural metanarrative. Paul characteristically appeals to individual scriptural stories rather than to the scriptural story as a whole, and he appeals to them with the sole aim of uncovering their testimony to a divine act that lies beyond the scope of human storytelling. Paul is certainly a theological interpreter of scriptural narrative, but it is a mistake to understand him as a 'narrative theologian'. It is significant that, with the exception of Galatians 1–2, Paul in his extant writings never actually tells a story. This is not just an accidental deficiency that can be put right by reconstructing some kind of 'narrative substructure'. The only 'narrative substructure' in Paul is the scriptural narrative or narrative collection from which he draws in order to elucidate an essentially nonnarratable gospel.

# Abbreviations

| | |
|---|---|
| *CBQ* | *Catholic Biblical Quarterly* |
| *CurBS* | *Currents in Research: Biblical Studies* |
| *ExpTim* | *Expository Times* |
| ICC | International Critical Commentary |
| *JBL* | *Journal of Biblical Literature* |
| *JJS* | *Journal of Jewish Studies* |
| *JSNT* | *Journal for the Study of the New Testament* |
| JSNTSup | Journal for the Study of the New Testament Supplement Series |
| *JTS* | *Journal of Theological Studies* |
| *NovT* | *Novum Testamentum* |
| *NTAbb* | *Neutestamentliche Abhandlungen* |
| *NTS* | *New Testament Studies* |
| *RevExp* | *Review and Expositor* |
| SBLSymS | Society of Biblical Literature Symposium Series |
| *SJT* | *Scottish Journal of Theology* |
| SNTSM | Studiorum Novi Testamenti Societas |
| SNTW | Studies of the New Testament and Its World |
| *ZTK* | *Zeitschrift für Theologie und Kirche* |

# Contributors*

*Edward Adams*
Lecturer in New Testament Studies
Department of Theology and Religious Studies, Kings College London

*John M.G. Barclay*
Professor of New Testament and Christian Origins
Department of Theology and Religious Studies, University of Glasgow

*Douglas A. Campbell*
Lecturer in New Testament Studies
Department of Theology and Religious Studies, Kings College London

*James D.G. Dunn*
Lightfoot Professor of Divinity
Department of Theology, University of Durham

*Morna D. Hooker*
Lady Margaret's Professor Emerita
Faculty of Divinity, University of Cambridge

*David G. Horrell*
Senior Lecturer in New Testament Studies
Department of Theology, University of Exeter

*Andrew T. Lincoln*
Portland Professor of New Testament
School of Theology and Religious Studies, University of Gloucestershire

243

*Bruce W. Longenecker*
> Lecturer in New Testament Studies
> Faculty of Divinity, University of St Andrews

*I. Howard Marshall*
> Honorary Research Professor
> School of Divinity and Religious Studies, University of Aberdeen

*R. Barry Matlock*
> Lecturer in New Testament Studies
> Department of Biblical Studies, University of Sheffield

*Graham N. Stanton*
> Lady Margaret's Professor of Divinity
> Faculty of Divinity, University of Cambridge

*Francis Watson*
> Professor of New Testament Exegesis
> School of Divinity and Religious Studies, University of Aberdeen

---

*Authors retain copyright for their chapters.

# Index of Scriptural Citations

# Index of Modern Authors